The Houston Mama's Handbook

Melanie A. Williams
Jamie L. Williams

Thank You

The Houston Mama's wish to thank all those who have helped in bringing this book together.....

Our sweet bald husbands who have worn so many "hats" throughout this process.

Melanie's precious baby girls who have watched way to many Disney movies.

Erika our beloved editor and babysitter.

And all those who have supported us and given us words of encouragement along the way.

Thank You!

Dedicated to: Our babies

Table of Contents

Cover Illustration by Alison Jay

Chapter 1

Places to Go and Things to Do

Chapter 1

Places to Go and Things to Do

There is so much to do in the Greater Houston area. We couldn't possibly name them all but we have tried to find activities that will involve both parents and children. Our goal is to encourage family togetherness and help make parenting just a little easier. In this chapter you will find activities listed by areas so they will be easy to find. We have also included FREE activities as well as the Big Attractions. Remember to check the other chapters of the book for more specific activities like "The Great Outdoors" or "Sports".

Freebies

FREE Activities

Home Depot Children's Workshops

www.homedepot.com - check the website for a location near you.
Hours: Every 1st Saturday of the month from 9:00am – 12:00pm at all store locations.

Price: FREE

Children accompanied by an adult construct projects from pre-fabricated kits. In addition your child will receive a kids size orange apron and an achievement pin. These projects are best for children ages 4-12 years. A sign-up sheet is posted 3 weeks in advance and early sign-up is recommended.

Toy's R Us – Camp Geoffrey

www.toysrus.com - check website for a location near you.
Hours: Summer Program select Saturday's from1:00pm to 3:00pm

Price: FREE

Children participate in a variety of arts and craft projects. These activities are best for children between the ages of 3-10 years of age. Check your local store for participation.

Libraries- (See Chapter 8 Libraries and Books)

www.hcpl.net

Don't forget to visit your local library for FREE children's activities throughout the year.

Local Fire Station

Take your kids to see a fire engine up close. Call your local fire station to set up a tour! They usually provide a badge and plastic fire hat for kids!

FREE Animals

Kemp's Ridley Sea Turtle Research Center

4700 Avenue U
Galveston, TX
409-766-3670
www.galveston.ssp.nmfs.gov
Hours: FREE tours are given on Tuesday, Thursday, and Saturday at 10:00am 11:00am 1:00pm and 2:00pm.

Price: FREE

Families can experience one on one interaction with the turtles. There is no glass between you and the animals. You can also learn about ongoing research and about different turtle species. Parties of 9 or more need to make an appointment.

Sea Center Texas

300 Medical Dr.
Lake Jackson, TX
979-292-0100
www.tpwd.state.tx.us
Hours: Tuesday-Friday 9:00am– 4:00pm
Saturday 10:00am-5:00pm
Sunday 1:00pm-4:00pm

Price: FREE

This is a state-of-the-art marine fish hatchery and aquarium. The center includes an aquarium; touch tanks full of crabs, clams, snails, and even sea anemones. See up close how the fish hatchery works. Call to schedule an appointment to fish in their half-acre pond.

The Houston Zoo

1513 N. McGregor in Hermann Park
Houston, TX
713-533-6500
www.houstonzoo.org
Visit the zoo for FREE on Martin Luther King Day, Memorial Day, July 4th, Labor Day, and the day after Thanksgiving.

FREE Museums

Art Car Museum

140 Heights Blvd.
Houston, TX
713-861-5526
www.artcarmuseum.com
Hours: Wednesday through Sunday
11:00am-6:00pm

Price: FREE

Your kids will love this museum! They rotate their exhibits throughout the year and every November they have a Children's Workshop where they can build their very own art car.

The Children's Museum of Houston

1500 Binz
Houston, TX
713-522-1138
www.cmhouston.org
FREE Family Thursdays from 5:00pm-8:00pm

The Heritage Society's Museum of Texas History

1100 Bagby St. in Sam Houston Park
Houston, TX
713-655-1912
www.heritagesociety.org
Hours: Monday through Saturday 10:00am to 4:00pm and Sunday 1:00pm to 4:00pm

Price: Admission into the museum gallery is FREE

They also provide historic house tours, an old store, children's programs, lectures and special events. Please contact for pricing.

Holocaust Museum Houston
5401 Caroline
Houston, TX
713-924-8000
www.hmh.org
Hours: Open Monday through Friday 9:00am-5:00pm

Saturday and Sunday from 12:00pm-5:00pm
Price: FREE

This museum has a 30-minute presentation that tells the stories of Houstonians that survived the Holocaust.

Houston Museum of Natural Science
One Circle Dr. Hermann Park
Houston, TX
713-639-4629
www.hmns.org
FREE admission on Tuesdays from 2:00pm- closing
(5:00pm or 8:00pm in the summer)

John P. McGovern Museum of Health and Medical Science
1515 Hermann Dr.
Houston, TX
713-521-1515
www.museumofhealth.org
FREE Family Thursdays from 2:00pm-5:00pm

The Menil Collection
1515 Sul Ross St.
Houston, TX
713-525-9400
www.menil.org
Hours: FREE admission Wednesday through Sunday from 11:00am-7:00pm
Art displays from the Byzantine Period and even some Picasso.

Museum of Fine Arts, Houston
1001 Bissonnet St.
Houston, TX
713-639-7300
www.mfah.org
Hours: FREE admission on Thursdays from 10:00am to 9:00pm
FREE weekends for kid's ages 6-18 years with a public Library card.

Pioneer Memorial Log Home Museum
1510 N MacGregor Way in Hermann Park
713-522-0369
Hours: Open Monday through Friday 9:00am to 5:00pm.

Price: FREE

Come explore and discover some interesting Texas history!

San Jacinto Battlegrounds State Historical Site
1 Monument Cr.
La Porte, TX
281-479-2421
www.sanjacinto-museum.org
The monument, museum, and battlegrounds are FREE. Other activities have a minimal cost. The Battleship is FREE to kids 12 and under.

Hours: Open 7 days a week from 9:00am to 6:00pm

Price: FREE

FREE Parks and Nature Centers

Edith L. Moore Nature Sanctuary
440 Wilchester Blvd.
Houston, TX
www.houstonaudubon.org
Hours: Open 7 days a week from 7:00am to 7:00pm

Price: FREE

This park runs along a creek and has a restored log cabin that offers a variety of educational programs. Bird watching is the most popular past time here and you can print off a bird checklist from the website.

Hermann Park
6001 Fannin St.
Houston, TX
One of the largest parks in the Houston area, it is home to the Houston Zoo, The Miller Outdoor Theatre, Museum of Natural Science, and the Japanese Garden. Other areas of the park include a water playground, picnic pavilions and FREE unlicensed fishing for kids 12 and under. This is a great place to spend the day!

Houston Arboretum and Nature Center
4501 Woodway
Houston, TX
713-681-8433
www.houstonarboretum.org
Hours: Open 7 days a week from 8:30am to 6:00pm

Price: FREE

Walk more than 5 miles of trails and experience nature in the middle of Houston.

Jesse H. Jones Park and Nature Center
20634 Kenswick Dr.
Humble, TX
281-446-8588
www.hcp4.net
Hours: Park is open 7 days a week: March through October from 8:00am-7:00pm
December and January from 8:00am-5:00pm
November and February from 8:00am-6:00pm
Nature Center is open daily all year round from 8:00am to 4:30pm

Price: FREE

Mercer Arboretum
2306 Aldine Westfield Rd.
Humble, TX
281-443-8731
www.hcp4.net
Hours: Open Monday through Saturday 8:00am to 7:00pm and Sunday 10:00am to 7:00pm

Price: FREE

You might think this is just a place for plant lovers but anyone can appreciate this beautiful botanical garden. See rare species of plants like the carnivorous insect eating plants. See the butterfly nursery and the hundreds of fish in the Koi ponds. Don't forget your camera, and bring your insect repellant!

Nature Discovery Center

7112 Newcastle
Bellaire, TX 77401
713-667-6550
www.naturediscoverycenter.org
You do not want to miss a chance to visit this place. It is in Russ Pitman Park in the middle of Bellaire. The center has a hands-on approach designed to spark an interest in children for nature and science. They have a discovery room with boxes, fashioned after those in the Smithsonian, where kids can explore a crystal cave, or reconstruct a turtle skeleton. Kids are also delighted when they get to see the baby chicks, frogs, snakes, and other animals here.

Hours: Open Tuesday through Sunday 12:00pm-5:30pm

Price: FREE

FREE Performing Arts

Concerts in the Parks Series

League Park
200 N. Park Ave
League city, TX
281-554-1184
281-554-1181
www.ci.league-city.tx.us
Hours: Select Saturdays at 7:00pm May through September.

Price: FREE

See local bands perform as well as the League City Symphony. Check the website's calendar page for details.

Cynthia Woods Mitchell Pavilion

2005 Lake Robbins Dr.
The Woodlands, TX
281-363-3300
www.pavilion.woodlandscenter.org
FREE on the Lawn (tickets are required)

Most of the FREE lawn events are productions by the Houston Symphony. Check the website for show times and details.

Miller Outdoor Theatre

100 Concert Dr. in Hermann Park
Houston, TX
713-284-8350 (recorded information)
713-284-8352
www.milleroutdoortheatre.com
There are so many types of performances held here all throughout the year. They are all FREE and open to the public on a first come first serve basis. Please check the website for details.

Other Freebies

Bolivar Ferry

409-795-2230
www.dot.state.tx.us/MNT/ferryops/ferryops.htm
This is a FREE ferry ride from Galveston Island to the Bolivar Peninsula. Bring some crackers to feed the Seagulls and maybe you'll even see a dolphin.
Hours: This ferry runs 24 hours seven days per week. During the daylight hours there is about a 20 minute wait between trips. 8:00pm to Midnight there is about a 30-minute wait. Midnight through dawn there is about 1 hour between trips.

Downtown Tunnel System

713-222-9255
There are about 7 miles of underground tunnels connecting downtown Houston. The tunnels house a variety of shops, hotels, restaurants, and even link the downtown Theatre District. FREE maps are available at the Central Library (501 McKinney). The Wells Fargo Plaza offers direct access to the tunnels.
Hours: Open Monday through Friday 7:00am to 6:00pm
Price: FREE. Tours are made available through www.discoverhoustontours.com for $5.00 per person.

Old Town Spring

123 F. Midway
Spring, TX
281-353-9310
www.oldtownspringtx.com
You will love this small town atmosphere built around a historic abandoned railroad track. There are over a hundred small shops and restaurants here. Cute is about the only word to describe it. Admission in FREE! Don't forget to check their events calendar.

Hours: Tuesday through Saturday 10:00am-5:00pm
Sunday 12:00pm-5:00pm
Monday closed

Port of Houston

713-670-2416
www.portofhouston.com
This is a FREE public boat tour through the port. The ride lasts about an hour and a half.

Hours: Tuesday, Wednesday, Friday and Saturday at 10:00am and 2:30pm
Thursday and Sunday at 2:30pm only
You must call or register online before taking the tour.

Big Attractions

Adventure Bay

13602 Beechnut St.
Houston, TX 77083
281-498-7946
www.adventurebay.com
This water park includes slides, a lazy river, tube slides, a children's activity center, and a wave pool.

Hours: Open May through September approximately 10:00am–7:00pm. Hours subject to change.

Admission: General $21.50
48"and under $15.99
3 and under FREE
** Print a coupon from the website**

Bayou Wildlife Park
5050 F.M. 517
Alvin, TX, 77511
281-337-6376
www.bayouwildlifepark.com
A safari in Houston? Who would have thought? Read on! Included with admission is a guided tram ride across the prairie where you learn about all the animals. Llamas, white rhinos, giraffes, deer and zebras just to name a few. Feed the animals along the way, a bucket of feed is only $2.00. Also included with your admission are the petting zoo and pony rides. Bring a lunch to enjoy in their picnic area.

Hours: Open Tuesday through Sunday 10:00am-4:00pm

Price: Adults $10.95, Children 3-11yrs $5.50

Downtown Aquarium
410 Bagby St.
Houston, TX 77002
713-223-FISH
www.downtownaquarium.com
Besides the wonderful tanks full of exotic fish inside the restaurant, the Aquarium has a number of other attractions. Like the Shark Voyage, the White Tiger Exhibit, the Touch and Feel Tanks, or carnival like rides, this place has it all! Bring the kids' bathing suits and they can play in the Dancing Fountains for FREE.

Hours: Sunday through Thursday 10:00am-10:00pm
Friday and Saturday 10:00am-11:00pm

Admission: Attractions are priced individually or you can get an all day pass for $15.99 that includes all the rides and exhibits.

Kemah Boardwalk
Kemah, TX
www.kemahboardwalk.com
Just 20 miles from downtown Houston this has become the perfect family get-a-way. At the heart of the boardwalk are some great restaurants but they also have carnival rides and concerts every Thursday night at 6:30pm. Some select Mondays are "Kid Krazy" with half price kid's meals and half price ride wristbands. Please see the website for details.

Moody Gardens
Galveston, TX
800-582-4673
www.moodygardens.com
Come see the Aquarium Pyramid, the Discovery Pyramid, the Rainforest Pyramid, IMAX theatre, Ride Film theatre, Colonel Paddlewheel Boat, and many other seasonal attractions.

Hours: Open Sunday through Friday 10:00am-6:00pm, Saturday 10:00am-8:00pm
Summer hours 10:00am-9:00pm daily

Admission: Attractions are individually priced from $4.95 - $14.95 per person
We recommend a day pass good to see all the attractions for $35.95 per person
3 and under are FREE

Six Flags Astroworld
9001 Kirby
Houston, TX 77054
713-799-1234
www.sixflags.com
Located off Loop 610 at the Fannin exit.
This theme park includes many awesome rides but also a FREE family water park with admission.

Hours: Open March through October approximately 10:00am-8:00pm

Summer Hours are usually 10:00am-9:00pm See website for specific hours.
Admission: General $41.99
48" and under 24.99
2 yrs and under are FREE
Print your tickets online and go straight to the gate. Get your online coupon for $24.99 per person
See ad in back

Six Flags Splashtown
21300 I- 45 N.
Spring, TX 77373
281-355-3300
www.sixflags.com
A refreshing water park full of slides and rides!

Hours: Open May through September 10:00am-7:00pm Hours are subject to change.

Admission: General $29.99
48" and under $19.99
2 yrs. and under FREE

See ad in back

Space Center Houston

1601 Nasa Parkway
Houston, TX 77058
281-244-2100
www.spacecenter.org
This is the official visitors center of the NASA/Johnson Space Center. There are live presentations as well as fun exhibits. Attractions include the Kids Space Place, a five-story plaza that models a full-size shuttle, computer simulators, tours of the astronauts training center, and a giant screen theatre. The original Mission Control room is also open for viewing. This is an activity both parents and kids will love!

Hours: 10:00am-5:00pm weekdays
10:00am-7:00pm weekends

Admission: Adults $17.95
4-11yrs $13.95
3 and under are FREE
Print a $2.00 off admission coupon online

The Houston Zoo

1513 N. McGregor in Hermann Park
Houston, TX
713-533-6500
www.houstonzoo.org
This live animal adventure is a great place to spend the day with your kids. Exhibits include over 700 species of animals like tigers, elephants, giraffes, monkeys, and even sea lions. There is also a children's petting zoo, and a water park!

Hours: March through September 9:00am-6:00pm

October through February 9:00am-5:00pm
Admission: Adults 12 and up $8.50
Children 2-11 yrs. $4.00
2 and under are FREE

Big Museums

The Children's Museum of Houston

1500 Binz
Houston, TX
713-522-1138
www.cmhouston.org
Come and experience 14 hands-on fun exhibits in the areas of science and technology, history and culture, health and human development, and the arts. Don't forget to check out their special events and exhibits.

Hours: Tuesday through Saturday 9:00am-5:00pm
Sunday 12:00pm-5:00pm
Monday 9:00am-5:00pm

Admission: $5.00 per person
2 and under are FREE

Battleship Texas State Historical Park

3527 Battleground Rd.
La Porte, TX 77571
281-479-2431
www.tpwd.state.tx.us/park/battlesh/battlesh.htm
This is the only surviving battleship to have fought in both World Wars. Make sure you check out the website's special events page.

Hours: Open 7 days a week from 10:00am-5:00pm

Price: Adults ages 13 and up $7.00
Children 12 and under are FREE

Houston Fire Museum

2403 Milam St.
Houston, TX 77006
www.houstonfiremuseum.org
This museum is housed in the historic former City of Houston Fire Station No. 7. Exhibits include the evolution of firefighting, a collection of 19th-century fire service equipment and a hands-on educational Junior Firehouse used to teach kids fire safety and prevention.

Hours: Tuesdays through Saturday 10:00am-4:00pm

Admission: $3.00 for adults and $2.00 for kids

Houston Museum of Natural Science
One Hermann Circle Dr. in Hermann Park
Houston, TX 77030
713-639-4629
www.hmns.org
This museum includes three floors of exhibits, the Cockrell Butterfly Center, the Burke Baker Planetarium, and the Wortham IMAX Theatre. For children there is a hands-on exhibit called the Fondren Discovery Place. There is so much to learn and enjoy here!

Hours: Permanent Exhibits Monday through Saturday 9:00am-5:00pm
Tuesday 9:00am-8:00pm
Sunday 11:00am-5:00pm

Admission: Adults $6.00
Children 3-11 $3.50
2 and under are FREE

Other attractions and special exhibits have their own hours and prices. See their website for details and purchase your tickets online.

Museum of Fine Arts, Houston
1001 Bissonet St.
Houston, TX
713-639-7300
www.mfah.org
This is one of the premiere art lover's destinations. This museum includes two museum buildings, two art schools, two decorative arts centers, and a sculpture garden. Sundays are Family days at the museum and you can participate in a drop-in creation station. You can make your own sculpture, paintings, photographs, and more. Please check their website for exact Family Days creation projects.

Hours: Tuesday and Wednesday 10:00am-5:00pm
Thursdays 10:00am-9:00pm FREE admission all day
Friday and Saturday 10:00am-7:00pm
Sunday 12:15pm-7:00pm

Admission: Adults $7.00
Children $5.00
** FREE weekends for kids with a Public Library Card ages 6-18 yrs.**

Activities

NORTH

Celebration Station
180 W. Rankin Rd.
Houston, TX 77090
281-872-7778
www.celebrationstation.com
Activities: Arcade games, Batting cages, Bumper boats, Go-karts, Miniature golf, Playland rides, and a Restaurant.

Hours: Monday through Friday 10:00am-10:00pm
Friday and Saturday 10:00am-Midnight
Sunday 12:00pm-10:00pm

Price: Miniature golf $6.00 for adults; $4.00 for children 3-12 yrs
Go-karts, and bumper boats $6.00 per ride
Playland rides $2.00 per ride; parents ride FREE
Unlimited pass is $22.00 per person

Jumpin Jak's
3403 F.M. 1960 W.
Houston, TX 77068
281-537-8833
www.jumpinjaks.qpg.com
This is an indoor play place where you can beat the heat or rain. They also offer birthday party packages.

Hours: Monday through Thursday 9:30am-9:00pm
Friday 9:30am-5:30pm

Price: Ages 1-3 - pay your age
Ages 4-12 - $4.00

See ad in back

Lazerrage

612 Spring Cypress
Spring, TX 77373
In Old Town Spring
281-355-8900
www.lazerrage.com
Activities: Arcade games, Laser Tag, Makoto, and Pool. Birthday packages are available.

Hours: Monday through Thursday 12:00pm-10:00pm
Friday 12:00pm-11:30pm
Saturday 10:00am-11:30pm
Sunday 12:00pm-9:00pm

Price: Laser Tag for ages 5 and up $6.50 per game
Pool: $3.50 per hour
See website for weekly specials and to print a coupon

Main Event – The Woodlands

19441 I-45 North
Shenandoah, TX
281-355-5511
www.maineventusa.net
Activities: Billiards, Bowling, Games, and Laser Tag. Birthday party packages available.

Hours: Sunday through Thursday 11:00am-Midnight
Friday 11:00am-2:00am
Saturday 10:00am-2:00am

Price: Please call for pricing.
Check out half price Tuesdays

Pump it Up

536 Sawdust Rd.
Spring, TX 77380
281-465-4747
www.pumpituphouston.com
Activities: Open playtime sessions, Birthday Party Packages, and Mommy and Me. All indoor bounce center.

Hours: Vary; Mommy + Me Monday, Thursday and Friday from 9:30am-11:00am

Price: $5.00 per child; please call for Birthday Party Packages

See ad in back

NORTHWEST

Go-Kart Raceway

2800 W. Mount Houston Rd.
Houston, TX
281-447-7378
www.go-kartraceway.com
Activities: Arcade games, Go-karts, Super-karts, and Two seater-karts. Birthday party packages available.

Hours: Sunday through Thursday Noon-Midnight
Friday and Saturday Noon-2:00am

Price: Go-karts $4.00 per ride
Super-karts $6.00 per ride
Two seater $7.00 per ride
Check website for specials and coupons

Gymboree Play and Music

17776 Tomball Parkway #35-A
Houston, TX 77064
713-953-0444
www.playandmusic.com
Play classes range from 1 month to 5 years of age. Music classes range from 6 months to 5 years. Art classes range from 18 months to 5 years of age. Classes run for 11 weeks. Please call for a schedule and to inquire about Birthday parties.
Prices: $110.00 - $230.00; One time enrollment of $20.00

Mountasia Family Fun Center

17190 Sate Hwy. 249
Houston, TX 77064
281-894-9791
www.mountasia.com
Activities: Batting Cages, Bumper Boats, Gameroom, Go-karts, and Miniature Golf.

Hours: Monday through Thursday 10:00am-10:00pm
Friday and Saturday 10:00am-11:00pm
Sunday 12:00pm-10:00pm

Price: Miniature Golf adults $6.00; children 12 and under $4.95
*Go-karts and bumper boats $4.50 per ride*Print a buy 1 get 1 FREE coupon online**

Oil Ranch
#1 Oil Ranch Rd.
Hockley, TX 77447
281-859-1616
www.oilranch.com
Activities include pony rides, milking a cow, dairy educational barn, baby animal farm, train rides, hayrides, an Indian village, summer swimming, playground, and even a miniature golf course. They also have special events all throughout the year like FREE snow cones and a FREE pumpkin in October.

Hours: Tuesday through Friday 10:00am-4:00pm
Saturday 10:00am-6:00pm

Price: $7.99 per person
2 and under are FREEGroup discounts available
See ad in back

Pump it Up (2 Locations)

Cy-Fair
10910 W. Sam Houston Pkwy. N. Suite 100
Houston, TX 77064
281-469-4205
www.pumpitupparty.com

Katy
923 S. Mason Rd.
Katy, TX 77450
281-829-5711
www.pumpituphouston.com

Activities: Open play time, Mommy and Me, Birthday party packages, Church Group activities, and day care outings.
Hours: Vary throughout the year; Mommy and Me – Monday, Thursday, and Friday from 9:30a.m. – 11:00a.m.
Price: Mommy and Me $5.00 per child; Please call for birthday party and group information.
See ad in back

NORTHEAST

Mountasia Family Fun Center
26000 Hwy.59 N.
Kingwood, TX 77339
281-359-4653
www.mountasia.com
Activities: Batting Cages, Bumper Boats, Gameroom, Go-karts, and Miniature Golf.

Hours: Monday through Thursday 10:00am-10:00pm
Friday and Saturday 10:00am-11:00pm
Sunday 12:00pm-10:00pm

Price: Miniature Golf adults $6.00; children 12 and under $4.95
Go-karts and bumper boats $4.50 per ride
Print a buy 1 get 1 FREE coupon online

Old MacDonald's Farm
3203 F.M.1960 E.
Humble, TX
281-446-4001
www.eieiohumble.com
Activities: 12 separate petting zoos, Birthday parties, and in October a pumpkin patch.

Hours: March through October open daily 10:00am- 1hr. before dusk
November through February only open on weekends.
December and January closed

Price: $5.75 per person. Includes all activities.

SOUTHWEST

Celebration Station
6767 Southwest Frwy.
Houston, TX 77074
713-981-7888
www.celebrationstation.com
Activities: Arcade games, Batting cages, Bumper boats, Go-karts, Miniature golf, Playland rides, and a restaurant.

Hours: Monday through Friday 10:00am-10:00pm
Friday and Saturday 10:00am-Midnight
Sunday 12:00pm-10:00pm

Price: Miniature golf $6.00 for adults; $4.00 for children 3-12 yrs
Go-karts, and bumper boats $6.00 per ride
Playland rides $2.00 per ride; parents ride FREE
Unlimited pass is $22.00 per person

Gymboree Play and Music (3 Locations)

www.playandmusic.com

1990 Post Oak Blvd.
Houston, TX 77056
713-953-0444

14623 Memorial Suite B
Houston, TX 77079
713-953-0444

3340 F.M. 1092 Suite 120
Missouri City, TX 77459
713-953-0444

Play classes range from 1 month to 5 years of age. Music classes range from 6 months to 5 years. Art classes range from 18 months to 5 years of age. Classes run for 11 weeks. Please call for a schedule and to inquire about Birthday parties.
Prices: $110.00 - $230.00; One time enrollment of $20.00

Laserzone

4125 S. Hwy 6
Sugar Land, TX 77478
281-277-2900
www.laserzoneusa.com
Activities: Arcade games, and Laser Tag. This facility has a 3-story laser tag arena with ramps leading to different levels. Each game lasts 20 minutes and at the end you will receive a scorecard.

Hours: Monday through Thursday 1:00pm-10:00pm
Friday 1:00pm-Midnight
Saturday Noon-Midnight
Sunday Noon-10:00pm

Price: $7.50 per person; $6.50 for members
Check out the website for weekly specials

Putting Edge

7620 Katy Frwy. Suite 406
Houston, TX 77024
713-263-7051
www.puttingedge.com
This facility is an indoor glow-in-the-dark miniature golf course.
Hours: Monday – Thursday 10:00am – 11:00pm
Friday and Saturday 10:00am – 12:00am
Sunday 10:00am – 9:00pm
Prices: 4 and under are FREE with a paid admission
5-6 yrs $6.00
7-12 yrs $7.50
General $8.50

SOUTHEAST

The Little Cedar Bayou Wave Pool
600 Little Cedar Bayou Dr.
La Porte, TX 77571
281-470-1966
www.laportetx.gov
This is a great wave pool complete with FREE inner tubes and a sand volleyball court.

Hours: Monday through Thursday 11:00am-8:00pm
Friday through Sunday 11:00am-6:00pm
Open Memorial Day through Mid August. Then weekends through Labor Day.

Price: Residents $3.00; Non-residents $5.00; 2 and under are FREE.

Putt-Putt FunHouse
806 E. Nasa Rd.1
Webster, TX 77598
281-333-0579
www.puttputtfunhouse.com
Activities: Arcade games, Batting cages, Bumper boats, Laser tag, Miniature Golf, and a FREE Kid's Space play center. Also offer birthday party packages.

Hours: Sunday through Thursday 10:00am-11:00pm
Friday and Saturday 10:00am- Midnight

Price: Bumper boats: $4.50/5-minute ride
Batting cages: Tokens 4 for $1.00
Laser Tag: $5.00 per person for 7.5-minute game
Miniature Golf: $5.00 per person per game or 3 games for $7.00

US Golf and Games
10106 Thermon St.
Houston, TX 77075
713-943-2299
Activities: All indoors this facility offers batting cages, miniature golf, an arcade, billiards, and birthday party packages.
Price: Golf $3.00 per person under 6yrs $1.50

Ballon Rides

Air Texas Balloon Adventures
15714 Downford Dr.
Tomball, TX 77377
713-554-6044
www.airtexsballoons.com

Airventure Ballooning
713-774-2359

Bear Creek Balloons
16840 Clay Rd. Suite 112
Houston, TX 77084
281-463-0080

Soaring Adventures
713-524-5940

Bowling

AMF Bowling Centers
www.amfcenters.com
This is a national bowling chain with a good reputation. They offer open play and league bowling. For kids they have bumper bowling in every lane as well as arcade games. Birthday party packages are available. Parents can have fun here too!

Hours: Sunday through Thursday
11:00am-11:00pm
Friday and Saturday 11:00am-2:00am

Price:
Monday-Friday before 6:00pm
After 6:00pmWeekends
Children $2.75/game
Children $3.50/game
Children $4.00/game
Adults $3.00/game
Adults $4.00/game
Adults $5.00/game

Shoe rentals are $3.00 for children and $4.00 for adults

NORTH

AMF-Diamond lanes
267 N. Forest Blvd.
Houston, TX 77090
281-440-9166
www.diamondlanes.amfcenters.com

AMF-Woodlands Lanes
27000 I-45 N.
Conroe, TX 77385
281-367-1277
www.woodlandslanes.amfcenters.com

NORTHWEST

AMF-Willow Lanes
19102 State Hwy. 249
Houston, TX 77070
281-955-5900
www.willowlanes.amfcenters.com

AMF-Windfern Lanes
14441 Northwest Frwy.
Houston, TX 77040
713-466-8012
www.windfernlanes.amfcenters.com

AMF-West Houston Lanes
19936 Saums Rd.
Katy, TX 77449
281-578-9292
www.westhoustonlanes.amfcenters.com

NORTHEAST

AMF-Humble Lanes
19214 Eastex Hwy.
Humble, TX 77338
281-446-7184
www.humblelanes.amfcenters.com

SOUTHWEST

AMF-Bunker Hill Lanes
925 Bunker Hill Rd.
Houston, TX 77024
713-461-1207
www.bunkerhilllanes.amfcenters.com

AMF-Stafford Lanes
4919 S. Main
Stafford, TX 77477
281-491-2856
www.staffordlanes.amfcenters.com

SOUTHEAST

AMF-Clear Lake Lanes
16743 Diana Ln.
Houston, TX 77062
281-488-1331
www.clearlakelanes.amfcenters.com

AMF-Alpha Lanes
318 W. Bay Area Blvd.
Webster, TX 77598
281-338-1272
www.alphalanes.amfcenters.com

Museums

NORTH

Heritage Museum of Montgomery County
1506 I-45 N.
Conroe, TX 77305
936-539-6873
www.heritagemuseum.us
This museum is housed in the historic Grogan/Chochran home built in 1924. It has three galleries, "Glimpses of Montgomery County", "Towns, People, and Events", and a "Hands-on Children's Room". Here kids can explore a log cabin and an old general store. Special summer programs allow children to churn butter, dip candles, wash clothes on rub boards, play pioneer games, and saw logs.

Hours: Open Wednesday through Saturday 9:00am-4:00pm

Price: FREE

NORTHWEST

Forbidden Gardens
23500 Franz Rd.
Katy, TX 77493
281-347-8000
281-347-8096
www.forbidden-gardens.com
Come and explore the wonders of Imperial China without leaving Texas. This is mostly an outdoor museum with exhibits like the Terra Cotta Army, a replica of the Forbidden City, a weapons room, and an architecture room.
Hours: Friday through Sunday 10:00am-5:00pm
Tours are required and begin at 11:00am, 12:00am, 1:00pm, 2:00pm, and 3:00pm.
Price: $10.00 for adults
$5.00 for kids 6-18yrs
$3.00 for kids 5 and under
One child under 5 is allowed FREE with one paid adult admission.

Military Museum of Texas

8611 Wallisville Rd.
Houston, TX
713-673-1234
www.texasmuseum.org
This big museum is dedicated to the collection, restoration, and preservation of military vehicles, artillery pieces, and other military support equipment. It is their goal to see that they instill a greater appreciation for those who serve our country. The collection includes operational tanks, armored personnel carriers, jeeps, helicopters, and so much more. This museum is a little boy's paradise but girls will appreciate it as well.

Hours: Saturday 9:00am-4:00pm
Sunday 10:00am-3:00pm

Price: FREE, Donations accepted

NORTHEAST

Houston Police Museum

17000 Aldine Westfield
Houston, TX 77073
281-230-2360
www.houstontx.gov/police/history.htm
This is the Houston Police Department museum. It has more than 7000 artifacts both from the past and present. Included in the tour is a police car that kids can climb in and out of, a helicopter hanging from the ceiling, old badges, guns, and even a drug display. Don't forget about police week held in May.

Hours: Monday through Friday 8:00am-3:30pm; Tours are given at 10:00am everyday.

Price: FREE

SOUTHWEST

Fort Bend Museum

500 Houston St.
Richmond, TX 77464
281-342-6478
www.fortbendmuseum.org
This beautiful museum complex includes the Long Smith Cottage, the 1883 John Moore Home, and the McFarlane House. Their goal is to "preserve and interpret the regional history of Fort Bend County". The kids might also enjoy the Morton Cemetery where Jane Long is buried. You can get a map, paper, and charcoal to do grave rubbings, from the museum. Visit their website for special events throughout the year.

Hours: Tuesday through Friday 9:00am-5:00pm
Saturday 10:00am-5:00pm
Sunday 1:00pm-5:00pm

Price: Adults $5.00
Children $3.00 ages 5-15yrs
4 and under are FREE

George Ranch Historical Park

10215 F.M. 762
Richmond, TX 77406
281-343-0218
www.georgeranch.org
This is a 23,000-acre working cattle ranch where you can experience everything from the Texas Revolution to World War II. Learn and see something new every time you visit! Displays include an authentic chuck wagon, a frontier cabin, or a giant tree house. Maybe you'll even get to see a historical re-enactment. Costumed presenters make this place come to life. Don't forget to check out their Campfire Christmas held in December.

Hours: Open every day from 9:00am-5:00pm

Price: Adults $9.00
Children $5.00 ages 5-15 yrs
4 and under are FREE

SOUTHEAST

West Bay Common School Children's Museum
210 N. Kansas
League City, TX
281-554-2994
www.oneroomschoolhouse.org
This museum is an exhibit of buildings and artifacts from the turn of the century. The museum includes the One-room Schoolhouse, the Barn Museum, and the Ice House Museum. They also offer an award-winning program for children, of all ages, to experience an 1898 learning environment.

Hours: Monday through Thursday 9:00am-4:00pm
Friday 9:00am-1:00pm

Price: $3.00 for everyone.

Paintball Facilities

NORTH

Paint Ball Mania
924 Butler Rd.
Conroe, TX 77303
936-588-3128
936-539-3202
www.paintball-mania.com
This facility has 7 fields, 3 hyperball, 3 woods, and an airball field.
Ages: 10 and up

Hours: Open Saturday and Sunday only 10:00a.m.- Dark

Price: $25.00-$65.00

NORTHWEST

Tanks World of Paintball

14820 Katy-Hockley Rd.
Katy, TX 77493
713-862-5555
www.tankspaintball.com
Ages: 10 and up

Hours: Saturday 9:00am-6:00pm and Sunday 9:00am-5:00pm

Price: $30.00 per person includes entry, equipment rental, and paintballs.

NORTHEAST

Survival Game of Texas

23903 Aldine Meadows
Houston, TX
281-370-GAME
www.paintballstoreinc.com
Fields include a 3000 sq ft. twin castle, speedball, Vietnam village, and a jungle field.
Ages: 10 and up with a signed release form.

Hours: Open 7 days a week; Morning session 8:30am-1:00pm
Afternoon session 1:30pm-6:00pm
Night session 6:30pm-10:30pm

Price: $15.00-$25.00 includes equipment rental, and all day use.

SOUTHWEST

Paint Ball Bonanza

Fields are located at S. Main and Chimney Rock
Please see website for a map
713-935-0552
www.paintballbonanza.com
Ages: 10 and up with a signed release form

Hours: Saturday 9:30am-5:00pm
Sunday 10:30am-5:00pm

Price: $8.00 up to $100.00 for 3 hr session
Get a season pass for $44.99

SOUTHEAST

Paintball Zone
2811 Dixie Farm Rd.
281-660-0663
www.paintballzone.net
Features a 2-story castle, fort field with a tower, spool field, hyperball, lego field, air-ball, and a maze field.
Ages: 10 and up with a release form

Hours: Saturday and Sunday 10:00am- dark

Price: $8.50 up to $58.50
Equipment rental $14.00

Skating Ice/Roller

NORTH

SK8 Town - Roller
846 Rayford
Spring, TX
281-292-22626

Hours and Price: Tuesday-Friday 1:00pm-4:30pm for $5.00
Friday Night 7:00pm-11:00pm for $6.50
Saturday 1:00pm-6:30pm for $5.00
Saturday Night 6:00pm-10:00pm for $6.50
Sunday Discount Day 1:00pm-4:00pm for $3.50

NORTHWEST

Aerodrome – Ice
8220 Willow Place N.
Houston, TX
281-84-SKATE
www.aerodromes.com

Hours: Public Skate times are subject to change without notice. Check website for details.

Monday-Wednesday 11:00am-2:10pm
Thursday 11am-2:10pm and 3:30pm-5:30pm
Friday 11am-2:10pm and 8:00pm-11:00pm
Saturday 12pm-3:30pm and 8:30pm-11:00pm
Sunday 1:00pm-5:00pm
Price: All admission is $7.00
Ice skate rentals $3.00
See ad in back

Bear Creek Roller Rink – Roller
5210 Hwy 6 N.
Houston, TX 77084
281-463-6020
www.bearcreekskate.com

Hours and Prices: Monday-Friday 1:00pm-4:30pm for $4.00
Tuesday Night 7:00pm-10:00pm for $4.00
Friday Night 6:00pm-11:00pm for $6.00
Saturday 12:00pm-6:00pm for $5.00 and 6:00pm-11:00pm for $6.00
Sunday 1:00pm-6:00pm for $4.00

Mason Road Family Skate Center - Roller
535 Apple White Dr.
Katy, TX
281-392-9555
www.katyinfo.com

Hours and Prices: Tuesday (2 skate for the price of 1) 1:00pm-9:00pm for $6.00
Wednesday and Thursday 1:00pm-5:00pm for $6.00
Friday skate 7:30pm-9:00pm dance 9:00pm-11:00pm for $6.00
Saturday 12:30pm-5:00pm and 7:30pm-11:00pm for $6.00
Sunday 1:00pm-5:30pm for $6.00

NORTHEAST

Great Time Skate - Roller
1447 Aldine Westfield
Houston, TX
281-442-0720

Hours and Prices: Tuesday-Thursday 1:00pm-3:00pm for $3.50
Thursday Family Night 7:00pm-9:00pm for $3.00
Friday and Saturday 7:00pm-12:00am for $6.00
Sunday 2:00pm-6:00pm for $5.00

SOUTHWEST

Sugar Land Ice and Sports Center – Ice
16225 Lexington Blvd.
Sugar Land, TX 77479
281-265-7465
www.sugarlandice.com

Hours: Please call for public skate times.

Price: $7.00 per person
Skate rental for $3.00

Polar Ice Galleria – Ice
5015 Westheimer Suite 1260
Houston, TX 77056
713-621-1500
www.polariceent.com

Hours: Monday-Thursday 11:00am-5:00pm and 8:00pm-10:00pm
Friday 11:00am-10:00pm
Saturday 12:30pm-10:00pm
Sunday 1:00pm-9:00pm

Price: Adults $7.00
Children 12 and under $6.50
Skate Rentals $4.00

SOUTHEAST

Funtime Skating Rink – Roller
1500 N. Texas Ave.
Webster, TX
281-332-4211
www.skatefuntime.com

Hours and Prices: Monday-Friday 11:00am-4:00pm for $5.00
Tuesday night 6:30pm-9:00pm for $.99
Friday night 6:30pm-11:30pm for $7.00
Saturday 11:00am-10:00pm for $6.00
Sunday Family Skate 1:30pm-5:00pm for $6.00

Pearwood Skate Center - Roller
1230 E. Broadway
Pearland, TX 77581
281-482-4060
www.pearwoodskate.com

Hours and Prices: Tuesday-Friday 11:00am-4:00pm for $5.00
Friday Night 7:00pm-11:00pm for $6.00
Saturday 12:00pm-5pm and Family Skate 7:30pm-10:30pm for $6.00
Sunday 1:00pm-4:00pm for $6.00

Space City Ice Station – Ice
18150 Gulf Frwy.
Houston, TX 77546
281-486-7979
www.spacecityicestation.com

Hours: Public skate times
Monday-Friday 11:00am-1:00pm and 3:00pm-5:00pm
Friday 7:30pm-9:30pm
Saturday 2:00pm-4:00pm and 7:30pm-9:30pm
Sunday 2:00pm-4:00pm

Price: All $6.00
Skate rental $4.00

The Sports Page Skating Rink – Roller (2 locations)

www.skateworlds.com

410 W. Pasadena Blvd.	2606 Cherrybrook
Deer Park, TX	Pasadena, TX
281-479-2816	713-943-8530

Hours and Prices: Friday 6:00pm-11:00pm for $6.00
Saturday 12:00pm-7:00pm and 6:00pm-11:00pm for $6.00 skate all day for $8.00

Chapter 2

The Great Outdoors

Chapter 2

The Great Outdoors

The wide-ranging health benefits of outdoor activities for both adults and children have been well noted. These benefits include, but are not limited to reducing tension and stress, stimulating the mind, and improving overall muscle tone and flexibility. Outdoor activities increase both your physical and mental health – all while appreciating the beauty of nature.

Today, American families spend more than 90% of their time inside. Sometimes, being in a natural outdoor setting can have more health advantages than being indoors. Seek out nature. Change your view and enjoy time with your family in the great outdoors.

General Resources

The following are some general outdoor websites for Houston Mama's to use in their quest for great family activities. Any of these websites will provide a wealth of knowledge concerning the outdoors. Find information on biking, bird watching, camping, canoeing, climbing, fishing, hiking, and more.

Dude Ranches in Texas

www.duderanches.com/texas.htm
Find all of the different Dude Ranches in the state of Texas on one site. Check out the different outdoor experiences available to your family. Saddle up partner!

Guide to Texas Outside

www.texasoutside.com

Find information on hiking, biking, camping, boating, canoeing, fishing, sailing, hunting, scuba diving, rock climbing, and so much more, all in the great state of Texas. This is one of the most extensive sites available in Texas. Plan your next great outdoor adventure with the help of this site. Texas is truly your backyard!

National Park Service

www.nps.gov

The National Park Service has a great website that takes you to wonderful maps and detailed information about the National Parks in the state of Texas. Start by searching through the Parks and Recreation area and you will be able to compare different locations for great outdoor family trips.

National Wildlife Federation

www.nwf.org/kids

This link is the "Just for Kids Ranger Rick" information area for your children ages 1-18. You can find all sorts of great activities to do in your own backyard that are very educational and fun. There is an area just for parents and one for educators about the wildlife information and activities that are happening.

Recreation.gov

www.recreation.gov

This extensive website has an organized way to help you look through each states outdoor recreation opportunities. You can find almost every outdoor activity category here and then find locations and information about those activities in your state. You might want to make this a regular stop before planning outdoor trips.

Wild Texas

www.wildtexas.com

Find over 400 Texas Parks and campgrounds with this site. You can learn how to beach camp at Padre Island or plan a road trip all from your home computer. While there you can get driving distances and even make reservations online. This is a great camping and outdoor recreation resource for your family to enjoy.

Texas Parks and Wildlife

www.tpwd.state.tx.us

The mission of TPWD is, " To manage and conserve the natural and cultural resources of Texas and to provide hunting, fishing, and outdoor recreation opportunities for the use and enjoyment of present and future generations." This is an extensive online guide to Texas State Parks. You can print a Texas State Park Guide, get licensing information and learn about conservation. This is a wonderful website and will be helpful with any of your outdoor activities.

Houston Wilderness

www.houstonwilderness.org

An organization dedicated to conservation of natural resources in an ever-expanding city. This site provides outdoor information specific to the Houston area. From hunting and fishing to biking and hiking this organization wants to help you find the best our Houston outdoors has to offer.

Texas State Parks Close to Home

Following is a guide to Texas State Parks close to the Houston area. All of these State Parks have outdoor recreation activities your family will enjoy. If you do not find the activities you are looking for listed in the other areas of this chapter, always refer back to this section and contact the State Park for a complete detailed list of their activities.

Brazos Bend State Park

21901 F. M. 762 Needville TX

979-553-5101

www.tpwd.state.tx.us/park/brazos

This park offers camping, fishing, biking, hiking trails, and bird watching. Watch out for the alligators that are a common site in this park! They also have the George Observatory for stargazers. Call for hours of observatory.

Open year round: Gates open from 7a.m. to 10p.m.

Admission: $3.00 per day per person. Children 12 and under are FREE.
Camping fees: Campsites w/electric and water $15.00 per night
Screened shelters $21.00 per night

Galveston Island State Park
14901 F.M. 3005
Galveston, TX
409-737-1222
www.tpwd.state.tx.us/park/galveston
Activities include camping, bird watching, hiking, mountain bike riding, fishing, and beach swimming.

Open year round: Gates open 8a.m. to 10p.m.

Admission: $3.00 per day per person. Children 12 and under are FREE.
Camping fees: Campsites w/electric and water $15.00 per night
Premium site $20.00 per night
Screened shelters $20.00 per night

Huntsville State Park
P.O. Box 508
Huntsville, TX
936-295-5644
www.tpwd.state.tx.us/park/huntsvil
Park offers camping, hiking, biking, miniature golf, horseback riding, fishing, swimming, and boat rentals.

Open year round: Gates open 7:30a.m. to 10:00p.m.

Admission: $3.00 per person per day. Children 12 and under are FREE
Camping fees: Campsite with water $10.00 per night
Campsite w/water and electric $13.00 per night
Screened shelters $20.00 per night

Lake Livingston State Park
300 Park Road 65
Livingston, TX
936-365-2201
www.tpwd.state.tx.us/park/lakelivi
Park offers camping, pick nicking, swimming pool, mountain biking, fishing, boating, and horseback riding.

Open year round: No gate.

Admission: $3.00 per person per day. Children 12 and under are FREE
Camping fees: Campsites range from $9.00 to $21.00 per night
Screened shelters $28.00 per night

To find a complete list of State Parks please visit www.tpwd.state.tx.us

Biking

Greater Houston Off-Road Biking Association

www.ghorba.org
Find out what's going on in Houston's world of mountain biking. There is information on special events, trails in Houston and surrounding areas as well as biking groups in your area. They also have a riding program for kids called Sprokids. They teach biking appreciation through clinics, mountain biking events, fun rides, and races. See site for details and a calendar of events.

Mountain Bike Texas

www.mountainbiketexas.com
Find a bike trail anywhere in the state of Texas. This site also provides information on Biking Organizations and Bike shops. Plan a special biking trip for your family!

Texas Parks and Wildlife

www.tpwd.state.tx.us/adv/101/biking.htm
Find a complete list of Texas State Park bike trails. State Parks in our area with bik include Brazos Bend SP, Galveston Isl Huntsville SP, and Lake Livingston SP. You can find annual biking events through the site as well.

City of Houston Parks Department

www.houstontx.gov/parks/park-trail-boundaries.htm
Bike and hike in any of Houston's 94 city parks. Check site for a complete listing of parks and trail information. Parks and trails are open from 6 a.m. to 11 p.m. daily.

Bird and Wildlife Watching

Texas Parks and Wildlife

www.tpwd.state.tx.us/adv/birding

There is a children's guide to bird watching in the State of Texas. It teaches children how to identify birds by their body shape, color of their feathers, and beaks. You can even print a field guide for kids to use on their next bird watching adventure. Information on "The Great Texas Coastal Birding Trail" that runs along the Texas coastline is found online. Find out about special birding activities like the Texas Birding Festival or the Great Texas Birding Classic. Birding is enjoyed by millions of people and would be a great hobby to start with your kids.

Houston Audubon Society

440 Wilchester blvd.
Houston TX
713-932-1639
www.houstonaudubon.org

This is a wonderful website for those just starting to bird watch as well as those experienced birders. There are 12 Houston Audubon Society wildlife sanctuaries in our area. All of which provide birding education programs as well as guided tours. The Audubon also sponsors summer bird camps for children ages 5 to 12. The Audubon Docent Guild offers birthday parties, owl prowls, and nature camps for children ages 4 to 11 years. Bird watching is an activity even the youngest children in the family can enjoy.

Camping

We have included some great resources to plan your next camping trip. From packing your gear to finding a campsite, you should find just about everything you need. Also refer back to Texas State Parks for more great camping spots.

Texas Parks and Wildlife

www.tpwd.state.tx.us/parkguide

This online version of the Texas State Park Guide is meant to help your family plan the best camping trip possible. This site includes maps and information on 120 parks and historical sites in Texas. Find camping fees, hours, locations, accommodations, and activities.

Kirkham's Checklist

www.kirkhams.com/checklists/camper_checklists.html
Whenever it is time to pack for a camping trip we all try to remember the items that we will need, as well as, the items we forgot last time. There is a great camping checklist that you can just print off the Kirkham's website. It is called the Camper's Checklist and is quite extensive. It will save you a lot of time before the family camping trip.

Great Family Campsites

NORTH

Castaways RV Park and Resort

12922 Longstreet rd
Willis, TX
800-828-2613 or 936-856-2949
www.castawaysrvpark.com
Located in a private cove on Lake Conroe this campground offers cabins, a boat launch, fishing, canoe rentals, swimming pool with slides, and many recreational activities.

Open year round: Sun – Thur. 9a.m. to 8p.m.
Fri. and Sat. 9a.m. to 9p.m.

Prices: Camp sites $25.00 to $35.00 per night two- night minimum
Cabins $45.00 to $125.00 per night two- night minimum

NORTHEAST

Chain-o-Lakes Resort Campground

235 Chain-o-Lakes Resort
Cleveland, TX
832-397-4000
www.colresort.com
Located 1 hr from Houston this resort offers 200 campsites, hiking, kayaking, hayrides, fishing (no license required), horseback riding, cabins, and even cooking classes.

Open year round: office hours 8a.m. to 5p.m.

Prices: Camping sites $22.00 to $35.00 per night

SOUTH

Lost Lake Campground
4411 C.R. 418
Rosharon, TX
281-431-1824
www.lostlakecampground.com
Only 15 minutes south of Houston this private lake offers fishing, camping, swimming, a petting zoo, biking, and cabins.

Open year round 10 a.m. to 10 p.m.

Prices: Camping $7.00 per person per night. Children 6 and under FREE. Cabins $35.00 per night

Canoeing, Rafting, & Kayaking

Bayou Preservation Association
www.bayoupreservation.org
This is a great organization dedicated to the preservation of Houston's waterways. Click on water access, within the site, for a listing of Houston's bayous and creeks. All of the waterways listed are accessible to canoes and kayaks. There are 22 paddling sites in and around Houston. This is a very detailed listing and will tell you exactly where to go and how to get there.

Houston Canoe Club
www.houstoncanoeclub.org
Established in 1964 the members of this club enjoy canoeing, kayaking, quiet water, whitewater, touring, and racing. Become a member and enjoy their special trips and events. This site also has a great listing of waters to paddle in and around Houston.

Climbing

Most climbing gyms offer camps, birthday parties, and activities for kids of all ages. Call for more details on events and programs at your climbing gym.

Houston Climbing

www.houstonclimbing.com
This site is the official home of the Houston Climbing Club. There are many resources available for individuals interested in climbing. Find climbing walls, Texas Rock climbing destinations, and much more. The climbing club can help those interested in climbing. Check out their site for details.

Texas Rock Gym – Memorial

9716 Old Katy Rd. Suite 102
Houston, TX
713-973-ROCK (7625)
www.texasrockgym.com

Texas Rock Gym – Clearlake

201 Hobbs Rd. Suite #A1
League City, TX
281-338-ROCK (7625)
www.texasrockgym.com
See advertiser index on pg 473

Stone Moves

6970 FM 1960 West
Houston, TX
281-397-0830
www.stonemoves.com
See advertiser index on pg 473

Sun and Ski Sports – Katy Mills Mall

5000 Katy Mills Circle
Katy, TX
281-644-6040

Fishing & Boating

Texas Parks and Wildlife

www.tpwd.state.tx.us/fish

Find any body of water in the state of Texas to fish in. You can check water conditions and find out what type of fish you can catch there. TPWD also offers the "Family Fishing Celebration". This program offers FREE fishing at Texas State Parks on certain days of the year. There will also be other events surrounding the celebration, including, kids fishing derbies, and "Learn to Fish" seminars. Some parks will even provide loaner equipment and bait. See site for complete details.

TX Fishing

www.txfishing.com

"The Weekly Fishing Report for the State of Texas" provides guides and destinations all over the state of Texas. Look up a fishing club in your area. Most have children sponsored programs. This is a great site to plan your next fishing trip.

Fisherman's Paradise

19582 Hwy 35
Alvin, TX
281-648-3474

This fish farm stocks catfish if you want an "easy catch" fishing experience for your children. This is a catch and keep facility and you pay by the pound. You can rent your rod and reel and buy your bait from them.

Open: Saturday 8a.m.-6p.m.

Sunday 8a.m.-5p.m.

Call for schedule if it is raining.

Hiking

Houston Happy Hikers

281-498-1365

www.houstonhappyhikers.org

H.H.H. is an organization that promotes health through outdoor exercise and hiking events. They host a weekend walk about once a month and other year round activities. The Happy Hikers also provide trail work for the Houston Arboretum. This group is open to all ages. Mothers can even bring children in strollers if the hike permits. See their site for details.

Horseback Riding

Most State Parks have horseback riding trails. Contact them individually for hours and pricing.

Houston Horses

www.houstonhorses.net
This is a directory of FREE resources for the equestrian enthusiasts in Houston and surrounding areas. Find information on horseback riding, boarding stables, vets, and more.

LESSONS

NORTH

Centerline at Buck Grass Stables

One Heritage Circle
Magnolia, TX
281-259-5736
Located minutes from the Woodlands on F.M. 1488 Centerline offers, "The English Riding Academy". Beginners learn to groom a horse, put on a saddle and bridle, and how to cool down and un-tack a horse. Lessons are offered to for ages 6 and up. They also offer a summer camp sessions.

Price: 50 Min. lesson ranges from
$45.00 to $60.00
Summer Camps are one week M-F
$300.00 per session.

NORTHWEST

Little Bay Farm

21403 Mueschke Rd.
Tomball, TX
281-516-0588
www.littlebayfarm.com
Little Bay Farm provides group and private lessons for Hunter and Jumping, as well as, summer camps. Ages 8 and up.

Lessons are given Monday-Saturday: A.M. and P.M. classes available. Call for exact times.

Price: $40.00/lesson

Circle Lake Ranch

1102 Circle Lake Dr.
Katy, TX
281-395-4311
www.circlelakeranch.com
This ranch offers English and Western style horseback riding lessons. They have summer day camps and summer overnight camps, as well. Please see site for details. Ages 7 and up.

Price: Lessons range $35.00 to $45.00 each. They offer a payment discount program. Summer camp: 1-week session $300.00 ages 6-15

NORTHEAST

Cypress Trails Stables

21415 Cypresswood Dr.
Humble, TX
281-446-7232
www.horseridingfun.com
Cypress Trails Stables offers basic riding lessons, western, endurance riding, English, pleasure, and trail riding.

Ages: 4 and up

Price Range: $35.00 per hour
$30.00 per hour for trail riding

SOUTHWEST

Albe Farm

9611 Gaines Rd
Sugar Land, TX
281-561-0607
albert@albefarm.com
This horseback riding facility offers hunter and jumper lessons to beginners through show levels. For children ages 6 and up.

Lessons offered Tuesday through Saturday

Price: $35.00 per 45-minute lesson.

Diamond C Training Center

16827 Old Richmond Rd
Sugar Land, TX
281-498-5958

SOUTH

D-Talk Ranch

3023 Miller Rd.
Rosharon, TX
281-431-9001
www.d-talkranch.com
They provide western riding lessons to all ages (private or group). They teach basic western horsemanship, bridal, tack and saddle care.

Outdoor Education Facilities

Anahuac National Wildlife Refuge

509 Washington St.
Anahuac, TX
409-267-3337
This is a 34,000-acre Wildlife Refuge. It provides wintering habitat for birds. The habitat also has a healthy population of American Alligators. Children can study the ecosystems of the grasslands, streams, and marshes. They provide salt- water fishing in East Galveston Bay.

Hours: Open daily during daylight hours.

Price: FREE to the general public

Armand Bayou Nature Center

8500 Bay Area Blvd.
Houston, TX
281-474-2551
Armand Bayou Nature Center is a 2500-acre preserve. They have indoor and out door exhibits, children's programs, guided tours, environmental education activities, and hands on experiences. Children can study the ecosystems of the tall grass prairies, and the hardwood forests. They have also recreated a 100 –year- old Gulf Coast farm that includes a fully restored house and barn.

Hours: Wednesday – Saturday 9:00a.m. To 5:00p.m. And Sunday 12:00p.m. To Dusk

Price: Children 5-17, $1.00
Adults 18-61, $2.50
4yrs. and under are FREE

Galveston Island State Park

14901 F.M. 3005
Galveston, TX
409-737-1222
This State Park offers a view of a barrier island ecosystem, a coastal prairie, mudflats, and the wetlands. The areas of study are forest, grasslands, desert, marshes, canyons, beaches, caves, and man made structures. They have a museum, campfire programs, environmental education activities, and interactive displays.

Hours: 8a.m. to 5p.m. daily

Price: $.50 per person

Texas Parks and Wildlife

713-203-2915

www.tpwd.state.tx.us/edu/major-metro-houston.phtml

The Texas Parks and Wildlife division has many outdoor education programs. In Houston we have a program called the Houston Urban Outdoor Program, or HUOP. They will come to your child's school and give a presentation on wildlife and outdoor activities in our area. Our area representative is Dawn Bello. She offers special monthly outdoor programs, like fishing, at places like Gander Mountain. She will also set up a program for your child's school. Please contact her with any questions and she will be happy to help you.

Scenic Drives

Texas Escapes

www.texasescapes.com/Texas-Drives

Find a scenic drive anywhere you want to go in the state of Texas. Drives are sorted by region. For example, there is a 10.6-mile drive between New Braunfels and Canyon Lake Dam, which crosses the Guadalupe River four times. So much to see! Enjoy Texas on your next road trip.

Scouting

Boy Scouts of America

Sam Houston Area Council
2225 N. Loop West
Houston, TX

The Boy Scouts of America was incorporated to provide a program for community organizations that offers effective character, citizenship, and personal fitness training for youth.

Boy Scouting is one of three membership divisions of the BSA. The other two are Cub Scouting and Venturing. The Boy Scout program is available to boys who have earned the Arrow of Light Award, have completed the fifth grade, or who are age 11 through 17 years old. They must also subscribe to the Scout Oath and Law. The program achieves the BSA's objectives of developing character, citizenship, and personal fitness qualities among youth by focusing on a vigorous program of outdoor activities.

Call the Sam Houston Area Council to find a den or troop in your area.

Girl Scouts of Texas

San Jacinto Council
Houston, TX
713-292-0300
800-392-4340
Girl Scouts was integrated before the civil rights movement and went international before the United Nations was formed. They had a conservation program before Earth Day and hiked in the wilderness before women wore trousers. Girl Scouts of Texas is a statewide organization. They are committed to developing character and citizenship in young girls, as demonstrated in their program, "Texas Girls Grow Strong". Every adult who shares this dream is welcome to join.

Call the San Jacinto Council to find a troop in your area.

Chapter 3

Community Recreation

Chapter 3

Community Recreation

Throughout Houston there are many opportunities for children of all ages to participate in youth sports and recreation. Most of the sports programs offered through these community recreation programs are recreational and non-competitive in nature, although some recreation programs do offer competitive leagues.

Community Recreation

The City of Houston runs a large recreation program, with 56 community recreation facilities that offer a wide range of recreation programs. Other cities around Houston also offer recreation programs through their community centers. We have also included YMCA facilities in the area. This section was created as a quick reference to compare each center and what they have to offer. We tried to include as many recreation programs in this section as possible, but many centers offer many more programs than are listed in this section. We could also not list every Community Center in Houston. We hoped instead to try and include the centers with the most amenities and the most programs. If you are interested in everything a center has to offer, contact them and they can provide more complete information. Please note that programs and activities are changing constantly, and most programs are seasonal, or could be terminated at any time due to the lack of participants, changing program coordinators, etc.

Program Fees

Any Youth Sports program offered through the City of Houston is FREE of charge. City community centers will be noted with the website **www.houstontx.gov/parks** . Sometimes there will be a nominal fee for special classes and activities. However other city community centers will charge fees for services. Fees are usually affordable and some offer reduced rates for those with lower incomes. Each center can provide the specific fee information for everything they offer.

Also remember to check with your subdivision and Homeowners association for your communities programs.

Parent Involvement/Coaching

Getting involved in your child's sports and activities is so important in helping them succeed. Recreation departments are always in need of parents who will be willing to volunteer to coach many of the sports they offer. Two or three hours each week for practice, game (which you're probably attending anyway), and contacting the team members weekly is usually all it takes. You can also team up with friends to help coach a team so you can share the responsibility.

Traditional vs. Nontraditional Sports and Recreation

The traditional sports such as basketball, baseball, soccer, and football are the popular sports that a majority of the recreation departments offer. However, nontraditional sports are also becoming more popular, such as bowling, gymnastics, horseback riding and fencing. It's great to get your child involved in different programs and activities to give them an opportunity to try new things.

Outdoor Activities / Summer Camps

Different centers offer a variety of outdoor activities and summer day camps for kids. There was such a variety that all of the outdoor activities and summer camps had to be crammed under one title, "outdoor activities". Contact the centers that offer these activities to find out more details about what they offer in the summer.

Recreation Center Amenities	
BP = Basketball Pavilion	P = Playground
HBT = Hike and Bike Trail	RC = Racquetball Courts
IG = Indoor Gym	SP = Swimming Pool
LSF = Lighted Sports Field	TC = Tennis Court

Youth Sports	
BB = Baseball	SB = Softball
BSK = Basketball	TB = T-Ball
FF = Flag football	TN = Tennis
G = Golf	TF = Track & Field
S = Soccer	V = Volleyball

Classes/Activities	
AC = Arts & Crafts	GT = Gymnastics/Tumbling
B = Boxing	MA = Martial Arts
C = Cheerleading	OA = Outdoor Activities/Camps
CY = Cycling	SC = Sports Camps
D = Dance	SW = Swimming Lessons

NORTH

Conroe Branch – YMCA
10245 Owen Dr., Conroe TX 77304
936-441-9622
www.ymca.com
Youth Sports: BB, BSK, S, SB, TB, V
Classes/Activities: AC, G, SW

North Harris County – YMCA
17125 Ella blvd., Houston TX 77090
281-444-3550
www.ymca.com
Youth Sports: BB, BSK, S, SB, TB, V
Classes/Activities: AC, SW

Oscar Johnson JR. Community Center
100 Park Place, Conroe TX
936-494-3860
www.sportslineup.com
Amenities: IG, RC, SP
Youth sports: BSK, FF, SB, TN, TF, V
Classes/Activities: AC, C, GT, MA, OA

South Montgomery County - YMCA
6145 Shadow Bend, The Woodlands TX
281-367-9622
www.ymca.com
Youth Sports: BB, BSK, S, SB, TB, V
Classes/Activities: AC, G, SW

The Woodlands Community Center
5310 Research Forest Dr. ,
The Woodlands TX
281-210-3950
www.thewoodlandsassociations.org
Amenities: SP, IG, TC
Youth Sports: TN, BSK,
Classes/Activities: D, GT, MA, SC

NORTHWEST

Carverdale Community Center
9801 Tanner, Houston TX 77041
713-895-6141
www.houstontx.gov/parks
Amenities: BP, HBT, P, TC
Youth Sports: BB, T
Classes Activities: AC, OA, SC

Clay Road Family – YMCA
10655 Clay rd, Houston TX 77041
713-467-9622
www.ymca.com
Youth Sports: BB, BSK, S, SB, TB,V
Classes/Activities: AC, G, SW

Cypress Creek – YMCA
19915 State Hwy 249, Houston TX 77070
281-469-1481
www.ymca.com
Youth Sports: BB, BSK, S, SB, TB, V
Classes/Activities: AC, G, SW

Freed Community Center
6818 Shady Villa, Houston TX 77055
713-682-4467
www.houstontx.gov/parks
Amenities: HBT, IG, LSF, P
Youth Sports: BB, BSK, FF, G,
Classes/Activities:

Independence Heights Community Center
603 East 35th, Houston TX 77022
713-867-0373
www.houstontx.gov/parks
Amenities: BP, LSF, P, SP, TC
Youth Sports: BSK, S
Classes/Activities:

Lincoln Community Center
979 Grenshaw, Houston TX 77007
281-447-0158
www.houstontx.gov/parks
Amenities: HBT, BP, LSF, SP, TC
Youth Sports: BSK, S, TN
Classes/Activities:

Love Community Center
1000 West 12th, Houston TX 77008
713-867-0497
www.houstontx.gov/parks
Amenities: BP, HBT, IG, LSF, P, SP
Youth Sports: BB, BSK, TN
Classes/Activities:

Montie Beach Community Center
9311 E. Ave. P, Houston TX 77012
713-928-4803
www.houstontx.gov/parks
Amenities: HBT, LSF, P, TC
Youth Sports: BB, BSK, TN
Classes/Activities:

Northwest Branch – YMCA
1234 W. 34th St, Houston TX 77018
713-869-3378
www.ymca.com
Youth Sports: BB, BSK, S, SB, TB, V
Classes/Activities: AC, G, SW

Stude Community Center
1031 Stude, Houston TX 77009
713-867-0496
www.houstontx.gov/parks
Amenities: HBT, IG, LSF, P, SP, Water Park
Youth Sports: BB, BSK,
Classes/ Activities:

Woodland Community Center
212 Parkview, Houston TX 77009
713-867-0401
www.houstontx.gov/parks
Amenities: BP, IG, LSF, TC
Youth Sports: BB, BSK, TN
Classes/ Activities:

NORTHEAST

Clinton Community Center
200 Mississippi, Houston TX 77029
713-673-0955
www.houstontx.gov/parks
Amenities: BP, HBT, LSF, P, SP, TC, 9-hole Golf Course
Youth Sports: BB, BSK, S, TN, V
Classes/Activities: OA, SC

Finnigan Community Center
4900 Providence, Houston TX 77020
713-678-7385
www.houstontx.gov/parks
Amenities: HBT, IG, LSF, P, SP, TC
Youth Sports: BB, BSK,V
Classes/Activities: AC, OA, SC

Lake Houston – YMCA
2420 W. Lake Houston Pkwy., Kingwood TX 77339
281-360-2500
www.ymca.com
Youth Sports: BB, BSK, S, SB, TB, V
Classes/Activities: AC, G, SW

Melrose Community Center
1001 Canino, Houston TX 77076
173-895-6141
www.houstontx.gov/parks
Amenities: LSF, P, TC, Volleyball Courts, Water Park, 18-hole Golf Course
Youth Sports: T
Classes/Activities: OA, SC

Moody Community Center
3725 Fulton, Houston TX 77009
713-692-6925
www.houstontx.gov/parks
Amenities: HBT, IG, LSF, P, SP, TC
Youth Sports: BSK, S
Classes/Activities: OA, SC

Northeast Branch – YMCA
7901 Tidwell rd, Houston TX 77028
713-633-0530
www.ymca.com
Youth Sports: BB, BSK, S, SB, TB, V
Classes/Activities: Ac, G, SW

Perez Selena Community Center
6402 Market, Houston TX 77020
713-675-2151
www.houstontx.gov/parks
Amenities: HBT, IG, LSF, P, SP, Volleyball courts
Youth Sports: BSK, V
Classes/Activities: OA, SC

Robinson Sr. Community Center
1422 Ledwicke, Houston TX 77029
713-674-2401
www.houstontx.gov/parks
Amenities: BP, HBT, SP, TC
Youth Sports: BSK, TN
Classes/Activities: OA, SC

Hobart Taylor Community Center
8100 Kenton, Houston TX 77028
713-674-3959
www.houstontx.gov/parks
Amenities: BP, HBT, LSF, P, SP
Youth Sports: BB, BSK, S
Classes/Activities: OA, SC

Tidwell Community Center
9720 Spaulding, Houston TX 77016
713-636-8221
www.houstontx.gov/parks
Amenities: BP, IG, LSF, P, SP, TC
Youth Sports: BSK, TN
Classes/Activities: OA, SC, SW

Tuffly Community Center
3200 Russell, Houston TX 77026
713-674-2355
www.houstontx.gov/parks
Amenities: BP, HBT, LSF, SP
Youth Sports: BSK, FF, S, V
Classes/Activities: OA, SC

SOUTHWEST

Alief Branch – YMCA
7850 Howell Sugar Land rd, Houston TX 77083
281-495-9100
www.ymca.com
Youth Sports: BB, BSK, S, SB, TB, V
Classes/ Activities: AC, G, SW

Alief Community Center
11903 Bellaire, Houston TX 77072
281-983-8137
www.houstontx.gov/parks
Amenities: IG, LSF, P, SP, TC
Youth Sports:
Classes/Activities:

Burnett Bayland Community Center
6200 Chimney Rock, Houston TX 77081
713-668-4516
www.houstontx.gov
Amenities: BP, HBT, LSF, P, Water Park
Youth Sports: BSK
Classes/Activities:

Emancipation Community Center
3018 Dowling, Houston TX 77004
713-284-1977
www.houstontx.gov/parks
Amenities: BP, IG, LSF, P, SP, TC
Youth Sports: BSK
Classes/Activities:

Marian Community Center
11101 South Gessner, Houston TX 77071
713-773-7015
www.houstontx.gov/parks
Amenities: BP, HBT, IG, LSF, P, TC
Youth Sports: BSK
Classes/Activities:

Sharpstown Community Center
6600 Harbor Town, Houston TX 77036
713-988-5328
www.houstontx.gov/parks
Amenities: P, SP, TC, Golf Course
Youth Sports: BSK
Classes/Activities:

Sunnyside Community Center
3502 Bellfort, Houston TX 77051
713-734-5061
www.houstontx.gov/parks
Amenities: BP, HBT, IG, LSF, P, SP, TC
Youth Sports: BSK
Classes/Activities:

T.W. Davis Memorial – YMCA
911 Thompson Rd., Richmond TX 77469
281-341-0791
www.ymca.com
Youth Sports: BB, BSK, S, SB, TB, V
Classes/Activities: AC, G, SW

Windsor Village Community Center
14441 Croquet, Houston TX 77085
713-726-7113
www.houstontx.gov/parks
Ameitites: BP, LSF, P, SP, TC
Youth Sports: BSK, TN
Classes/Activities:

Four Corners Recreation Center
15700 Old Richmond Rd, Sugar Land TX 77478
281-983-9294
www.co.fort-bend.tx.us
Amenitites: BP, HBT, LSF, Volleyball court
Youth Sports: N/A
Classes/Activities: Summer Camp

SOUTHEAST

Beverly Hills Community Center
9800 Kingspoint, Houston TX 77075
713-948-9065
www.houstontx.gov/parks
Amenities: HBT, LSF, P, SP, TC
Youth Sports: BB, BSK, TN
Classes/Activities: AC, D, MA, OA, SW

C.V. Vic Coppinger Family – YMCA
2700 YMCA Dr., Pearland TX 77581
281-485-6805
www.ymca.com
Youth Sports: BB, BSK, S SB, TB, V
Classes/Activities: AC, G, SW

Eastwood Community Center
5020 Harrisburg, Houston TX 77011
713-928-4801
www.houstontx.gov/parks
Amenities: BP, HBT, LSF, P, SP, TC
Youth Sports: BB, BSK, S
Classes/Activities: AC, OA, SW

Edgewood Community Center
5803 Bellfort, Houston TX 77033
713-734-8434
www.houstontx.gov/parks
Amenities: BP, HBT, IG, LSF P, Water Park
Youth Sports: BB, BSK, FF, S, V
Classes/Activities: OA

Ingrado Community Center
7302 Keller, Houston TX 77012
713-643-4764
www.houstontx.gov/parks
Amenities: BP, HBT, LSF, P, TC
Youth Sports: BB, G, S, TN
Classes/Activities: OA

MacGregor Community Center
5225 Calhoun, Houston TX 77021
713-747-8650
www.houstontx.gov/parks
Amenities: BP, HBP, LSF, P, SP, TC, 18-hole golf course
Youth Sports: BB, BSK, G, S, TF, TN
Classes/Activities: AC, D, OA, Roller Hockey

Mason Community Center
541 South 75th, Houston TX 77023
713-928-2118
www.houstontx.gov/parks
Amenities: HBT, IG, LSF, SP, TC, 9-hole golf course
Youth Sports: BB, BSK, G, S
Classes/Activities: AC, D, MA, OA

San Jacinto – YMCA
1716 Jasmine Dr., Pasadena TX 77503
713-473-9441
www.ymca.com
Youth Sports: BB, BSK, S, SB, TB, V
Classes/Activities: AC, G, SW

Settegast Community Center
3000 Garrow, Houston TX 77003
713-238-2200
www.houstontx.gov/parks
Amenities: BP, LSF, P, TC, water park
Youth Sports: BB, BSK, TN
Classes/Activities: OA, SW

The City of Friendswood Community Services
910 S. Friendswood dr.
2nd floor in City Hall
281-996-3220
www.ci.friendswood.tx.us
Youth Sports: BB
Classes/Activitites: OA, SW

Kermet H. Applewhite Sports & Rec. Complex
16511 Diana ln., Houston TX
281-488-0360
www.clcca.org
Youth Sports: Can give referrals
Classes/Activities: MA, SW, Yoga

Pearland Parks and Recreation
2947 E. Broadway suite 300
281-652-1673
www.leisureexpress.com
Youth Sports: BB, BSK, FF, G, S, SB, T, V
Classes/Activities: AC, D, MA, OA, SC

GALVESTON

Galveston County – YMCA
1707 23rd St., Houston TX 77253
409-763-4607
www.ymca.com
Youth Sports: BB, BSK, S, SB, TB, V
Classes/Activities: AC, G, SW

Wright Cuney Park
718 41st St., Galveston TX
409-766-2140
www.cityofgalveston.org
Youth Sports: BSK, V
Classes/Activities: AC, G, MA, Boxing

NORTH - Swimming Pools	Indoor	Outdoor
Conroe Branch – YMCA 10245 Owen Dr., Conroe TX 77304 **936-441-9622**	X(heated)	
North Harris County – YMCA 17125 Ella blvd., Houston TX 77090 **281-444-3550**	X	
Oscar Johnson JR. Community Center 100 Park Place, Conroe TX **936-494-3860**	X	
South Montgomery County – YMCA 6145 Shadow Bend, The Woodlands TX **281-367-9622**	X	X
The Woodlands Community Center 5310 Research Forest Dr. ,The Woodlands TX **281-210-3950**	X	

NORTHWEST – Swimming Pools	Indoor	Outdoor
Clay Road Family – YMCA (2 pools) 10655 Clay rd, Houston TX 77041 **713-467-9622**	X(heated)	
Cypress Creek – YMCA 19915 State Hwy 249, Houston TX 77070 **281-469-1481**	X	X
Independence Heights Community Center 603 East 35th, Houston TX 77022 **713-867-0373**	X	

Lincoln Community Center 979 Grenshaw, Houston TX 77007 **281-447-0158**	X	
Love Community Center 1000 West 12th, Houston TX 77008 **713-867-0497**	X	
Northwest Branch – YMCA 1234 W. 34th St, Houston TX 77018 **713-869-3378**	X	
Stude Community Center 1031 Stude, Houston TX 77009 **713-867-0496**	X	

NORTHEAST – Swimming Pools	Indoor	Outdoor
Clinton Community Center 200 Mississippi, Houston TX 77029 **713-673-0955**	X	
Finnigan Community Center 4900 Providence, Houston TX 77020 **713-678-7385**	X	
Lake Houston – YMCA 2420 W. Lake Houston Pkwy. Kingwood TX 77339 **281-360-2500**	X	
Moody Community Center 3725 Fulton, Houston TX 77009 **713-692-6925**	X	
Northeast Branch – YMCA 7901 Tidwell rd, Houston TX 77028 **713-633-0530**	X	

Perez Selena Community Center 6402 Market, Houston TX 77020 **713-675-2151**	X	
Robinson Sr. Community Center 1422 Ledwicke, Houston TX 77029 **713-674-2401**	X	
Hobart Taylor Community Center 8100 Kenton, Houston TX 77028 **713-674-3959**	X	
Tidwell Community Center 9720 Spaulding, Houston TX 77016 **713-636-8221**	X	
Tuffly Community Center 3200 Russell, Houston TX 77026 **713-674-2355**	X	

SOUTHWEST – Swimming Pools	Indoor	Outdoor
Alief Branch – YMCA 7850 Howell Sugar Land rd, Houston TX 77083 **281-495-9100**	X	
Alief Community Center 11903 Bellaire, Houston TX 77072 **281-983-8137**	X	
Emancipation Community Center 3018 Dowling, Houston TX 77004 **713-284-1977**	X	
Sharpstown Community Center 6600 Harbor Town, Houston TX 77036 **713-988-5328**	X	

	Indoor	Outdoor
Sunnyside Community Center 3502 Bellfort, Houston TX 77051 **713-734-5061**	X	
T.W. Davis Memorial – YMCA 911 Thompson Rd., Richmond TX 77469 **281-341-0791**	X(heated)	
Windsor Village Community Center 14441 Croquet, Houston TX 77085 **713-726-7113**	X	

SOUTHEAST - Swimming Pools	Indoor	Outdoor
Beverly Hills Community Center 9800 Kingspoint, Houston TX 77075 **713-948-9065**	X	
C.V. Vic Coppinger Family – YMCA 2700 YMCA Dr., Pearland TX 77581 **281-485-6805**	X(heated)	
Eastwood Community Center 5020 Harrisburg, Houston TX 77011 **713-928-4801**	X	
MacGregor Community Center 5225 Calhoun, Houston TX 77021 **713-747-8650**	X	
Mason Community Center 541 South 75th, Houston TX 77023 **713-928-2118**	X	

San Jacinto – YMCA 1716 Jasmine Dr., Pasadena TX 77503 **713-473-9441**	X	
The City of Friendswood Community Services 910 S. Friendswood dr. 2nd floor in City Hall **281-996-3220**	X	
Kermet H. Applewhite Sports & Rec. Complex 16511 Diana Ln., Houston TX **281-488-0360**	X	X
Pearland Parks and Recreation 2947 E. Broadway suite 300 **281-652-1673**	X	X

GALVESTON - Swimming Pools	Indoor	Outdoor
Galveston County – YMCA 1707 23rd St., Houston TX 77253 **409-763-4607**	X	

Chapter 4

Sports

Chapter 4

Sports

Participation in sports promotes healthy development in young children, and helps to teach cooperative play, teamwork, good sportsmanship, and fair play. Sports help kids to develop their social competence, their ability to get along and be accepted by friends, family, teachers, and coaches. Children also learn to give and accept feedback and evaluate themselves and their performance.

When helping your child choose a sport consider their personality. Would they do better in an intense team sport with more competition, or one that allows more autonomy like swimming or gymnastics? Set your child up for success by finding a good fit for their personality and talents.

Nevertheless, let the child choose. It is important to offer constant support and love, while trying no to spread them too thin. While we all want our children to achieve great feats of success, it is important to remember that they are still children and need freedom to learn and explore at their own pace.

The key is that parents support their children and provide positive feedback. Emphasize fun while de-emphasizing competition. In order to encourage a child in sports they need to feel comfortable, no matter what their skill level. Sports teach children about themselves. Since our children watch our responses, and those of their coaches, for signs of approval or disapproval of their behavior, it is critical that we offer as much positive feedback as possible.

Stay actively involved in your children's sports experiences. Provide support and feedback, attend games and talk about them afterwards. Have realistic expectations of your child; learn about the sport your child is involved in. Help your child handle disappointments and most importantly model positive and respectful behavior.

The most important thing of all: HAVE FUN!

Read on to find out about leagues and sports opportunities in your area. Remember to check with your local community Recreation Center for different leagues and programs. (Community Recreation – Chapter 3)

Encouraging Girls in Sports

Nike came out with a commercial in 1996 that promoted girl's participation in sports. The ad moves from one girl to another as each gives a reason why young girls should play sports. They said:

If you let me play sports... *I will like myself more*
If you let me play sports... *I will have more self-confidence*
If you let me play sports... *I will be 60% less likely to get breast cancer*
If you let me play sports... *I will be more likely to leave a man who beats me*
If you let me play sports... *I will be less likely to get pregnant before I want to*
If you let me play sports... *I will learn what it means to be strong*
If you let me play sports...

Eteamz

www.eteamz.active.com

This is a great resource to find any sports team in your area. They have a database of thousands of local teams. Just click " Search Here", pick what sport you need information on and then enter your zip code. It is so easy to use!

Baseball

Little League

www.littleleague.org

This website has every baseball district in the U.S. To find a league in Houston and surrounding areas click on "Find a Local League". Then click on the eteamz link, click on Texas, and you will have a complete list of teams.

The following listings are ALL of the little league baseball teams in our area listed by their district. There are 7 districts in this area. We are providing you with the district information and from their website you can access the individual team information.

NORTH

Texas District 25

2500 Frick Rd., Houston TX 77038

www.eteamz.active.com/aldinell

Teams: 10 Teams in district 25

- Aldine district LL
- Denver Harbor LL
- Heights-Norhill LL
- Huffman LL
- Lindale LL
- North Houston American LL
- North Houston National LL
- Northside National LL
- Northwest National LL
- Parkwood National LL

Texas District 28

1002 Woodchurch, Houston, TX 77073

www.eteamz.active.com/district28

Teams: 7 teams in district 28

- Conroe LL
- Magnolia LL
- Montgomery LL
- Northwest 45 LL
- ORWALL American LL
- ORWALL National LL
- Tomball LL

Spring Klein Sports Association

P.O. Box 12022 Spring TX 77391

www.sksa.com

This association offers Spring and Fall Baseball programs as well as Summer Camps and Tournaments. You can register for teams online. Program offers baseball programs to children ages
5 yrs. to 14 yrs.

NORTHWEST

Texas District 16

Houston TX, 77043
Contact: Charlie Fox
713-462-0002
www.eteamz.active.com/texasdistrict16
Teams: 16 teams in district 16

- Bayland Park LL
- Bear Creek LL
- Bellaire LL
- Breas Bayou LL
- First Colony American LL
- First Colony National LL
- Katy American LL
- Katy National LL
- Memorial-Ashford LL
- Misssouri City LL
- Neartown LL
- Post Oak LL
- Spring Branch American LL
- West Oaks LL
- West University LL
- Westbury LL

Cy-Fair Sports Association

P.O. Box 841751 Houston TX 77284
www.cy-fairsports.org
This is one of the largest sports associations in the Houston area. Baseball is offered to children ages 4 – 18 years old. They also offer Basketball, Cheerleading, Drill Team, Football, Volleyball and Wrestling.

Price: Baseball - $100.00 per player

SOUTHWEST

Texas District 18
Bay City, TX 77414
979-245-2247
www.eteamz.active.com/texasdistrict18
Teams: 25 teams in district 18

- Alvin LL
- Angelton LL
- Baycity LL
- Boling Newgulf Youth LL
- Brazoria LL
- Brazos LL
- Clute LL
- Danbury Tri Bayou LL
- East Bernard LL
- El Campo LL
- Freeport LL
- Lake Jackson American LL
- Lake Jackson National LL
- Lamar American LL
- Lamar National LL
- Needville LL
- Palacious LL
- Rosenburg National LL
- Sugar Land LL
- Sweeney LL
- Tidehaven LL
- Van Vleck LL
- West Columbia LL
- West Sugar Land LL
- Wharton LL

SOUTHEAST

Texas District 14
408 Brookdale Dr.
League City, TX 77573
281-316-2232
www.eteamz.active.com/texasdistrict14
Teams: 18 teams in district 14

- Bayshore LL
- Bayside Area LL
- Bayside LL
- Baytown East LL
- Baytown North LL
- Baytown West LL
- Dickinson LL
- Galveston West-Isle LL
- Hitchcock LL
- Island LL
- La Marque-West Texas City LL
- League City American LL
- League City National LL
- Nasa Area East LL
- Nasa Area West LL
- Santa Fe LL
- Texas City American LL
- Texas City National LL

Texas District 15

Contact: Ferris M. Maness

281-489-9646

www.eteamz.active.com/td15

Teams: 9 teams in district 15

- Dixie LL
- Friendswood LL
- Houston East End LL
- Magnolia National LL
- OFA LL
- Pearland Maroon LL
- Pearland White LL
- Sagemont Beverly Hills LL
- South Central LL

Texas District 17

Galena Park, TX 77547

Contact: Darla DiStefano

713-455-9261

www.eteamz.active.com/catchthestinggalenaparkll

Teams: 13 teams in district 17

- Barbers Hill LL
- Channelview LL
- Deer Park LL
- Galena Park LL
- Highlands LL
- North Channel LL
- North Shore LL
- Pasadena Deepwater LL
- Pasadena International LL
- Sheldon LL
- South Houston LL

Basketball

(Check out recreation centers for more information)

Eteamz

www.eteamz.active.com

Find a basketball league in your area by clicking on " Find a Team", select basketball, and then enter your zip code. It's that easy!

Football

NORTH

All American Youth Football and Drill Team

P.O. Box 11148, Spring, TX 77391

www.aayfdt.org

This football league serves residents in Tomball, Klein and the Spring area. Find your attendance zone and the website will direct you to the team you will play for. Click on your team and all of their contact information will be listed.

North Harris County Pee Wee Football League

www.leaguelineup.com/nhcpwfl

This league serves North Harris County and offers football programs to children ages 5 to 12 years. They have freshman through Senior Varsity football teams.

South County Football League

P.O. Box 7882, The Woodlands, TX 77381

713-801-3515

www.scfootball.org

This football league serves residents of Montgomery County and North Harris County. This league offers football and cheerleading programs to children ages 5 through 12 years.

NORTHWEST

Cy-Fair Sports Association

P.O. Box 841751, Houston, TX 77284

www.cy-fairsports.org

This is one of the largest sports associations in the Houston area. Football is offered to children ages 4 – 18 years old. They also offer Baseball, Basketball, Cheerleading, Drill Team, Volleyball and Wrestling.

Price: Football - $105.00-$140.00 per player

Katy Youth Football

P.O. Box 5543, Katy, TX 77491

713-331-1907

www.katyyouthfootball.com

You can find any youth football team in the Katy area by using this website. This football program offers flag football as well as tackle.

NORTHEAST

Humble Area Football League

www.humblefootball.org

This league provides football and cheerleading.

Ages: 5-12 yrs.

Price: Football $105.00 and $120.00 required raffle ticket sales
Cheerleading $135.00 and $120.00 required raffle ticket sales.

SOUTHWEST

Fortbend Youth Football League

P.O. Box 1428
Missouri City, TX 77459
281-261-2222
www.eteamz.active.com/fbyfl

This league serves residents of Fortbend County and Southwest Houston. The league consists of 16 teams located throughout Fortbend and Southwest Houston. They offer contact football and cheerleading.

Ages: 7-12yrs.

Price: Contact for more information.

SOUTHEAST

Bay Area Football League

www.bayareafootball-league.com

This league provides football and drill activities to the youth of Southeast Houston. They have over 15 teams all over the Southeast area. Check the link to individual teams through the leagues website.

Lacrosse

Houston Youth Lacrosse Organization
Contact: Steve
281-997-8377
www.hylax.org
This organization makes lacrosse available to youth all over the Houston area. On their website simply click "links" and it will direct you to a team in your area. Leagues are available to boys in the 5th through 8th grades. They do provide summer camps to girls as well as boys.

Texas Rugby Union
www.texasrugbyunion.com
Through this website you can find information about youth rugby programs in your area as well as all across the state of Texas.

Houston Rugby Club
Westland Family YMCA
10402 Fondren Rd. Houston, TX 77096
Contact: Will Wornardt-President
281-467-3814
www.houstonrugby.org
This club meets at Westland YMCA. They provide instruction and organized games for girls and boys in the Houston area. Please see their website or contact someone in the community for more information.

Woodlands Rugby Football Club
www.woodlandsrugby.com
This leagues games run form January through March and they have a summer season of 7 games. Learn to play with this league but also play other rugby teams across the area. Scholarship programs are available through this club.

Ages: 12-19yrs.

Price: $55.00 per year

Soccer

All soccer programs in Southeast Texas are under the direction and guidelines of the South Texas Youth Soccer Association. In Houston there are four major Soccer Associations and their contact information is listed below. Within these associations they have member clubs, or soccer clubs. These clubs are the soccer teams your child will participate in. Each association offers recreational soccer to children ages 4-16 yrs. They also participate in competitive leagues and tournaments. You will find a complete listing below with each club's website address. Any questions can be directed to the Soccer Association or the individual teams.

NORTH, NORTHWEST, NORTHEAST

Timberline Youth Soccer Association
www.timberlinesoccer.com
Soccer Club Members:

- Aldine United Soccer Club
- Bear Creek Soccer Club – **www.bearcreeksoccer.org**
- Cy-Fair Soccer Club – **www.cyfairsoccer.org**
- Kingwood Alliance Soccer Club – **www.kingwoodalliance.com**
- Klein Soccer Club – **www.kleinsoccerclub.org**
- Texas Heatwave Soccer Club – **www.txheatwave.com**
- Texas Rush Soccer Club – **www.texasrush.com**

NORTHWEST

Katy Youth Soccer Association
P.O. Box 5206
Katy, TX 77491
www.kysa.com
Soccer Club Member:

- Katy Youth Soccer Club – www.kysa.com

SOUTHWEST

Houston Youth Soccer Association
President Chris Delay
www.hysa.us
Soccer Club Members:

- Albion Soccer Club – **www.albionhurricanes.org**
- Bellaire Soccer Club – **www.bellairesoccerclub.org**
- First Colony Soccer Club – **www.firstcolonysoccer.com**

- Lamar Soccer Club – **www.lamarsoccerclub.org**
- New Territory Soccer Club – **www.newterritorysoccer.org**
- Quail Valley Soccer Club – **www.qusa.com**
- St. Francis Soccer Club – **www.saintsoccer.com**
- St. Thomas Soccer Club – **www.stes.org**
- St. Thomas Moore Soccer Club – **www.stmoorenews.com**
- Sugar Land Soccer Club – **www.sugarlandsoccer.org**
- Westbury Soccer Club – **www.westburysoccer.org**
- Westside Soccer Club – **www.westsidesoccer.org**
- West Houston Soccer Club – **www.westhoustonsoccerclub.org**
- West University Soccer Club – www.westusoccer.org

SOUTHEAST, GALVESTON

Bay Area Youth Soccer Association
17511 El Camino Real # 114
Houston, TX 77058
281-990-8887
www.baysa.org
Soccer Club Members:

- Alvin Youth Soccer Club – **www.alvinsoccer.org**
- Baytown Saints Youth Soccer Club – **www.baytownsaints.com**
- Clear Lake United Youth Soccer Club – **www.clearlakeunited.org**
- Dickinson Youth Soccer Club – **www.dickinsonyouth.org**
- Friendswood Soccer Club – **www.eteamz.active.com/fwsoccer**
- Galveston Youth Soccer Club – **www.galvestonyouthsoccer.org**
- League City Youth Soccer Club – **www.leaguecitysoccer.org**
- Manuel Youth Soccer Club – **www.geocities.com/manuelsoccer**
- North Channel Youth Soccer Club – **www.northchannelsoccer.com**
- Pearland Youth Soccer Club – **www.pearlandsoccer.com**
- Quest Youth Soccer Club – **www.questyouthsoccer.org**
- South Belt Youth Soccer Club – **www.auspex-inc.com/sbysc**
- Texas City Youth Soccer Club – **www.tcsoccer.org**

Solo Sports

Aircraft School

Civil Air Patrol Cadet Programs

www.level2.cap.gov

The Civil Air Patrol (CAP) Cadet Program provides our youth with many opportunities to develop leadership skills through an aerospace program. The minimum age to join a cadet program is 12 years old, and the maximum age to join is 18 years. However, cadets can continue in the program until they are 21 years of age. The best way to learn about the cadet program is to contact a local squad unit in your area. Squads are listed by area below.

NORTH

Unit Name: HQ GROUP 13
20803 Stuebner Airline Rd # 23
Spring, TX 77379
Meets Saturdays at 10:00am
Unit Contact(s):
www.grp13txwgcap.org
COMMANDER: Maj Dennis Cima
PHONE: 281-392-9572

Unit Name: 7-6 AIR CAVALRY COMPOSITE SQDN
4724 South Parkway
Conroe, TX 77303
Meets Tuesdays at 7:00pm
4724 South Parkway US Army Reserve Center
Conroe, TX 77303
Unit Contact(s):
COMMANDER: Maj Stephen Dicker
PHONE: 281-541-1725

Unit Name: DELTA COMPOSITE SQDN
20803 Stuebner Airline Rd # 23
Spring TX 77379
Meets Tuesdays at 7:00pm
David Wayne Hooks Memorial Airport 20803 Stuebner Airline Dr.
Spring, TX 77379
Unit Contact(s):
URL http://delta.txwg.cap.gov/index.html
COMMANDER: Capt Daniel Katen
PHONE: 281-367-2450

NORTHWEST

Unit Name: THUNDERBIRD COMPOSITE SQDN 18000 Groesechke Rd 1-E-C
Houston, TX 77084
Meets Tuesdays at 6:45pm
Unit Contact(s):
COMMANDER: Maj Michael Hopkins
EMAIL: michael.hopkins@pathfinderlwd.com

Unit Name: SHELDON CADET SQDN
King Middle School 8530 CE King Parkway
Houston, TX 77044
Meets Wednesdays at 2:00pm
Unit Contact(s):
COMMANDER: Capt Roger Stafford
PHONE: 281-272-4374

NORTHEAST

Unit Name: MARAUDER COMPOSITE SQDN
P O Box 5144
Kingwood, TX 77325
Meets Mondays at 6:30pm
3803 W Lake Houston Parkway- Christ the King Lutheran Church
Kingwood, TX 77339
Unit Contact(s):
COMMANDER: Capt James Bryant
PHONE: 281-689-7499

Unit Name: HOUSTON COMPOSITE SQUADRON
1442 Kingwood Dr #198
Kingwood, TX 77339
Meets Mondays at 7:00pm
20300 Cypreswood Dr.
Humble, TX 77338
Unit Contact(s):
COMMANDER: Lt Col Gary Westphal
PHONE: 281-443-2826

SOUTHWEST

Unit Name: SUGARLAND COMPOSITE SQDN
7414 Belle Glenn Dr.
Houston, TX 77072
Meets Tuesdays at 7:00pm
Sugar Land Airport, Hangar 108 Far side of airport/behind tower
Sugar Land, TX 77478
Unit Contact(s):
COMMANDER: Lt Col Denver Radford
PHONE: 281-561-7043

Unit Name: WEST HOUSTON S.A.B.R.E. SQDN
PO Box 941784
Houston, TX 77094
Meets Thursdays at 7:00pm
West Houston Airport- 18200 Groschke Rd.
Houston, TX 77084
Unit Contact(s):
URL http://flashpages.prodigy.net/houston/TX447
COMMANDER: 1Lt Martin Padilla
PHONE: 713-463-5582

SOUTHEAST

Unit Name: TRINITY BAY COMPOSITE SQDN

7222 Shoshone Dr.
Baytown, TX 77521
Meets: Tuesdays at 7:00pm
111 W Wye Dr.
Baytown, TX 77521
Unit Contact(s):
COMMANDER: Capt Joel Marsalis
PHONE: 281-421-5585

Unit Name: BAYTOWN SENIOR SQDN

5100 Kendall Rd.
Baytown, TX 77520
Meets Mondays at 7:00pm
Cedar Bayou Community Bldg.- 7711 Hwy 146
Baytown, TX 77520
Unit Contact(s):
COMMANDER: Lt Col Don Fisher
PHONE: 281-383-1443

Golf

Most every golf course has a junior league. Contact your local golf course to find out about their junior league or their summer camps. Visit **www.golfhouston.com** to find a list of the best golf courses in the Greater Houston area.

Matt Swanson's School of Golf (2 locations)

www.houstongolfschool.com

Wild Cat Golf Club
12000 Almeda Rd.
Houston, TX 77045
281-440-1308

Sellingers Classic 3
6224 Theall Rd.
Houston, TX 77066
281-440-1308

Matt Swanson offers regular Jr. Camps to children ages 6-17yrs. These camps include 12 hours of instruction and are 3 days in length. Children can certify for the "Southern Texas PGA Little Linksters Program". They also have advanced Jr. Camps for those serious Jr. Golfers. This school also provides an after school weekly program for children in the 1st through 8th grades. Children will learn the fundamentals of golf.

Ages: 6-17 yrs for Junior camps

Price: Jr. Camp $150.00
Advanced Jr. Camps $250.00

After school program meets on Mondays and Wednesdays or Tuesdays and Thursdays from 5:00p.m. to 6:00p.m.

Ages: 1st – 8th grades

Price: $75.00 per month

Memorial Park Golf Academy
713-862-4033 ext. 4
www.memorialparkgolfacademy.com
This is a summer golf program designed to teach kids about the game of golf. There are 3 day classes held each week in the months of June and July. Hurry space is limited!

Ages: 7-14yrs.

Price: $95.00 per child.

Gymnastics

Contact the facilities for current schedules. Prices are subject to change.

NORTH

Achims Gymnastics, Inc.
22820 I-45 North
Spring, TX 77378
281-651-0933
www.achimsgymnastics.com
Classes: Super babies (6mos-2.5 yrs), Pres-school, School Age classes, Pre-team, Team, and Tumbling.

Fees: $50.00 per month for 1 class per week

Time: 60-minute classes

Basel's All Star Gymnastics and Cheer
4963 Louetta Rd.
Spring, TX 77379
281-370-2882
www.texaselitecheer.com
Classes: Mommy & Me, Pre-school, Trampoline and Tumbling, Dance, Gymnastics.

Ages: 18 months and up

Fees: $60.00 per month for 1 class per week.

Time: 40-60 minute classes.

See ad in back

International Gymnastics Academy
20100 B Holzwarth Rd.
Spring, TX
281-528-6050
www.igagym.com
Classes: Parent & Tot, Pre-school, Trampoline and Tumbling, Gymnastics.

Ages: 18 months and up

Fees: $55.00 per month

Time: 60-minute classes

Maximum Athletic Center
1500 Wilson Rd.
Conroe, TX 77304
936-539-3547
www.maximumathletics.com
Classes: Parent and Tot, Pre-school, Gymnastics, Recreational, Team, and Traveling Team.

Ages: 18 months and up

Fees: start at $52.00 per month for 1 class per week.

Time: 60-minute classes

JW Tumbles
6777 Woodlands Pkwy. Suite 208
The Woodlands TX 77382
281-298-7755
www.jwtumbles.com
Classes: Tumbles Tykes, JWT kids, Specialty
Programs, Personal Training,
Birthday parties, and Kids Night Out.
Ages: 4 months to 9 years
Fees: One time membership $35.00. Sessions begin at
$110.00. Please call
for details.
Time: 45 min – 60 minThe Little Gym of Spring

16442 Champion Forest Dr.
Spring, TX 77379
281-370-3031
www.tlgspringtx.com
Classes: Developmental Gymnastics (4mos-3yrs), Pre- school level (3-5yrs), Advanced Gymnastics (6-12yrs).

Ages: 4 months through12 yrs.

Fees: 21 week semester $282.00 per semester paid in full. 5 payments of $64.00.

Time 40-60 minute classes. Monday through Saturday

Woodlands Elite Cheer
1067 Pruitt Rd.
The Woodlands, TX 77380
281-681-1253
www.woodlandselite.com
Classes: Pre-school, Cheer, Tumbling, and Dance

Ages: 3 and up

Fees: $60.00 per month for 1 class per week

Time: 60-minute classes

NORTHWEST

Champion Gymnastics Academy
15740 Park Row Suite 500
Houston, TX 77084
281-578-2420
www.champgym.com
Classes: Mom & Me, Pre-school, Levels 1-3, Tumbling, Boys and girls Team, Recreational Team.

Ages: 18 months and up

Fees: $55.00 per month

Time: 40-60 minute classes

Cypress Academy of Gymnastics
11707 Huffmeister
Houston, TX 77065
281-469-4599
www.cypressacademy.com
Classes: Mom & Me, Pre-school, Kindergym, Developmental, Accelerated, Advanced gymnastics.

Ages: 18 months and up

Fees: $61.00 per month

Time: 45 min to 1 hour 10 minute classes

Houston North Gymnastics and Tumbling Center
11037 F.M. 1960 W.
Houston, TX 77065
281-894-8400
www.houstonnorthgym.com
Classes: Pre-school, Cheer/tumbling, Competitive teams, and Recreational classes for boys and girls.

Ages: 2 and up

Fees: Prices vary depending on type of instruction and program. Check with the office staff.

Northwest All-Star Gymnastics, Cheerleading and Dance
5701 Bingle Rd.
Houston, TX
713-681-4154
www.nwallstars.com
Classes: Mom & Me, Tots/Tumbleweeds, Cheerleading, After school program, Gymnastics, Tumbling, and Dance.

Ages: 18 months and up

Fees: $200.00 per semester. August through December

Time: 60-minute classes

Texas Star Gymnastics of Tomball
1230 Ulrich Rd.
Tomball, TX
281-255-9997
www.texasstargymnastics.com
Classes: Pre-school, Recreational, Levels1-4, Team, Cheer/Tumbling, and Dance.

Ages: 2 and up

Fees: $59.00 per month for 1 class per week.

Time: 60-minute classes

Westwood Gymnastics and Cheer
20212 Franz Rd.
Katy, TX
281-599-7030
www.westwoodgymnastics.com
Classes: Mom & Me, Pre-school, and Cheerleading

Ages: 18 months and up

Fees: $61.00 per month for 1 class per week

Time: 60-minute classes

NORTHEAST

Juergen's Gymnastics Academy
1550 Wilson Rd.
Humble, TX
281-548-1588
www.juergensgymnastics.com
Classes: Pre-school, Tumbling, Cheerleading, and Competitive Team.

Ages: 3 and up

Fees: $59.00 per month for 1 class per week

Time: 45-60 minute classes

SOUTHWEST

Biron Gymnastics
1322 Dairy Ashford
Houston, TX 77077
281-497-6666
www.birongym.com
Classes: Pre-school, School aged gymnastics, Advanced gymnastics and Cheerleading.

Ages: 12 months and up

Fees: Start at $44.00 per month

Time: 60 minute –1 hour 15 minute classes

Gymnastics Factory
2520 Albans St.
Houston, TX 77005
713-527-8753
www.gymnastfactory.com
Classes: Mommy & Me, Bridge Classes, Levels, Tumbling, Boys and Girls Team, and Cheerleading.

Ages: 16 months and up

Fees: $289.00 per semester. 1 class per week. Semester is August through December.

Time: 55-85 minute classes

The Little Gym of Houston Memorial
14090 B Memorial Dr.
Houston, TX 77079
281-558-9500
www.tlghouston-memorialtx.com
Classes: Developmental Gymnastics (4mos-3yrs), Pre- school level (3-5yrs), Advanced Gymnastics (6-12yrs).

Ages: 4 months through12 yrs.

Fees: 21 week semester $282.00 per semester paid in full. 5 payments of $64.00.

Time: 40-60 minute classes. Monday through Saturday

See ad in back

The Little Gym of Sugar Land/ Missouri City
3571 Hwy.6 South
Sugar Land, TX 77478
281-277-5470
www.tlgsugarlandtx.com
Classes: Developmental Gymnastics (4mos-3yrs), Pre-school level (3-5yrs), Advanced Gymnastics (6-12yrs).

Ages: 4 months through 12 yrs.

Fees: 21 week semester $282.00 per semester paid in full. 5 payments of $64.00.

Time: 40-60 minute classes. Monday through Saturday

See ad in back

Sugarwood Gymnastics Academy
4791 Lexington blvd.
Missouri City, TX
281-403-3400
Classes: Mom & Me, Pre-school, Kindergym, Levels, Trampoline and Tumbling.

Ages: 18 months and up

Fees: $59.00 per month for 1 class per week

Time: 45-60 minute classes

SOUTHEAST

AcroSports Gymnastics
1800 W. Nasa Blvd.
Webster, TX 77598
281-332-4496
www.acrosports.com
Classes: Pre-school, School-aged Academy, Tumbling, Cheer, Team, and Dance

Ages: 12 months and up

Fees: $55.00 per month

Time: 55-60 minute classes

Dynamic Gymnastics
3923 A Pansy St.
Pasadena, TX
281-487-8455
www.dynamicgym.org
Classes: Pre-school, School age, Tumbling, Cheerleading, and Competitive Gymnastics.

Ages: 3 and up

Fees: $45.00 per month for 1 class per week
$65.00 per month for 2 classes per week

Time: 50-minute classes

Gulf Gymnastics

1306 W. Sealy
Alvin, TX 77511
281-331-0844
www.gulfgymnastics.com
Classes: Tiny Tots, Beginners Gymnastics, Teams, and Cheer/Tumbling

Ages: 3 and up

Fees: $50.00 per month for 1 class per week.
$75.00 per month for 2 classes per week

Time: 60-minute classes

Reflex Gymnastics/Cheerleading Academy

2530 Garden rd. Building I
Pearland, TX 77581
281-412-3550
www.reflexgymnastics.com
Classes: Mom/Dad & Me, Transitional, Pre-school. School-age beginner, Advanced, Cheer/Tumbling, Dance, and Competitive Teams.
Ages: 12 months and up
Fees: $46.00 per month

Time: 40-60 minute classes

The Cheer Factory

11460 I-10 East
Baytown, TX 77520
281-704-2433
www.thecheerfactory.com
Classes: Gymnastics, Cheer/Tumbling, and Tumbling Tots.
Ages: 3 and up
Fees: $52.00 per month for 1 class per week

Time: 50-minute classes

GALVESTON

Acrofit Gymnastics Cheer and Dance

2103 Anders Ln.
Kemah, TX
281-535-2244
www.acrofitgymnastics.com
Classes: Mom & Me, Pre-school, Teams, Cheerleading, Tumbling, and Dance.

Ages: 18 months and up

Fees: $60.00 per month for 1 class per week
$85.00 per month for 2 classes per week

Time: 60-minute classes

Martial Arts

NORTH

Olympia Tae-kwon-do Training Center

5503 F.M. 2920
Spring, TX 77080
281-350-5599
Classes: Tae-kwon-do

Ages: 4 and up

Fees: $99.00 for 6 weeks: $ 50.00 registration fee includes uniform.

Toshido Karate International
13843 Hwy 105 W. Suite 101
Conroe, TX 77304
936-447-5900
www.toshidokarate.net
Classes: They run a full scale Martial Arts program.

Ages: 4 and up

Fees: $80.00-$200.00 per month

NORTHWEST

American Black Belt Academy
4978 Hwy 6 N Suite A
Houston, TX 77084
281-859-9566
www.abbahouston.com
Classes: Karate, Tae-kwon-do, and Kickboxing

Ages: 6 and up

Fees: Please call for pricing

Bear Creek Tae-kwon-do
16125 Timber Creek Place Ln.
Houston, TX 77084
281-463-1549
www.lstkd.com
Classes: Tae-kwon-do

Ages: 4 and up

Fees: $70.00 per month

Milbergers Martial Arts
10762 Grant Rd.
Houston, TX 77070
281-894-5555
www.karatehouston.com
Classes: Tiny tots, Kids program in Soo Bahk Do.

Ages: 3 and up

Fees: Please call for pricing

NORTHEAST

Battenbergs Black Belt Academy, Inc.

2910 Mills Branch Dr.
Kingwood, TX 77345
281-360-5460
Classes: Tiny Tigers, Karate for Kids, Tae-kwon-do, and Kickboxing

Ages: 4 and up

Fees: Please call for pricing

Kook Sul Won of Kingwood

23976 Hwy 59 W.
Humble, TX 77339
Classes: Children's Martial Arts program

Ages: 3 and up

Fees: $65.00 per month.

Tae-kwon-do Academy

7040 F. M 1960 E.
Atascocita, TX 77346
281-852-9002
www.hiromstkd.com
Classes: Tiger Cubs, and Junior's program

Ages: 4 and up

Fees: Please call for pricing

SOUTHWEST

American Martial Arts Academy

12280 Westheimer # 230
Houston, TX 77077
281-597-0580
www.martialartshouston.com
Classes: Kung Fu, Martial Arts, Kickboxing, Self Defense, and Kenpo

Ages: 4 and up

Fees: $120.00 per month includes a uniform. FREE trial class.

Kim's Karate Academy
15000 Bellaire Blvd.
Houston, TX 77083
281-933-1091
Classes: Tiny tots, Tae-kwon-do

Ages: 3 and up

Fees: $175.00 for 3 months for 3 classes per week. Includes a FREE uniform.

Safety America
2595 Cordes Rd.
Sugar Land, TX 77478
281-980-3030
www.safety-america.com
Classes: Karate, Aikido, Brazilian Jiu-Jitsu, and Self Defense.

Ages: 4 and up

Fees: $120.00 per month. One time registration $150.00 includes uniform.

SOUTHEAST

Bay Area Self Defense
2424 Falcon Pass
Clear Lake, TX
281-486-9626
www.bayareaselfdefense.com
Classes: Chi Soo TE

Ages: any

Fees: $50.00 per month or 3 months for $100.00

Clear Lake Tae-kwon-do USA
16532 Sealark Rd.
Houston, TX 77062
281-480-1500
www.blackbeltacademy.biz
Classes: Tea-kwon-do

Ages: 3 and up

Fees: $79.00 per month for 2 classes per week. Includes a free uniform.

Kuk Sool Won Martial Arts
2827 N. Alexander Dr.
Baytown, TX 77520
281-428-4930
www.ourbaytown.com/ksw/
Classes: Tiny Tigers, Children's program

Ages: 3 and up

Fees: $65.00 per month and up

Martial Arts America
2047 W. Main St. Suite C9
League City, TX 77573
281-332-5425
www.algarza.com
Classes: Tiger Tots, Junior Karate, Teen Karate, Private lessons, and Karate Camps.

Ages: 3 and up

Fees: $100.00 per month for 2 classes per week. Includes a uniform.

Running

Houston Striders, Inc.
713-797-8601
www.houstonstriders.com
This is a running club in the Houston area that your whole family can join. They participate in local running events as well as volunteer work for other Houston marathons. You can also find a list of local running events on their website.

Price: Family membership $25.00 per year.

Inside Texas Running

www.insidetexasrunning.com

Running events are listed on this website for the whole state of Texas. We have included some family friendly races specific to the Houston area. These events happen throughout the year. Please see site for race details.

- April-October Runners High Club Track and Trading at Memorial Park Track
- June- Deer Park 5K/Kids Mile in Deer Park Texas
- July- Freedom 5K and Family/Youth walk (1.5 miles) in Sugar Land Texas
- July- Run Wild 5K Run/Walk and Kids Run in Uptown Park Houston Texas
- August- Lazy-Hazy-Crazy Days of Summer 5K and Kids Run - Downtown Aquarium
- September- Fired Up 5K and Family/Youth Walk Sugar Land Fire Department
- October- D'Feet Breast Cancer- A Family Event in Galveston 5K, 10K, and 1K Kids Run

Scuba Diving Instruction

NORTH

Sea Sports Scuba (2 locations)

www.seasportsscuba.com

Spring
16300 Kuykendahl
Houston, TX 77068
281-367-6664

The Woodlands
25701 I-45 N.
The Woodlands, TX
281-367-6664

Class: Jr. open water certification

Ages: 10 and up

Fee: $300.00

Time: Certification requires 2 weekends out of a month. Classes are usually held on a Friday and Saturday and then a Saturday and Sunday class.

They also provide a Discover Scuba program for ages 8 and up. This is a FREE class held once a month to introduce people to the world of scuba diving.

NORTHWEST

Scuba Houston

14609 Kimberly Lane
Houston, TX 77079
281-497-7651
www.scubahouston.com
Classes: Scuba Rangers a program designed to introduce students to scuba diving and water safety. Swimming classes ages 3 and up. Star Rangers a snorkeling program for ages 5-7 yrs. All classes are held in an indoor heated pool.

Ages: 8 to 12 yrs.

Fee: $295.00 includes books and a 1year membership into Scuba Rangers.

Time: Classes usually held on Friday's from 6:00p.m. to 8:00p.m.

Classes: Jr. open water certification

Ages: 12-15yrs.

Fee: 3 week program $160.00; $195.00 for weekend program.

Sea Sports Scuba

9564 F.M. 1960 W
Houston, TX 77070
281-894-4488
www.seasportsscuba.com
Class: Jr. Open water certification

Ages: 10 and up

Fee: $300.00

Time: Certification requires 2 weekends out of a month. Usually held on a Friday and Saturday and then a Saturday and Sunday class.

They also provide a Discover Scuba program for ages 8 and up. This is a FREE class held once a month to introduce people to the world of scuba diving.

SOUTHWEST

Houston Scuba Academy
12505 Hillcroft
Houston, TX
713-721-7788
www.houstonscubaacademy.com
Houston's premiere family scuba diving facility. Open year round in an indoor heated pool.
Classes: Scuba Rangers a program designed to introduce students to scuba diving and water safety.

Ages: 8 and up

Fees: $295.00 includes membership

Time: Meet 1 time a week for 5 weeks. Each class is approximately 3 hours in length.

Sea Sports Scuba
7543 Westheimer
Houston, TX 77063
713-977-0028
www.seasportsscuba.com
Class: Jr. open water certification

Ages: 10 and up

Fee: $300.00

Time: Certification requires 2 weekends out of a month. Classes are usually held on a Friday and Saturday and then a Saturday and Sunday class.

They also provide a Discover Scuba program for ages 8 and up. This is a FREE class held once a month to introduce people to the world of scuba diving.

SOUTHEAST

Sport Divers of Houston, Inc.
20710 Gulf Freeway #50
Webster, TX
281-338-1611
Classes: Summer Camp and Jr. open water certification.

Ages: 8 and up for summer camp
Jr. open water ages 10 and up

Fees: $450.00 for Summer camp

Time: Summer Camp hours are Monday-Friday 8:30a.m. -5:00p.m.

Other Online Resources:

www.huscuba.org
www.bayareadivers.org

Swimming Instruction

Gulf Swimming
www.gulfswimming.org
This organization is the leading body for competitive swimming in the Southeast portion of Texas. They have a complete listing of swim clubs in and around the Houston area. On their website click on "Teams" then click on "Complete Team Listings". This will bring up a list of all the swim clubs. All of their contact information is included there. These clubs offer competitive swimming as well as learn to swim programs. They accept ages 6 months through 18 yrs.

Other Online Resources:

www.tsaswim.org - Texas Swimming Association

www.usaswimming.org - USA Swimming

www.swimmingworldmagazine.com

Tennis Courts

Houston Tennis Association
713-973-7636
www.houstontennis.org
This Association has all types of information for the world of tennis. Everything from leagues to a list of tennis courts around the Greater Houston area. Just about everything you need to know about tennis can be found here.

Wakeboard/Waterskiing

M2 Waterskiing School – located in south Houston
15200 Nautique Way
Houston, TX 77047
713-433-4475
www.m2ski.com
Classes: Wakeboard and waterskiing classes as well as Summer camps. The school accepts beginners through advanced students.

Ages: Any age but student should be able to swim very well.

Fees: Waterskiing begins at $35.00 per lesson
Wakeboarding begins at $40.00 per lesson

Mike Munn's International Ski School
713-515-6494
www.munnski.com
Classes: Lessons offered in slalom, tricks, jump, barefoot, and wakeboarding. This school provides its own private lake in Northeast Houston. They accept beginners through advanced students.

Ages: Student must have excellent swimming skills.

Fees: Single lesson: $40.00
Full day $150.00
Beginner private lesson $50.00

Time: Ski school runs Monday or Friday from 9:00a.m. -3:00p.m. Year round.

Other Online Resources:

www.waterskimag.com
www.wakeworld.com

www.wakeboardingmag.com

Spectator Sports

The Houston Astros – Baseball

www.houston.astros.mlb.com
Tickets: 1-877-9-ASTROS or purchase online through website.

Price Range: $5.00-$45.00. Outfield deck tickets are $1.00 for youth 3-14 yrs.

Check out the discount ticket offers through the website. Kids can also join the Astros Buddies Club for only $10.00 per season. This club is for children 12 and under and they receive all kinds of FREE goodies.

Houston Rockets – Basketball

www.nba.com/rockets
Tickets: 1-866-446-8849 or at **www.toyotacentertix.com**

Price Range: $10.00 and up

Kids can join the Rockets Kids Club! To join please visit their website. Registration begins in October of each year. Also register for the Team MAC- the Houston Rockets Youth Basketball League. This program is FREE and open to boys and girls ages 4-18 yrs. For more information call **713-226-4459**.

Houston Comets – Women's Basketball

www.wnba.com/comets
Tickets: 713-627 WNBA. You can also purchase tickets at Houston area Randall's stores.

Price Range: $8.00 and up

Houston Texans NFL Football

www.houstontexans.com
Tickets: **www.ticketmasters.com** or call **832-667-2002**

Price Range: $35.00 and up

Checkout their community page to find information on different community events happening throughout the year. Kids can also join the Houston Texan's Kids Club.

Houston Aeros – Ice Hockey

www.aeros.com

Ticket: 1-866-GO-AEROS

Price Range: $11.00-$55.00

Join the Houston Aeros Kid's Club. This membership includes 1 FREE ticket to a specific game, t-shirt, a membership card and discount on other game tickets.

Check out this leagues "Street Fleet" roller hockey program. It is sponsored through the Aeros and the Parks and Recreation Department. For more information call **713-974-PUCK**

Want to have a Birthday party with the Aeros? Please call 713-974-7825 for more information.

Houston Wranglers

www.houstonwranglers.net

Tickets: 713-783-1620

Price Range: $15.00 -$75.00

Houston's first premiere tennis league. Gates open at 5:30 before each game and include music, food and drinks before each match. They have scheduled Kid's Days throughout the season. This includes rides and games prior to the match, a racquet give-a-way and a free book for all kids. Check out the website's schedule for specific dates.

RICE University

www.riceowls.com

Tickets: 713-522-OWLS

Texas Southern University

www.tsu.edu

Tickets: www.ticketmasters.com **or 713-313-7271**

University of Houston

www.uhcougars.collegesports.com

Tickets: 1-877-COUGAR-5 or buy online through the website.

Chapter 5

Music

Chapter 5

Music

The Magic of Music

The Secret Great Parents Know About Raising Their Kids

Few things can be more valuable to a child than the opportunity of studying music during their youth. Besides giving them a love and appreciation for this great art form, it increases their quality of life, and prepares them in ways that cannot be done with any other activity. The research has been stunning and clearly indicates that music gives young people the skills they need to enjoy supper-success in life. A short list of these skills includes:

- Creative Thinking
- Concentration
- Self-Esteem
- Performing Under Pressure
- Motor Skill Development
- Imagination
- Analytical Thinking
- Discipline
- Self-Expression
- Increased Intelligence
- Problem Solving
- Coordination

Music Study and Intelligence

- A research team exploring the link between music and intelligence reported that music training is far superior to computer instruction in dramatically enhancing children's abstract reasoning silks, necessary for learning math and science. *–Neurological Research, Vol. 19, February 1997*

- A child's intelligence is increased by playing a musical instrument because 80-90% of the brain's motor-control capabilities are devoted to the hands, mouth and throat. By developing highly refined control in those areas, a child is stimulating almost the entire brain, thereby increasing its total capabilities. – *Frank R. Wilson, MD, Clinical Professor of Neurology, University of California, San Francisco School of Medicine*

- The musician is constantly adjusting decisions on tempo, tone, style, rhythm, phrasing, and feeling- training the brain to become incredibly good at organizing and conducting many activities at once. Dedicated practice of this orchestration can have a great payoff for lifelong attentional skills, intelligence, and an ability for self-knowledge and expression. *– John J. Rately, MD, "A User's Guide to the Brain"*

Music Study and Academics

- High school music students have been shown to hold higher grade point averages (GPA) than non-musicians at the same school. In a study conducted in California, music students had an average GPA of 3.57; non-musicians averaged 2.91. Further, 16% of the music students held a 4.0 GPA while only 5% of the non-music students did.
- Students involved in the arts score up to 125 points higher than the national average on the SAT.
- A Rockefeller foundation study found that college music majors have the highest admittance rate into medical school (66%). By contrast, only 44% of biochemistry majors were admitted.
- In a study by the *Norwegian Research Council for Science and the Humanities*, a connection was found between students having musical competence and high motivation to achieve success in school.

Hungary is one of the poorest nations in the world, yet they rank highest in academic excellence. In that country, there is a mandatory music requirement for grades one through nine. The first four hours of each day are set aside for music, orchestra, and choir. In fact, each of the top three nations in the world have mandatory music requirements for their students in the lower grade levels. By contrast, America spends 29 times more money than any other nation on education, yet does not share this commitment to music and ranks 14th out of 17 countries in academic excellence.

Music Study and Success in Society

- Secondary students who participated in band and orchestra reported the lowest lifetime use of all substances (alcohol, tobacco, illicit drugs). –Texas Commission on Drug and Alcohol Abuse Report
- The very best engineers and technical designers in the Silicon Valley industry are, nearly without exception, all practicing musicians. *–Grant Venerable, "The Paradox of the Silicon Savior"*

Music Study and Life

- Learning to play a musical instrument enhances coordination, concentration and memory, improves eyesight and hearing, teaches discipline, fosters self-esteem, stimulates imagination and self-expression and develops the motor systems of the brain in a way that cannot be done by any other activity.
- Students who participated in arts programs in selected elementary and middle schools in New York City showed significant increase in self-esteem and thinking skills. – *National Arts Education Research Center*
- Studying music encourages self-discipline and diligence. These traits carry over into intellectual pursuits and lead to effective study and work habits. Creating and performing music promotes self-expression and provides self-gratification while providing pleasure to others. *-Michael E. Blakely, MD*
- Music is about communication, creativity, and cooperation, and, by studying music in school, students have the opportunity to build on these skills, enrich their lives, and experience the world form a new perspective. – *Bill Clinton, former President of the United States of America*
- Personal expression is encouraged through the arts. This develops flexible and fluent thinking abilities, as well as, skills of close scrutiny and careful evaluation. – *Oklahoma State Department of Education*

Music study gives young people an edge that they can't get anywhere else. Congratulations on your desire to provide this vital opportunity for your children. It will be one of the most important things you ever do as a parent. Good luck in the magical journey of music study and life.

This information has been provided by *The Art City Music Academy of Utah.*

Find A Teacher

Music Teachers National Association

www.mtna.org

The Music Teacher's National Association (MTNA) offers a wide variety of benefits and services to professional music teachers and family's nation wide. If you are searching for a nationally certified teacher, their site features a comprehensive database of instructors searchable by zip code and instrument.

Suzuki Music Association

www.suzukiassociation.org

The Suzuki Association of the America's (SAA) provides programs and services to members throughout North and South America. Go to the "Parents" icon and click on "Teacher Location". Follow the instructions and a list of teachers in your area will appear. There are Suzuki programs for: Violin, Viola, Cello, Bass, Piano, Guitar, Flute, Harp, Recorder, and ECC.

Summer Suzuki Institutes are special camps that provide an intense musical experience for families and children who currently study an instrument through the Suzuki Method.

These institutes are located through out the U.S. and Canada. Summer camps offer activities for students, parents and teachers in one-week sessions through out the summer. For more information on summer institutes visit their website under the "Parents Link" then click on "Summer Institutes".

Kindermusik

www.kindermusik.com

Kindermusik is the Nation's premiere early childhood music and movement program. This program is a magical place where children can dance, sing, play instruments, share a story, create, compare, and explore the world around them. Each class level is carefully designed to enhance your child's musical language, as well as, their mental, physical, social, and emotional development. Family involvement lets you learn and enjoy music with your child. From dancing and singing with your baby, to helping them read the notes of their first musical composition, this is an activity both of you will enjoy! There are several certified Kindermusik teachers in Houston. We have included a few for each area. If the one you are looking for is not listed see the Kindermusik website click on " Find a Class" enter your zip code and it will list additional teachers.

Ages: Birth oto age 7

Fees: Please call teacher for pricing.

Kindermusik Instructors

NORTH

Julie Evans
Phone: 281-384-4507
Houston, TX 77090

Vicki Bull
Phone: 281-379-4020
Spring, TX 77379

Ana Schoellman (2 Locations)
www.kindermusikbyanaschoellman.com
Phone: 713-471-0496
Spring, TX 77373 & The Woodlands, TX 77380

Nancy Hall (2 locations)
www.kindermusikofthewoodlands.com
Phone: 281-367-0545
The Woodlands, TX 77380 & Magnolia, TX 77354

Cathy Swick
Phone: 281-363-9021
The Woodlands, TX 77381

NORTHWEST

Nancy Johnston (3 locations)
www.msnancysmusic.com
Phone: 281-855-8855
Houston, TX 77095 (Copperfield), Cypress, TX 77429, & Katy, TX 77450

Carolyn Timm
Phone: 281-693-5064
Katy, TX 77492

St. Peter's United Methodist Church
Phone: 281-492-8031
Katy, TX 77450

NORTHEAST

Debbie Wenter
Phone: 281-361-4965
Kingwood, TX 77345

SOUTHWEST

Rita Widener
Phone: 713-392-1765
Stafford, TX 77477

Siri Vann
Phone: 281-242-3017
Sugar Land, TX 77479

Zing Allsopp (2 locations)
Phone: 281-389-3258
Sugar Land, TX 77479 & Missouri City, TX 77459

SOUTHEAST

Sarah Hames
www.friendswoodmusic.com
Phone: 281-993-1279
Friendswood, TX 77546

Susan Brown
Phone: 713-933-9816
Webster, TX 77598

Sing and Play Fine Arts Studio
Phone: 281-997-7271
Pearland, TX 77581

Terri Hart
Phone: 713-557-3517
Pearland, TX 77584

Kathy Smith (2 locations)
Phone: 832-656-8422
Webster, TX 77598 & League City, TX 77573

Melissa Magdaleno
www.kindermusikwithmissy.com
Phone: 281-557-0411
League City, TX 77573

GALVESTON

Margarita Sims
Phone: 409-741-0328
Galveston Island, TX 77551

H&H Music Company
www.brookmays.com
H&H Music Company is a reputable instrument shop here in the Houston area. They are part of the Brooks Mays Music Group and provide quality music lessons to all ages. Following is a listing of their stores and the private lessons they offer. They also have a list of private music teachers in your area. Go to your local store and request the list.

H&H Music Company

NORTH

H&H - F.M. 1960 W.
713 F.M. 1960 West, Houston TX 77090
281-580-8000
www.brookmays.com
Lessons offered: piano, and guitar. Half-hour lessons one time per week.
Ages: 6 and older

Fees: $15.00 registration
$75.00/month; dependant upon teacher and instrument

NORTHWEST

H&H – Willowbrook
17776 F.M. 249, Houston TX 77064
281-890-0272
www.brookmays.com
Lessons offered: guitar, piano, violin, and voice. Half-hour lessons one time per week.
Ages: 6 and older

Fees: $80.00 per month for piano, violin, and voice
$76.00 per month for guitar

H&H – Katy
1220 Fry Rd. Houston TX 77084
281-531-0996
www.brookmays.com
Lessons offered: guitar, and piano.

Ages: Depends on teacher

Fees: This store refers to teachers in the area. Contact the store for teacher information.

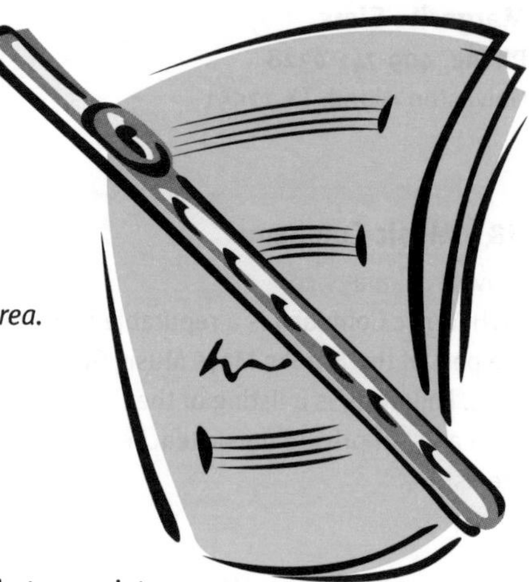

H&H – I-10
10303 Katy Freeway, Houston TX 77024
281-531-9222
www.brookmays.com
Lessons offered: This store has teachers that come into the store to give lessons. Contact the store for more information.

Ages: Dependant upon teacher

Fees: Dependant upon teacher

SOUTHWEST

H&H – Sugar Land
15415 Southwest Frwy., Sugar Land, TX 77478
281-242-3915
www.brookmays.com
Lessons offered: flute, saxophone, clarinet, piano, guitar, and bass.

Ages: all ages

Fees: $20.00 per half-hour one time per week

H&H – Meyerland
8715B West Loop South, Houston, TX 77096
713-666-2090
www.brookmays.com
Lessons offered: piano, guitar, drums, woodwinds, and trumpet

Ages: 6 and older

Fees: $25.00 per half-hour one time per week

SOUTHEAST

H&H – Friendswood
18980A Gulf Freeway, Friendswood, TX 77546
281-486-0082
www.brookmays.com
Lessons offered: guitar, bass, drums

Ages: 6 and older

Fees: $20.00 per half-hour for guitar
$23.00 per half-hour for bass, and drums

H&H – Pasadena
6025 Fairmount Parkway, Pasadena, TX 77505
281-487-6204
www.brookmays.com
Lessons offered: piano, violin, woodwinds, and guitar

Ages: 6 and up

Fees: $20.00 per half-hour one time per week

Music Schools/Studios

NORTH

Arbor Music
33219 Egypt Ln. Magnolia, TX
Contact Eric Williams 281-259-5585
www.arbormusic.com
This school provides private lessons in guitar, banjo, bass guitar, violin, cello, viola, woodwinds, and brass instruments. They also provide music summer camps and on the first Saturday of every month they jam to Blue Grass.

Ages: 6 and up

Fees: $80.00 per month for 1 lesson per week

Landes Music
25210B Grogans Mill, The Woodlands, TX 77380
281-364-9707
www.landesmusic.com
This music store also provides private music lessons in guitar, bass, drums, piano, band, and orchestra instruments.

Ages: Open to all ages and levels of ability

Fees: $15.00 per half hour for guitar and bass
$20.00 per hour for all other instruments

NORTHWEST

Katy Music Teachers Association
www.katymusicteachers.com
This is a website full of information for parents and students in the Katy area. Click on their "Membership List" and you can find a teacher specific to your instrument, and their contact information.

Ms. Nancy's Music Studio (3 Locations)

Copperfield
15450 F.M. 529
Houston, TX 77095
281-855-8855

Cypress-St. Mary's Episcopal
15415 N. Eldridge Pkwy.
Cypress, TX 77429
281-829-ARTS

Katy Visual Performing Arts
2501 S. Mason rd. Suite 290
Katy, TX 77450

www.msnancysmusic.com
This studio has three convenient locations and offers a variety of music genre. They specialize in Kindermusik, an early development program for babies through age 7. They also provide music summer camps as well as birthday parties. Private lessons are available in piano, voice, guitar, and bass.

Ages: Birth to age 7 for Kindermusik
Private Lessons age 5 and up

Fees: Please call for pricing

St. Mark Music Conservatory

1515 Hillendahl Blvd., Houston, TX 77055
Kathy Gresham – Director
713-468-2623 Ext.369
www.stmarkhouston.org
St. Marks provides private music lessons to both members and non-members. Lessons are available in piano, voice and most other instruments. The cost is very affordable yet they offer superb quality. They also have an orchestra department for beginners through advanced players.
Ages: Pre-K and up

Fees: $18.00 and up per lesson

NORTHEAST

Atascocita School of Music

5746 F.M. 1960 E., Humble, TX 77346
281-852-7086
www.atascocitamusic.com
This is a musical school teaching private lessons for guitar, voice, piano, drums, violin, viola, and bass guitar. All lessons are half-hour in length. The school also provides performance classes, music theory, pre-school music and even a digital recording studio.
Ages: All ages and levels.

Fees: $75.00 per month. Includes 1 lesson per week. Usually 4 or 5 classes per month.

Music from Nothing

17031 Atlanta St., Humble, TX 77396

281-441-1404

This private music lesson company will come to your home. They are located in Humble but are willing to travel a reasonable distance. They provide lessons for all instruments including voice. Price of lessons is dependent upon where you live.

Ages: 3 and up

Fees: $18.00 to $20.00 per half hour

SOUTHWEST

ABC School of Music

9183 Katy Freeway Suite 100, Houston TX 77024

713-365-9154

www.abcschoolofmusic.com

This school provides private lessons for guitar, piano, voice, bass, orchestra, and band instruments. You can even pay for your lessons online through their website.

Ages: All ages and abilities

Fees: $100.00 for 4 to 5 lessons per month. $10.00 per hour for group lessons.

Colony Music Studio

2859 Dulles Ave., Missouri City, TX 77459

281-208-0900

www.ColonyMusicStudio.com

Provide private lessons for piano, guitar, voice, violin, string bass, and cello. Twice a year they have a recital so parents can see their children's progress.

Ages: All ages

Fees: $25.00 per half hour lesson.

Tempo School of Music

13505 Westheimer, Houston, TX 77077

281-293-8880

www.temposchoolofmusic.com

This school is a great resource for private music lessons. Instrument lessons are offered for piano, guitar, bass, voice, saxophone, clarinet, flute, violin, and drums. Lesson rates are the same regardless of instrument or teachers qualifications.

Ages: All ages

Fees: $18.00 per half hour
$36.00 per hour

SOUTHEAST

Allegro Music Company

3144 Nasa Rd. 1, Seabrook, TX 77586

281-326-6874

www.nasamusic.com

Nasa Music is the home of Allegro Music Company. They provide quality music lessons for piano, guitar, voice, trumpet, saxophone, drums, clarinet, and flute. Lessons are usually 30 to 45 minutes in length.

Ages: 2 and up

Fees: call for details

Sing and Play Fine Arts Studio

4205 W. Broadway, Pearland, TX 77581

281-997-7271

Lisa Arriaga Director

www.singandplayfinearts.com

This studio provides both private and class lessons in piano, guitar, voice, and violin. They also have percussion, art, drama, Spanish, and creative movement classes. They also specialize in Kindermusik the nations leading early development musical program. You can even have your child's musical birthday party here.

Ages: Birth to age 7 for Kindermusik
All ages for other lessons

Fees: Prices dependant upon class taken.
Start at approximately $150.00/semester

GALVESTON

Island Music
2401 45th St., Galveston, TX 77550
409-763-6197
This music company provides private music lessons in piano, guitar, bass, and voice.

Ages: 5 and up

Fees: $15.00 per half hour lesson

Music Preparatory Programs

Rice University - The Shepard School of Music
P.O. Box 1892, Houston TX 77251
Contact: Virginia Nance
713-348-5753
This preparatory program offers private music lessons to children ages 5 through seniors in high school. The courses are non-credited and taught by both the university staff and graduate students. Please contact the school for information on instruments and pricing.

University of Houston – Moores School of Music
Rebecca and John Moores School of Music Building
4800 Calhoun, Houston TX 77204
Dawn Padula (Director)
713-743-3398
www.music.uh.edu
The University of Houston offers a preparatory program for young students. Private and group lessons are available for orchestral instruments, piano, guitar, saxophone, Suzuki violin, voice, music theory, composition, flute and percussion. Please contact the school for exact pricing information.

Chapter 6

Theatre, Dance and Creative Arts

Chapter 6

Theatre, Dance and Creative Arts

The arts are much more than just fun "extra" activities for kids. Participation in the arts opens up children's minds, and offers them the skills they need for a bright future.

Did you know that . . .

- The arts teach kids to be more tolerant and open.
- The arts allow kids to express themselves creatively.
- The arts promote individuality, bolster self-confidence, and improve overall academic performance.
- The arts can help troubled youth, providing an alternative to delinquent behavior and truancy while providing an improved attitude towards school.

Young artists, as compared with their peers, are likely to:

- Attend music, art, and dance classes nearly three times as frequently.
- Participate in youth groups nearly four times as frequently.
- Read for pleasure nearly twice as often.
- Perform community service more than four times as often.
- (Living the Arts through Language + Learning: A Report on Community-based Youth Organizations, Shirley Brice Heath, Stanford University and Carnegie Foundation For the Advancement of Teaching Americans for the Arts Monograph, November 1998)

Kids involved in the arts are more likely to be class officers, participate in math and science, and excel in academic involvement.

Encourage your child to try new things and explore new interests continually. You may stumble upon a passion for acting, dance, art, or even sewing! The arts, in their many forms, enrich our children's lives and broaden their horizons.

Young Audiences of Houston

1800 St. James Place, Suite 600
Houston, TX 77056
713-520-9267

www.yahouston.org

This is a non-profit organization dedicated to the education of Houston's children through the arts. YA offer programs for Pre-K through the 12th grade. Programs include live performances, workshops, and professional development programs in the schools. Some featured events are a summer theatre arts program for students, FREE performances, and FREE movies at the Miller Outdoor Theatre. Please see their website for specific times and dates. This is a very fun and affordable way for your children to experience the arts.

DOWNTOWN

Houston Theatre District

www.houstontheatredistrict.org

Located in the heart of downtown lies the world famous theatre district. The district is home to 8 world-class performing arts organizations. Houston is one of only five U.S. cities that permenantly houses professional companies in all of the major arts, opera, ballet, and theatre. There are 4 performance centers that make up the heart of the theatre district. Information about each theatre is listed below as well as how to purchase tickets and find out what is playing there.

Alley Theatre

615 Texas Ave., Houston, TX 77002
Box Office Phone: 713-228-8421

www.alleytheatre.org

Check their website for performances and show times. You can purchase tickets online through the website or by phone at the box office.

Family events: This theatre offers a "Family Night Out" where kids can attend a creative drama workshop while their parents attend a play. In the Spring they have a "Family Series" of plays that are kid friendly. Just in time for the holidays "A Christmas Carol" returns to the stage November 26th through December 26th. This is a Christmas treat your whole family will enjoy.

Hobby Center for the Performing Arts

800 Bagby St., Houston, TX 77002
713-315-2400
Box Office Phone: 713-315-2525

www.thehobbycenter.org
The Hobby Center is the official home to:

- Broadway in Houston – **www.broadwayacrossamerica.com**
  Family Events: This theatre company has wonderful shows for the whole family like Annie January 3-15th 2006
  The Lion King July 9th-August 13th 2006
- Theatre Under the Stars – **www.tuts.com**
  Family Events: Come see great family productions like
  Cats December 6th-18th 2005
  Doctor Dolittle January 17th-29th 2006
  Beauty and the Beast March 14th-26th 2006
- Check out these websites to find show times and ticket information.

Jones Hall

615 Louisiana St., Houston TX 77002
713-227-3974
www.joneshall.org
Jones Hall is home to:

- The Society for the Performing Arts - **www.spahouston.org**
  Family Events: H.E.B. presents a Family Series with shows like
  Bowfire November 12th 2005 at 7pm
  Peking Acrobats April 1st 2006 at 7pm
  Break! The urban Funk Spectacular April 28th 2006 at 7pm
- The Houston Symphony - **www.houstonsymphony.org**
  Family Events: The Time Warner Family Season consists of 4 concerts on Saturday morning at 10:00am and 11:30 am. Concerts include:
  Peter and the Wolf October 22nd 2005
  Holiday Traditions Around the World December 10th 2005
  Happy 250th Birthday Mozart February 11th 2006
  Dr. Seuss's Gertrude McFuzz April 15th 2006
  - Check these websites for ticket information and show times.

Wortham Theatre Center
501 Texas St., Houston, TX 77002
Box Office Phone: 713-237-1439

www.worthamcenter.org
The Wortham Center is the official home of:

- Houston Grand Opera - **www.houstongrandopera.org**
- The Houston Ballet - **www.houstonballet.org**
  Family Events: Join the Ballet for their wonderful Christmas tradition "The Nutcracker" November 10th- 13th 2005.
- DaCamera of Houston - **www.dacamera.com**

Please visit these websites for more information.

Miller Outdoor Theatre
100 Concert Dr. Houston, TX 77030
Located in Hermann Park
713-284-8350 (recorded information)
713-284-8325

www.milleroutdoortheatre.com
This is literally an outdoor theatre where families can enjoy FREE entertainment. Shows like Macbeth, Seussical the Musical, performances by the Houston Symphony, and Rumpelstiltskin, just to name a few. There are usually no tickets required, but on some occasions, tickets might be required for the covered seating area. You can obtain those tickets at the box office between 11:30a.m. and 1:00 p.m. on the day of the performance. Concessions are offered at the theatre to support the FREE performances. Check their website for a detailed list of shows and dates.

NORTH

Cynthia Woods Mitchell Pavilion

2005 Lake Robbins Dr., The Woodlands TX 77380

281-363-3300

www.pavilion.woodlandscenter.org

Every fall they host The Children's Festival. This is a live event designed to educate and entertain elementary through intermediate aged children. Shows include story telling, music performances, dancing, puppetry, and theatre. This is a wonderful event for the whole family. Weekdays are reserved for schools but weekends are open to the public.

The festival is usually held in November, but check their website for detailed information. Also check other family friendly events by clicking on "Events", and then use the drop down menu to select Children/Family.

Playhouse 1960

6814 Gant Rd., Houston, TX 77070

281-587-8243

www.playhouse1960.com

This theatre offers children's theatre matinee performances every Saturday and Sunday. Some of their shows include, Charlie and the Chocolate Factory, Pocahontas, and The Wizard of OZ.

Show times: 3:00 p.m. every Saturday and Sunday

Tickets: $5.00 per child

SOUTHWEST

The Company on Stage

536 Westbury Square, Houston, TX 77035

713-726-1219

www.companyonstage.com

This company offers children's theatre on Saturdays at 11:00 a.m. and 1:30 p.m. Shows for the 2005-2006 season are Frosty the Snowman, The Clown Who Ran Away, Pinocchio Commedia, and Cinderella. This theatre also has acting classes and activities for children.

Show times: 11:00a.m. and 1:30 p.m. Saturdays Only!

Tickets: $7.00 per person

Dinner Theatre

A Mystery to Me and Murder By Chocolate

Near the Boardwalk, Kemah, TX
281-992-1888
www.amysterytome.com
Come and enjoy a mystery while eating dinner or enjoying your favorite dessert. The dinner includes salad, entrée, drinks, and a dessert. Or you can choose to just have dessert and a drink with your mystery. This acting group will also travel to any other location near you entertaining up to as many as 250 people. All shows are "G" rated and appropriate for children. If that isn't enough they also have do-it-yourself mystery games that you can play at home with the kids, or at your next party. Great for Halloween!

Price: Mystery dinner $34.00 per person

Mystery dessert $18.00 per person

Hours: Open Friday and Saturday only. Check website for details.

Mystery Café

Marriott West Loop Hotel
1750 West Loop South at San Felipe
713-944-CLUE
www.mysterycafehouston.com
This mystery theatre is located inside the Marriott hotel. It is an interactive murder mystery comedy. It will have you bursting at the seams. This mystery includes dinner with salad, dessert, tea, and coffee. Each show is four acts in length and reservations are required.
Price: $49.95 per person
Open: Friday and Saturday seating begins at 7:30 p.m.

The Great Caruso

10001 Westheimer, Houston TX 77042
713-780-4900
www.houstondinnertheatre.com
Come for dinner and stay for the show! This is Houston's only dinner theatre. Dinner comes first and includes salad, main coarse, dessert and drink. The menu is viewable online. They also have a special holiday show that premieres in November. Performances are appropriate for children.
Price: $12.00 for dinner; $23.00-$28.00 for the show
Children are half price.
Hours: Open Wednesday – Saturday

Acting

DOWNTOWN

TUTS Humphrey's School of Musical Theatre
Hobby Center
800 Bagby St. Suite 100
Houston, TX 77002
713-558-8801
www.tuts.com
This school prides itself on providing the finest in year-round musical theatre education. They also have winter and summer performing arts camps. Students will learn singing, dancing, and acting techniques.

Ages: 4 and up

Price: Call for tuition pricing

NORTH

Class Act Productions
TWHS-McCullough Campus Auditorium
3800 S. Panther Creek, The Woodlands, TX
www.classactproductions.com
"Setting the stage for Young Performers". This theatre group provides Musical theatre classes for kid's ages 6 to 16 yrs. Students learn scenes from different plays and musicals. The teacher's will also address skills for the stage like auditioning and stage presence.

Ages: 6-16yrs.

Price: $220.00 per session. There are two sessions Sept to Dec. and Jan to April. All sessions are 12 weeks in length.

Applause Theatre
6608 F.M. 1960 W., Houston TX
281-852-8201
www.applausetheatre.com
This is a non-profit youth organization that features a musical theatre school and musical performances. Acting classes are for children in the 1st through the 12th grade. This school also has summer camps, a Broadway series, and workshops. Study throughout the year and then become a part of the show.

Ages: 1st – 12th grade

Price: $35.00 reg. Fee; $85.00 per month or $285.00 per semester.

The Actor Factory

16106 Waycreek, Houston, TX 77068
281-651-9885
www.theactorfactory.com
Classes meet at Progressions Performing Arts
5220 F.M. 2920, Spring, TX
This school provides private and group lessons in acting. They also have a musical theatre performing group, summer musical workshops, audition preparation, summer acting workshops and the children's drama club.

Ages: 5 and up

Fees: Group lessons start at $25.00 per hour and go up. Private lessons are $40.00 per hour.

NORTHWEST

Katy Visual and Performing Arts Center

2501 S. Mason Rd. Suite 290, Katy, TX 77450
281-829-2787
www.KVPAC.org
These classes meet at the Great Southwest Equestrian Center in Katy. KVPAC provides arts education through theatre, visual arts, and music. The performing arts program offers students instruction in stagecraft, acting, voice and choreography. Most classes are in the form of workshops, and summer camps. There are numerous opportunities with this organization.

Ages: Pre-school to High school aged children

Price: You can get a family membership for $50.00 per year. Workshops and camps have additional fees. Please see site for details.

HITS Theatre

311 W. 18th St., Houston, TX 77008
713-861-7408
www.hitstheatre.org
Located in the Height just Northwest of downtown Houston. HITS is a Musical Theater Performance arts school that teaches singing, dancing, and acting in a rehearsal like situation. Classes are for children 1st grade and up. Classes include Broadway Basics for children in Kindergarten through 3rd grade. Broadway kids 3rd through 6th grade. Broadway Teens for kids in 6th through 12th grade.

Ages: Kindergarten through the 12th grade.

Price: Tuition is based on age and classes taken. Call for pricing.

NORTHEAST

Centre Stage Theatrical School & Company

1320 Kingwood Dr., Kingwood TX

www.centrestagetheatre.org

Classes for this school are held at Roland Ballard School of Gymnastics and Dance. They specialize in acting, vocal training, musical theatre, movement, and choreography.

Classes meet Sundays only at the following times.
Ages: 4-6yrs. 2:00-3:30p.m.
6 to pre-teen 3:30-5:00p.m.
Teens 5:00-6:30p.m.

Price: 4-6yrs $55.00 per month
7-18 yrs. $65.00 per month

SOUTHWEST

The Company on Stage

536 Westbury Square, Houston, TX 77035

713-726-1219

www.companyonstage.com

Acting classes
Ages: Please call for exact pricing and other details.

Main Street Theatre

4617 Montrose Blvd. Suite 100, Houston, TX 77006

713-524-7998

www.mainstreettheatre.com

Houston Best Theatrical training for student's kindergarten through 12th grade. Classes run Fall, Winter, and Spring. Summer camp sessions are available. Check the website for registration information.

Ages: 5 through 18yrs

Price: Tuition begins at $120.00 per session. See site for more details.

Dance Instruction

NORTH

In-Step Dance and Performing Arts Center
449 Sawdust Rd., The Woodlands, TX 77380
281-298-7837

www.instepdancecenter.com
Classes: Ballet, Jazz, Tap, Modern and tumbling.
Ages: Pre-school and up
Fees: Annual registration $25.00

Special Events: Summer camps and birthday parties available. They also have a recital and a dance concert at the end of the semester.

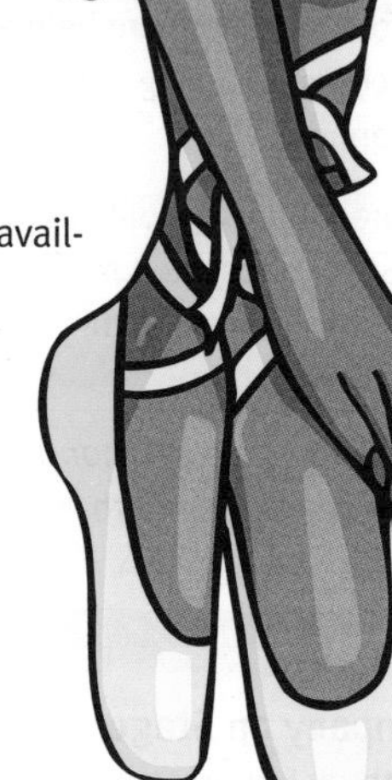

Studio of Dance
16668 Champion Forest, Spring, TX 77379
281-320-1120

www.studioofdance.net
Classes: Creative dance, Ballet, Jazz, and Pointe

Ages: 3 and up

Fees: Annual registration $30.00
Classes priced by the hour starting at $50.00 per month

NORTHWEST

Abbotts Performing Arts Center
8475-K Hwy 6 North, Houston, TX
281-550-1234

www.apackdance.com
Classes: Ballet, Jazz, Tap, Gymnastics, and a pre-school program.

Ages: 3 and up

Fees: 1 class per week is $50.00 per month. Cost goes up with more classes per week.

20% Family discount available.
Special Events: Every year they have a recital to show their family and friends what they have learned. They also have summer dance camps and compititions throughout the year.

DanMar Dance Studio
166 Applewhite Dr., Katy TX 77450
281-392-1150
www.danmarstudio.com
Classes: Flamenco, Belly dancing, Salsa, Hip-hop, Jazz, Ballet, Lyrical, and Tap classes

Ages: 4 and up

Fees: Please call for details

Events: There are many opportunities to perform with this group through out the area.

Fairfield Dance Center
15040 Fairfield Village Place Suite 180
Cypress, TX 77429
281-213-3200
www.fairfielddance.com
Classes: Ballet, Tap, Jazz, Combo, Modern, Technique, Cheer Dance, and Hip-hop.

Ages: 3 and up

Fees: Annual registration $30.00

Special Events: Summer camps and Birthday parties available. They have an annual recital, performance teams, and dance competitions.

Katy Dance and Gymnastics
3719 Fry Rd. Suite E, Katy, TX
281-492-0555
www.katydancegym.com
Classes: Ballet, Tap, Jazz, Gymnastics, Tumbling, and a pre-school motor movement class.
Ages: 2 and up (18 months for motor class)
Fees: Annual registration $35.00

$49.00 and up per month depending on length of class. Family discounts available.

Special Events: Each year they have a Nutcracker Ballet in December and a spring concert. They also have an elaborate dance recital. Summer camps are also available.

NORTHEAST

Atascocita Dance

8034 F.M. 1960 E., Humble, TX 77346
281-812-8114
www.atascocitadance.com
Classes: Ballet, Creative dance, Hip-hop, Lyrical, Tap, and Pointe.

Ages: 3 and up

Fees: Annual Registration $35.00 per family
Classes start at 45 minutes for $50.00

Special events: This is a fun group! They have a yearly recital as well as a parade team. They are involved in several workshops throughout the year, and have some fun parties!

Roland Ballard School of Dance and Gymnastics

1320 Kingwood Dr., Kingwood, TX 77339
281-358-4616
Classes: Ballet, Jazz, Tap, Lyrical, Hip-hop, and Creative dance.

Ages: 3 and up

Fees: $60.00 per month for a 1 hr. class once per week.

SOUTHWEST

Ann Moody Sill Dance Studio

11110 S. Highway 6, Sugar Land, TX 77478
281-498-8270
www.amsds.com
Classes: Ballet, Tap, Jazz, Lyrical, Character, Tumbling, and Hip-hop.

Ages: 3 and up

Fees: Please call studio for exact tuition.

Special events: They have bi-annual recitals held at Houston's beautiful Wortham Center.

Houston Academy of Dance

14520 Memorial Dr. Suite 78
Houston, TX 77079
281-497-4783
www.hadance.com
Classes: Ballet, Pointe, Jazz, Hip-hop, Performing modern, and Tap.

Ages: 3 and up

Fees: Prices start at $72.00. Tuition discounts available.

Houston Ballet's Ben Stevenson Academy

1921 W. Bell St., Houston, TX 77019
713-523-6300
www.houstonballet.org
Located just west of downtown Houston this is a very prestigious ballet school. The academy offers a program designed to take students from their first introduction to the art through a full coarse of ballet study. Their program begins with the pre-school division (ages 4 and 5) where they learn the fundamentals of ballet. The Main School Division is where students will continue learning and fine tuning their skills. Entrance into the Main School requires an audition and is for levels 1 through 7.

Ages: 4 and up

Fees: Tuition is for a full year. Preschool division $688.00 per year. Main School tuition begins at $988.00 per year and increases as student graduates to a different level.

Southwest Dance Academy

7867 S. Hwy. 6, Houston, TX 77083
281-564-6200
Classes: Ballet, Tap, Jazz, Modern, and Creative Movement for toddlers and pre-school.

Ages: 18 months and up

Fees: Tuition is per semester. $225.00 per semester for 1 class per week.

Special Events: They have a recital every June for students.

Studio 03- Owens Performing Arts Center

7002 Riverbrook Dr. Suite 400
Sugar Land, TX 77479
281-937-0090
www.studio03.com
Their goal is to provide quality dance education that is exciting, fun, and innovative.

Classes: Ballet, Tap, Jazz, Hip-hop and a Pre-Ballet class.

Ages: 3 and up

Fees: Annual registration $30.00
Classes are charged by the hour and start at $58.00.

Special Events: Every year they have a recital. They also have a dance company for ages 15-22 (auditions required).

SOUTHEAST

Friendswood Ballet

108 Hope Village Rd., Friendswood, TX 77546
281-482-1058
Frances Hawkins, Director
Classes: Ballet, Pre-school and elementary program, and 6 day per week program for students desiring a professional career.

Ages: Pre-school and up

Fees: Call director for pricing information.

Kennedy Dance Theatre

15210 Hwy. 3, Webster TX
281-480-8441
www.kennedydance.com
Classes: Ballet, Jazz, Tap, Tumbling, Pre-dance, Boys only classes, Hip-hop, Modern, Scottish, Irish, and Folk dance.

Ages: 2 and up

Fees: Please contact for exact pricing.

Special events: Summer cheer and dance camps available. Children's Dance Theatre and a Creative dance program for preschoolers. They participate in community events and have at least two major performances a year. They also have a recital once a year in The Grand Opera House in Galveston.

Rachal Dance Studio, Inc.
4012 Strawberry, Pasadena, TX 77504
281-487-1444
www.rachaldancestudio.cc
Classes: Ballet, Tap, Jazz, Tumbling, Hip-hop, and Mommy and Me classes.

Ages: All ages

Fees: Mommy and Me class-$50.00 per month
Other classes- $35.00 to $40.00 per month

The Houston Metropolitan Dance Company
1202 Calumet@ San Jacinto,Houston, TX 77004
713-522-6375
www.houstonmetdance.com
This studio is located just south of Downtown Houston.

Classes: Ballet, Jazz, Tap, Modern, Hip-hop, Primary Ballet, Primary Tap, and Creative dance.

Ages: 3-12 yrs.

Fees: Annual registration $15.00
1 class per week for 3 weeks is $36.00 up to 4 classes per week for 6 weeks is $216.00

Arts and Crafts

Toy's R Us, Camp Geoffrey
www.toyrrus.com
Hours: Summer program. 1:00p.m. -3:00p.m. Select days.

Price: FREE

Activities, crafts and more. Best for ages 3-9. See store for participation.

NORTH

Gardenridge

www.gardenridge.com

All throughout the year Gardenridge has FREE children's crafts and events. They vary season to season and are usually heavily advertised throughout all the stores in the Houston area. Contact the store for more details and events. All year long each store sponsors Wilton Cake Decorating classes. See your local store for details.

Gardenridge - Airtex
431 Airtex, Houston, TX 77073
281-821-7008
I-45 at Airtex

Gardenridge - The Woodlands
16778 I-45 North, Conroe, TX 77384
936-271-1300
2.5 miles north of The Woodlands Mall

Hobby Lobby

www.hobbylobby.com

This is a great craft store where your kids can truly enjoy arts and crafts! They have an array of classes that differ from store to store. Some examples of classes offered are beginning sewing, Wilton Cake Decorating classes, art classes, scrapbooking, oil painting, knitting, crocheting, drawing classes, calligraphy, jewelry classes, Kid's Summer Art Programs, and many more. Most classes are children approved, but you will want to check with the store to make sure. Remember not every store offers the same classes!

1217 W. Loop Hwy 336
Conroe, TX 77301
936-788-5556

2325 F.M. 1960 W.
Houston, TX 77068
281-444-4770

501 Sawdust
Spring, TX 77380
281-292-2382

Michael's

www.michaels.com

Your kids can join the Michael's Kid Club for FREE. Children ages 5-12 are invited to join. They will receive an official membership card, and a special gift. A personalized birthday card will be sent to them every year in their name. They will also receive a newsletter 6 times a year, and a free Imagination Activity coupon to participate in a fun craft on Saturday. Imagination Saturdays are held each week from 10:00a.m.to 12:00p.m. You can also find any craft online and do-it-yourself at home with the kids. Projects include materials needed and instructions.

Ages: 5-12

Fees: Saturday classes start at $2.00 and go up.

2218 I-45 N.
Conroe, TX 77301
936-539-9630

9075 I-45 N Ste.104
Conroe, TX 77385
936-271-0011

20626 I-45 N
Spring, TX 77373
281-353-5031

NORTHWEST

The Artist Within

12710 Grant Rd.
Cypress, TX 77429
281-370-9336
www.artistwithin.net
This school offers art classes to children, teens and adults. They also have fun summer camps and an arts program for homeschoolers.
Ages: 5 and up
Hours: After school art for children 4:30pm-6:30pm
Saturday Classes 10:00am-Noon
Price: $110.00 for 4 weeks. This includes supplies.

Please see ad in the coupon section

Gardenridge

www.gardenridge.com
All throughout the year Gardenridge has FREE children's crafts and events. They vary season to season and are usually heavily advertised throughout all the stores in the Houston area. Contact the store for more details and events. All year long each store sponsors Wilton Cake Decorating classes. See your local store for details.

Gardenridge – Katy

19411 Atrium place
Houston, TX 77084
281-578-2334
I-10 West at N Fry rd.

Hobby Lobby

www.hobbylobby.com

This is a great craft store where your kids can truly enjoy arts and crafts! They have an array of classes that differ from store to store. Some examples of classes offered are beginning sewing, Wilton Cake Decorating classes, art classes, scrapbooking, oil painting, knitting, crocheting, drawing classes, calligraphy, jewelry classes, Kid's Summer Art Programs, and many more. Most classes are children approved, but you will want to check with the store to make sure. Remember not every store offers the same classes!

26060 Hwy. 290 W.
Cypress, TX 77429
281-373-1070

4705 Hwy. 6 North
Houston, TX 77084
281-550-6411

10516 Old Katy Rd.
Houston, TX 77043
713-467-6503

10955 F.M. 1960 W.
Houston, TX 77070
281-894-9798

1787 Fry Rd.
Katy, TX 77449
281-578-7750

27706 Tomball Parkway Plaza
Tomball, TX 77375
281-255-6644

Michael's

www.michaels.com

Your kids can join the Michael's Kid Club for FREE. Children ages 5-12 are invited to join. They will receive an official membership card, and a special gift. A personalized birthday card will be sent to them every year in their name. They will also receive a newsletter 6 times a year, and a free Imagination Activity coupon to participate in a fun craft on Saturday. Imagination Saturdays are held each week from 10:00a.m.to 12:00p.m. You can also find any craft online and do-it-yourself at home with the kids. Projects include materials needed and instructions.

Ages: 5-12

Fees: Saturday classes start at $2.00 and go up.

7616 F.M. 1960 W.
Houston, TX 77070
281-894-4955

6823 Hwy 6 N.
Houston, TX 77084
281-463-9826

9666 Old Katy rd.
Houston, TX 77055
713-490-1796

NORTHEAST

Hobby Lobby

www.hobbylobby.com

This is a great craft store where your kids can truly enjoy arts and crafts! They have an array of classes that differ from store to store. Some examples of classes offered are beginning sewing, Wilton Cake Decorating classes, art classes, scrapbooking, oil painting, knitting, crocheting, drawing classes, calligraphy, jewelry classes, Kid's Summer Art Programs, and many more. Most classes are children approved, but you will want to check with the store to make sure. Remember not every store offers the same classes!

20325 Hwy 59 N.
Humble, TX 77338
281-540-4612

Michael's

www.michaels.com

Your kids can join the Michael's Kid Club for FREE. Children ages 5-12 are invited to join. They will receive an official membership card, and a special gift. A personalized birthday card will be sent to them every year in their name. They will also receive a newsletter 6 times a year, and a free Imagination Activity coupon to participate in a fun craft on Saturday. Imagination Saturdays are held each week from 10:00a.m.to 12:00p.m. You can also find any craft online and do-it-yourself at home with the kids. Projects include materials needed and instructions.

Ages: 5-12

Fees: Saturday classes start at $2.00 and go up.

226 F.M. 1960 Bypass Rd. E
Humble, TX 77338
281-446-9101

SOUTHWEST

Gardenridge

www.gardenridge.com
All throughout the year Gardenridge has FREE children's crafts and events. They vary season to season and are usually heavily advertised throughout all the stores in the Houston area. Contact the store for more details and events. All year long each store sponsors Wilton Cake Decorating classes. See your local store for details.
Gardenridge – Sugar Land
16960 Southwest Frwy.
Sugar Land, TX 77084
281-578-2334
SW Freeway exit Sweetwater

Hobby Lobby

www.hobbylobby.com
This is a great craft store where your kids can truly enjoy arts and crafts! They have an array of classes that differ from store to store. Some examples of classes offered are beginning sewing, Wilton Cake Decorating classes, art classes, scrapbooking, oil painting, knitting, crocheting, drawing classes, calligraphy, jewelry classes, Kids Summer Art Programs, and many more. Most classes are children approved, but you will want to check with the store to make sure. Remember not every store offers the same classes!
8715 W. Loop South
Houston, TX 77096
713-665-2666

Michael's

www.michaels.com
Your kids can join the Michael's Kid Club for FREE. Children ages 5-12 are invited to join. They will receive an official membership card, and a special gift. A personalized birthday card will be sent to them every year in their name. They will also receive a newsletter 6 times a year, and a free Imagination Activity coupon to participate in a fun craft on Saturday. Imagination Saturdays are held each week from 10:00a.m.to 12:00p.m. You can also find any craft online and do-it-yourself at home with the kids. Projects include materials needed and instructions.

Ages: 5-12

Fees: Saturday classes start at $2.00 and go up.

7560 Westheimer Rd.
Houston, TX 77063
713-490-1421

3904 Bissonet St.
Houston, TX 77063
713-662-0913

12556 Westheimer Rd.
Houston, TX 77077
281-558-1088

SOUTHEAST

Gardenridge

www.gardenridge.com
All throughout the year Gardenridge has FREE children's crafts and events. They vary season to season and are usually heavily advertised throughout all the stores in the Houston area. Contact the store for more details and events. All year long each store sponsors Wilton Cake Decorating classes. See your local store for details.
Gardenridge – Webster
20780 Gulf Frwy.
Webster, TX 77598
281-332-6526
I-45 South exit Nasa Rd. 1

Hobby Lobby

www.hobbylobby.com
This is a great craft store where your kids can truly enjoy arts and crafts! They have an array of classes that differ from store to store. Some examples of classes offered are beginning sewing, Wilton Cake Decorating classes, art classes, scrapbooking, oil painting, knitting, crocheting, drawing classes, calligraphy, jewelry classes, Kids Summer Art Programs, and many more. Most classes are children approved, but you will want to check with the store to make sure. Remember not every store offers the same classes!

4553 Garth Rd.
Baytown, TX 77521
281-420-3347

4200 Pasadena Blvd.
Pasadena, TX 77503
281-478-5770

20091 Gulf Frwy.
Webster, TX 77598
281-557-9385

Cooking Schools

NORTH

Culinary Institute – Alain and Marie Lenotre

7070 Allensby, Houston, TX 77022
713-692-0077
www.ciaml.com
This school is located just North of downtown Houston. They offer several week-long summer cooking camps through June and July. Provided in the price of the camp is lunch, tools, and a recipe book. Also provided are kitchen utensils, a chef's hat, and an apron. Classes are taught in meats, sauces, salad dressings, Italian cuisine, pastries, and chocolate desserts.

Hours: 9:00a.m.- 1:00p.m.

Cost: $350.00

SOUTHWEST

Le Leed's
3001 Fondren Rd., Houston, TX
713-339-4535
www.cheflee.com
Chef Lee offers private lessons throughout the year. He also has holiday cooking programs and Summer Cooking Camps. Contact the school for more details.

Ages: 6-12 yrs.

Cost: Private lessons are $35.00 per class. That includes the child and the parent/guardian.

Cookbooks for Kids

Check out these children's cookbooks and have fun in the kitchen.

The Healthy Body Cookbook – Over 50 Fun Activities & Delicious Recipes for Kids – *By Joan D'Amico and Karen Eich Drummond*

Betty Crocker's Kids Cookbook

Better Homes and Gardens New Junior Cookbook

Better Homes and Gardens Silly Snacks

Photography

Karen Barfield Photography
1312 Woodvine 1 mile from IKEA
Houston, TX 77055
713-688-0148
www.barfieldphotography.com
Karen teaches children one on one private lessons. She will show the student how to use a camera both automatically and manually. She teaches camera mechanics for any type of camera you have.

Ages: 8 and up

Price: $85.00 per hour. Multiple class discount available. Please call Karen for more details.

Sewing/Quilting

NORTH

Eastex Sewing Machine Co.
10874 F.M. 1960 W. Houston, TX 77070
281-970-5552
Classes: Summer Camp for kids. Make a short set, backpack, and a rag quilt.

Ages: 9 and up

Price: $350.00

Class registration includes a sewing machine and all materials used.
They also provide private individualized lessons.

Hancock Fabrics (2 locations)
2208 F. M. 1960 W.
Houston, TX 77090
281-440-5255
www.hancockfabrics.com
Instructor: Julianne

1408 West Loop 336
Conroe, TX 77304
936-788-1072
Classes: Children's Quilting Class
Price: $15.00 per class

Classes: Beginning sewing

Ages: 13 and up

Prices: $100.00 for 4 weeks. Classes run 2.5 hrs.

NORTHWEST

McDougal Sewing Machine Center
1837 Mason Rd., Katy, TX 77449
281-347-0453
www.mcdougals.com
Classes: Kid's camp levels 1,2 and 3. Make anything from a pillow to doll clothes (depending on sewing level). They provide a sewing machine for use.

Ages: 8-12 yrs.

Price: $90.00 includes fabric that will be used.

Hancock Fabrics
10896 F. M. 1960 W.
Jones Road Plaza
Houston, TX 77070
281-469-6881
www.hancockfabrics.com
Instructor: Julianne

Classes: Beginning sewing

Ages: 13 and up

Prices: $100.00 for 4 weeks. Classes run 2.5 hrs.

NORTHEAST

Sew Nice
8900 F.M. 1960 E. Bypass West, Humble, TX 77338
281-446-4050
www.home.earthlink.net/~sewnice
Classes: Young Sewers. Students get to choose their sewing projects. Examples are lounge pants, jackets, pillows, etc. Please bring you own machine if possible but they can provide you with one, if needed. All classes are taught on Saturday 10:30a.m. – 1:30p.m.

Ages: 8 and up

Price: $20.00 per session. Sessions are 3 hours in length.

Hancock Fabrics
9771 F.M. 1960 E., Humble, TX 77338
www.hancockfabrics.com
Instructor: Alice

Classes: Beginner sewing and quilting class.

Ages: 5 and up

Price: Quilting classes are $50.00 for 4-2 hr sessions.

SOUTHWEST

A Cinderella's Dream

888 W. Sam Houston Pkwy. Houston, TX

713-334-4646

Classes: Machine sewing, and introduction to patterns. Students will make a pillow, drawstring bag, and shorts.
Ages: 9 and up
Price: $165.00 for a 3-day session

$260.00 for a 5-day session

You pick what days you want to come. Price also includes a sewing kit and supplies.

Hancock Fabrics

4325 Hwy. 6, Sugar Land, TX 77478

281-980-4142

www.hancockfabrics.com

Classes: Beginner sewing and quilting classes. Taught on Thursdays and Saturdays.
Ages: 12 and up
Price: $20.00 per class

McDougal Sewing Machine Center

2645 Town Center Blvd., Sugar Land, TX 77479

281-347-0453

www.mcdougals.com

Classes: Kids camp levels 1, 2 and 3. Make anything from a pillow to doll clothes depending on sewing level. They provide a sewing machine for use.
Ages: 8-12 yrs.
Price: $90.00 includes fabric that will be used.

The Sewing Connection

Alice McKinney

713-668-7477

Alice will come to your home and teach you private one on one lessons. She commutes within the Southwest portion of Houston. Call her and she can give you more details. You must have your own sewing machine!
Ages: 7 and up
Price: $15.00 per hour with a minimum of 2 hrs.

Classes taught Monday through Thursday.

SOUTHEAST

Hancock Fabrics
16701 El Camino Real, Clear Lake, TX 77062
281-488-5102
www.hancockfabrics.com
Classes: Beginning sewing and quilting.
Ages: 12 and up
Price: Contact store for details.

Chapter 7

School and Educational Programs

Chapter 7

School and Educational Programs

A child's first teacher is their parent. Once a child is born, they begin to learn and this process continues throughout their lifetime. Parents must be pro-active in overseeing their child's education whether at home or school. In this chapter you will discover some of the many resources that are available for parents to help them achieve this goal.

Some Helpful Tips

Parents' willingness to contact their child's teacher regularly is probably the first step to becoming a parent who is actively involved in their child's education. With a clear understanding of your child's strengths and challenges, you will be better prepared with a plan to help your child succeed. Here are some helpful tips to aid in this process:

- Oversee your child's homework daily.
- At the beginning of the school year communicate with your child's teacher about his/her homework policy.
- Set aside time daily for a regular homework routine; allowing time to check for understanding and completeness.
- Monitor the amount of time spent watching television.
- Be pro-active in the decision and policymaking process by joining the PTA/PTO or attending school board meetings.
- Familiarize yourself with the state and national legislature proposed bills and let your voice be heard.

General Resources

Compare Texas Schools

www.greatschools.net/
This website provides parents with information about schools in their neighborhood and the surrounding area. This is a great resource to gain more information about the school your child will be attending.

"GreatSchools.net offers comprehensive school profiles, powerful school search and compare tools, and a wide range of advice to help parents navigate the challenges of K-12 education. GreatSchools.net is the nation's leading online guide to K-12 schools. Published by GreatSchools, Inc., a California nonprofit organization, GreatSchools.net provides parents with the information they need to choose schools, support their children's education and improve schools in their communities."

Texas Education Agency

1701 North Congress Avenue
Austin, Texas, 78701
512-463-9734
www.tea.state.tx.us/index.html
The mission of the Texas Education Agency is to provide leadership, guidance, and resources to help schools meet the educational needs of all students (as stated on their website). This agency works closely with the Texas State Office of Education in order to guide and monitor activities and programs related to public education in Texas.

Texas Education Network (TENET)

www.tenet.edu

www.tenet.edu/parents
The Texas Education Network (TENET) was established in August 1991. It was authorized by the 71st Texas Legislature and developed by the collaborative efforts of the Department of Information Resources, the Texas Education Agency, and The University of Texas at Austin. Its purpose was to advance and promote education in Texas by providing a communications infrastructure, which can be used to foster innovation and educational excellence in Texas. This website has educational information for administrators, parents, teachers, and students. It is a network of links that will aid in the goal of education, whichever role you play.

Texas PTA
408 W. 11th St., Austin, TX 78701-2113
512-476-6769 or 1.800.TALK.PTA
www.txpta.org/index1.html
The Texas PTA was formed in 1909 as grass-roots organization to speak and lobby in behalf of children in the state of Texas. This organization has currently grown to number over 650,000. On this official website for the Texas PTA, you can navigate through the various links to gain more information about how to become involved in your local chapter.

Texas State Office of Education
1701 North Congress Avenue, 5th Floor
Austin, TX 78701-1494
512-936-8400 local
888-863-5880 toll free
www.sbec.state.tx.us
This is where the Houston Mama can find information about the State Board, Curriculum & Instruction, No Child Left Behind, and Education Licensing.

Other Online Educational Resources

Here is a list of a few sites that contain useful educational material to enrich your child's education and learning.

Awesome Library
www.awesomelibrary.org

Enchanted Learning
www.enchantedlearning.com
This site has many activities for all areas of study. It has printable activity books by themes. By becoming a member to the site, you will get unrestricted access to the site. The cost of membership is $ 20.00 per year. Check the website for more details.

Fun Brain

www.funbrain.com

This site contains games for your school-aged children in math, reading, spelling, and science. There is even a link to games that you can play with your children who are under six. The games are entertaining and educational.

Kid Wizard

www.kidwizard.com

This site contains fun science experiments, games, puzzles, and active indoor and outdoor games. What a wonderful resource for you and your children to use anytime.

Kids Konnect

www.kidskonnect.com

Kids Konnect is a safe website that allows your children to find information for school projects or reports. Information can be found for biographies, science projects, literature, and many different countries.

Child Care Agencies

Parents want to make sure that their child is well-protected, happy and receiving quality service from their childcare provider. Take time to investigate your child's potential facility. Here are some tips in choosing a quality facility. The following information is provided by *Early Years Are Learning Years, NAEYC*

Low child-to-teacher ratios.

There should be at least one adult for every

- four infants
- five younger toddlers (12 to 24 months)
- six older toddlers (2 to 3 years)
- ten 3- or 4-year-olds

A well-trained staff.

Ask about the degrees and certificates held by the director and teachers, and find out what steps they take to provide staff with ongoing training.

Appropriate group size.

- In addition to low child-to-teacher ratios, the overall size of the program is important.
- Look for a program with fewer than six to eight infants in a group.
- There should only be 10 to 12 toddlers.
- no more than 18 or 20 preschoolers in a group.

Low staff turnover.

Teachers who have been in a program longer establish bonds with the children, and those relationships help children grow and learn.

A safe and healthy environment.

First, check that the program is licensed by the state. Make sure the facility looks clean, and that all children are under adult supervision at all times. Staff should be able to describe clear health and safety procedures, as well as policies for handling emergencies.

Additional Resources

National Association for the Education of Young Children

http://naeyc.org/

This website is a resource for parents searching for an accredited school and program. Go to the families' link and then start searching from there. NAEYC's mission is to serve and act on behalf of the needs, rights and well-being of all young children with primary focus on the provision of educational and developmental services and resources (NAEYC Bylaws, Article I., Section 1.1).

Child Care Aware

www.childcareaware.org/en/

The following information comes from the Child Care Aware website. Child Care Aware is a non-profit initiative that helps parents find the best and most reliable information for locating quality child care in their area.

"We do this by raising visibility for local child care resource and referral agencies nationwide, and by connecting parents with the local agencies best equipped to serve their needs."

On this website you will be able to search for a Child Care Resource & Referral (CCR&R) agency in your area. This site also provides information about the average cost of child care in your area. For both of these features you only need to type your zip code.

Child Care Facilities

NORTH

Children's World- The Woodlands

7253 E Capstone Circle, The Woodlands, TX 77381

Phone: 936-321-1330

www.knowledgelearning.com

Children's World offers childcare from 6 weeks to 12 years old. Some of their unique features include various summer programs and many locations to meet your needs. Learn more about what they can offer on their website, or call for a tour.

Forest Crossing KinderCare

9005 Forest Crossing Drive, The Woodlands, TX 77381

Phone: 281-296-2966

www.kindercare.com

KinderCare's website provides a detailed age-appropriate checklist to compare other childcare facilities to choose the best one for your child. KinderCare has programs specific for each age group in order to make every moment count as a learning experience. View their website for a more detailed description of their program.

NORTHWEST

Childtime Learning Center

9110 Jones Road, Houston, TX 77065

Phone: 281-897-9010

www.childtime.com

Childtime Learning Center cares for children from infancy to 12 years old. Their website has a quality checklist that you can use in order to find the best facility for your child. In the after school program children have the opportunity to work in various centers depending on their interests.

La Petite Academy

15255 Mason Rd, Cypress, TX 77429

Phone: 281-256-2811

www.lapetite.com

There are over 600 La Petite Academy centers across the United States. The center cares for children from 6 weeks to 12 years old. One feature about La Petite Academy is that they provide a daily-progress chart for toddlers to summarize your child's day. Learn more about them on their website.

NORTHEAST

Childtime Learning Center

3420 Tree Lane, Kingwood, TX 77339
Phone: 281-359-6650

www.childtime.com
Childtime Learning Center cares for children from infancy to 12 years old. Their website has a quality checklist that you can use in order to find the best facility for your child. In the after school program children have the opportunity to work in various centers depending on their interests.

Timber Forest KinderCare

19151 Timber Forest Drive, Humble, TX 77346-1817
Phone: 281-852-3888

www.kindercare.com
Kindercare's website provides a detailed age-appropriate checklist to compare other childcare facilities to choose the best one for your child. KinderCare has programs specific for each age group in order to make every moment count as a learning experience. View their website for a more detailed description of their program.

SOUTHWEST

Children's World- Stafford

12331 Murphy Rd., Stafford, TX 77477
Phone: 281-495-7920

www.knowledgelearning.com
Children's World offers childcare from 6 weeks to 12 years old. Some of their unique features include various summer programs and many locations to meet your needs. Learn more about what they can offer on their website, or call for a tour.

Childtime Learning Center

4935 Sandhill, Sugar Land, TX 77479
Phone: 281-494-4800

www.childtime.com
Childtime Learning Center cares for children from infancy to 12 years old. Their website has a quality checklist that you can use in order to find the best facility for your child. In the after school program children have the opportunity to work in various centers depending on their interests.

SOUTHEAST

Children's World- Silverlake

2325 County Road 90, Pearland, TX 77584

Phone: 281-485-8667

www.knowledgelearning.com

Children's World offers childcare from 6 weeks to 12 years old. Some of their unique features include various summer programs and many locations to meet your needs. Learn more about what they can offer on their website, or call for a tour.

La Petite Academy

3007 Invincible Dr., League City, TX 77573

Phone: 281-334-4289

www.lapetite.com

There are over 600 La Petite Academy centers across the United States. The center cares for children from 6 weeks to 12 years old. One feature about La Petite Academy is that they provide a daily-progress chart for toddlers to summarize your child's day. Learn more about them on their website.

Montessori School Resources Online

Listed below are links to find additional Montessori schools. Please visit the links to find additional schools in your area.

http://privateschool.about.com/cs/montessoriindex/a/montessoritx.htm

http://www.montessoriconnections.com

Montessori Unlimited

http://www.montessori.com/index_home.html

Montessori Unlimited consists of 29 Montessori schools, some of which are located in the greater Houston area.

NORTH

Cypresswood Montessori

18323 Kuykendahl, Spring, TX 77379
Phone 281-370-6100
www.cypresswoodmontessori.com
Ages: 6 wks – kindergarten; elementary- junior high (after school care)
Cypresswood Montessori was established in 2003. They offer after school care, tutoring, gymnastics and Spanish classes.

Greystone House (3 locations)

www.greystonehouse.com
Greystone House cares for children from birth to six years old. The first Greystone location opened in 1984 in north Houston.

Kuykendahl location

17710 South Cypress Villas Dr., Spring, TX 77381
Phone 281-251-3851

Willowbrook location

7554 FM 1960 West, Houston, TX 77070
Phone 281-890-0294

Evergreen location

1000 Evergreen Circle, The Woodlands, TX 77381
Phone 281-298-2444

NORTHWEST

Montessori Children's Cottage

4009 Sherwood Lane, Houston, TX, 77092
Phone: 713-686-5427
www.montessorichildrenscottage.com
Ages: 6wks- 1st grade
Montessori Children's Cottage was established in 1970 and offers Spanish, French, gymnastics, ballet and piano lessons. Some classes have additional cost.

Montessori Moments
19115 Spanish Needle, Houston, Texas 77084
Phone: 281-578-9838
www.montessorimoments.com
Ages: 18 months - 9 years
Montessori Moments is located in Northwest Houston, just north of I-10. The school was founded in 1993.

NORTHEAST

Kingwood Day School
21820 E. Memorial at Loop, Porter TX 77365
Phone: 281-354-5237
www.kingwooddayschool.com
Ages: 2 1/2 - 6 years
Kingwood Day School also offers summer camps designed with hands-on activities, as well as fieldtrips to enrich student understanding and learning.

Pines Montessori School
3535 Cedar Knolls
Kingwood, Texas 77339
Phone: 281-358-8933
www.pinesmontessori.com
Ages: 18 months- 12 years
Pines Montessori School serves ages 18 months to 12 years and is located along the Creekwood Nature Reserve. It has served the Kingwood area since 1977.

SOUTHWEST

Riverbend Montessori
4225 Elkins, Sugar Land, Texas 77479
Phone: 281-980-4123
www.riverbendmontessori.com
Ages: 18 months- 4th grade
Riverbend Montessori was founded in 1976 and has multilevel classrooms. Spanish is part of their regular curriculum. Explore their website to gain more information.

Westside Montessori School
13555 Briar Forest Drive, Houston, TX 77077
Phone: 281-556-5970
www.westsidemontessori.com
Ages: 18 months- 9 years
Westside Montessori School was established in 1977 and provides various classes during after school programs such as, Mad Science, dance, art, and sports activities. These classes have additional fees.

SOUTHEAST

Clear Lake Montessori (2 locations)
www.clmontessori.com
Ages: 18 months – 6th grade
Clear Lake Montessori began in 1973 and was Clear Lake's first Montessori school. Ages vary according to location. Part of their after school program, the Clubhouse, provides lessons in a variety of activities including, foreign languages, martial arts, cooking, dance, and more. The activities are changed twice a semester to provide variety.

Elementary at Sea Lark
16400 Sea Lark, Houston, TX 77062
Phone: 281-486-4971

Falcon Pass
2486 Falcon Pass, Houston, TX 77062
Phone: 281-486-4971

Country Meadows Montessori
607 S Friendswood Drive #10, Friendswood, TX 77546
Phone: 281-482-7117
www.countrymeadowsmontessori.net
Ages: 18 months- 6 years
Country Meadows also provides childcare from 6 weeks- 12 years. They offer free transportation to some area districts, as well as family discounts.

Public School Districts in the Houston Area

http://www.houston-texas-online.com/htoeducation.html
This website shows a map of the school districts in Houston and surrounding areas. The links will connect you to the individual websites for each district. It also lists some private schools in the Houston area.

Private/Parochial Schools

In Houston and the surrounding areas, there are many choices for enrolling your child in a private or parochial school. Many of these schools offer a smaller student-teacher ratio, specialized instruction, or religious based education. Listed below are a few websites to help you get started in this pursuit. Many of these schools offer tours of their campus and you can meet with some of their staff. When choosing a school make sure to ask about their accreditations, curriculum, philosophies, and policies to ensure that the school is what you desire.

Houston Area Independent Schools

www.houstonprivateschools.org
The HAIS website provides a way to search by category or by individual private school. Each school synopsis link opens in a new browser window and most provide a link to the individual school's website.

Houston's Web Source for Private Schools & Enrichment Programs

www.houstonprivateschools.com
This site allows you to search for schools based on their location in Houston. It provides an address and phone number for the school. Some of the listings provide a website for their school. If there is no website listed, you can call and ask if they have one.

Private/Parochial Schools by Location

Please see individual site for school information. We have listed a few for each location.

NORTH

The John Cooper School
One John Cooper Drive, The Woodlands, TX 77381
Phone: 281-367-0900
www.johncooper.org
Grades: K-12

The Woodlands Christian Academy
5800 Alden Woods Drive North, The Woodlands, TX 77384
Phone: 936-273-2555
www.twca.net
Grades: K - 12

Woodlands Academy Preparatory
10400 Gosling Road, The Woodlands, TX 77381
Phone: 281-292-2680
www.woodlandspreparatory.org
Grades: K - 12th

Abercrombie Academy (3 locations)
www.abercrombieacademy.com

Woerner Road Location
209 Woerner Road, Houston, TX 77090
Phone: 281-444-2038 email aaterry@ns1.main.com
Grades: 3 yrs old – 1st grade

Theiss Mail Preschool/Kindergarten
17102 Theiss Mail Road, Spring, TX 77379
Phone: 281-370-1975 email sherry@abercrombieacademy.com
Grades: preschool – kindergarten

Theiss Mail Elementary School
17102 Theiss Mail Road, Spring, TX 77379
Phone: 281-370-0663 email becky@abercrombieacademy.com
Grades: 1st –5th

NORTHWEST

Rosehill Christian School
19830 FM 2920, Tomball, TX 77377
Phone: 281-351-8114
www.rcseagles.org
Grades: PK3 yrs-12th

The Banff School
13726 Cutten Road, Houston, TX 77069
Phone: 281-444-9326
www.banffschool.org
Grades: PS-12

NORTHEAST

Christian School of Kingwood
2901 Woodland Hills, Kingwood, Texas 77339
Phone: 281-359-4929
www.cskw.org
Grades: Preschool - 7th Grade

Kingwood Christian Academy
1365 Northpark, Kingwood, Texas 77339
Phone: 281-354-1197
kingwoodchristianacademy.org
Grades: Pre-k 3yrs - 12th Grade

SOUTHWEST

Second Baptist School
6410 Woodway, Houston, TX 77057
Phone: 713-365-2314
www.sbseagles.org
Grades: Pre-K –12th

The Fay School
105 North Post Oak Lane, Houston, TX 77024
Phone: 713-681-8300
www.thefayschool.org
Grades: Early Childhood-Grade 5

SOUTHEAST

The Galloway School
3200 W Bay Area Blvd, Friendswood, TX 77546
Phone: 281-338-9510
info@thegallowayschool.org
Grades: 3 yrs- 6th grade

Westminster Academy
670 East Medical Center Boulevard, Webster TX 77598
Phone: 281-280-9829

www.westminsteracademy.org
Grades: Pre-K - 8th grade

GALVESTON

Trinity Episcopal School
720 Tremont St., Galveston, TX 77550
Phone: 409-765-9391

www.tesgalv.org
Grades: Pre-K – 8th grade

Satori Elementary School
2503 Sealy Avenue, Galveston, Texas 77550
Phone: 409-763-7022
satori@satorischool.net

Homeschooling

A to Z Home's Cool
www.homeschooling.gomilpitas.com
This site is a resource for parents who are homeschooling or are investigating the how's and why's of homeschooling. This site provides information about other helpful resources for families who are home schooling.

Homeschool Central
www.homeschoolcentral.com
Homeschool Central provides links and information for curriculum, how to get started, support groups and much more. One feature on this site provides links to additional state and regional resources.

Texas Home Educators
www.texashomeeducators.com
This website is designed to create a network of homeschooling resources for families to share ideas and information to better plan lessons for their children. To find local support groups navigate through the links on the page and find one that meets your needs.

Texas Homeschoolers

www.texashomeschoolers.com

Texas Homeschoolers provides information for homeschooling families regarding questions, curriculum, associations, articles, methods and materials. It has extensive information and is designed in an organized way.

Tutors / Learning Centers

Academic Resource Tutoring

Phone: 281-495-6600

www.artutoring.com

This site connects you with tutors serving the Houston area. Check their website for more information. They offering tutoring service for people ages 4 and up. It is a "pay as you go" program.

Huntington Learning Center

Phone: 1-800-226-5327

www.huntingtonlearning.com

Huntington Learning Center is designed to provide supplemental help to children ages 5- 17. Their website will allow you to find a center nearest you by imputing your zip code.

Kumon

Phone: 1-877-586-6673

www.kumon.com

The Kumon learning program was started 50 years ago to help children be successful in math and reading. Kumon serves children preschool age through secondary education. The site locates a center nearest you and gives you all the information you need to get started.

Sylvan Learning Center
1-888-EDUCATE
1-888-338-2283
www.educate.com
Sylvan Learning Center provides individualized instruction for your child in order for them to be successful. Sylvan will administer standardized tests to pinpoint your child's strengths and needed areas of concentration. The site directs you to a center nearest you to formulate a plan of action.

Top-Notch Tutoring
720-939-2804
www.texas.topnotchtutoring.net
Tutor@TopNotchTutoring.net
Top-Notch's offices are located in Colorado, but has tutors who are located throughout Houston. They will come to your home, or meet at a local library. There is a listing of tutors on the website and all arrangements are made by contacting the office. They also offer test preparation, music lessons, as well as academic tutoring.

Language Schools/ Adult Education

The following are listings for language schools and adult education resources for Houston and the surrounding area.

Berlitz
520 Post Oak Boulevard Suite 500, Houston, TX 77027
Phone: 713-626-7844
www.berlitz.us
This language school has one location in Houston near the Galleria. The school offers classes for children through adults. Their programs vary in session length and content. Look at their website for more information on pricing and specifics.

Crossing Borders
26519 North I-45, The Woodlands, TX 77380
Phone: 218-465-0899
www.crossingbordersgroup.com
Crossing Borders offers many different settings and classes in order to learn French and Spanish. They have specific classes geared for children to expose and immerse them in a foreign language. What better way to introduce another language to your family than through exposure while they are young? Crossing Borders also provides services for adults as well, such as, job specific and conversational Spanish, accent reduction and Mommy and Me Spanish.

Leisure Learning Unlimited
2990 Richmond, Suite 120 Houston TX 77098
Phone: 713-529-4414
www.llu.com
This organization provides access to numerous classes and trips in order to continue your quest for knowledge. You must be 17 years old to join. There is a yearly fee of $14 to be eligible for the classes. Classes may have additional cost for materials. See website for details.

Chapter 8

Libraries and Books

Chapter 8

Libraries and Books

Together with the school, the church and the hospital, a library is one of the cornerstones of a healthy community. Libraries give people the opportunity to experience new ideas, explore great minds, and experience great literature, while at the same time providing a sense of place for gathering.

Libraries reflect diversity and character, and give a greater sense of community to our neighborhoods. Libraries are available to school children and preschoolers in the evenings, over the weekends, and over summer vacation. They provide children with enriching activities and resources.

When parents help their children learn to read, they help open the door to a new world. The library is a partner in opening those new worlds for your children. As a parent you can begin an endless learning chain. You read to your children and they develop a love of stories and poems. They then want to read on their own. They practice reading and finally they read for their own information or pleasure. When they become readers, their world is forever expanded and enriched. The benefits to your child are immeasurable, and in the process you will find your world enriched as well. Having access to information through the printed world is an absolute necessity. Knowledge is the power and books are full of it!

Involve your kids in reading programs at you local libraries. The National Library picks a theme for their summer reading programs so they change each year. Your kids will love it! The programs are fun and, even better, they're free.

The programs offered at the libraries are listed under the library locations. Each branch may vary in what they have to offer. Please check with the library to find out the times and dates of the programs you're interested in.

HARRIS COUNTY LIBRARIES

www.hcpl.net

Locations:

Aldine Library
11331 Airline Drive, Houston, TX
281-445-5560
Hours: Mon 1-8, Tue & Thu 10-7, Wed 10-8, Fri 1-6, Sat 10-5

Atascosita Library
19520 Pinehurst Trails Drive, Humble, TX
281-812-2162
Hours: Mon & Thu 10-9, Tue 1-9, Wed 10-6, Fri 1-6, Sat 10-5, Sun 1-5

Baldwin Boettcher @ Mercer Park Library
22248 Aldine Westfield Road, Humble, TX
281-821-1320
Hours: Mon 1-8, Tue & Thu 10-7, Wed 10-8, Fri 1-6, Sat 10-5

Barbara Bush @ Cypress Creek Library
6817 Cypresswood Drive, Spring, TX
281-376-4610
Hours: Mon 1-9, Tue-Thu 10-9, Fri 10-6, Sat 10-5, Sun 1-5

Clear Lake City-County Freeman Branch
16616 Diana Lane, Houston, TX
281-488-1906
Hours: Mon-Thu 10-9, Fri 10-6, Sat 10-5, Sun 1-5

Cy-Fair Library
9191 Barker-Cypress Road, Cypress, TX
281-290-3210
Hours: Mon-Thu 7-10, Fri 7-4:30, Sat 8-6, Sun 1-6

Evelyn Meador Library
2400 North Meyer Road, Seabrook, TX
281-474-9142
Hours: Mon-Wed 10-6, Thu 1-8, Fri 1-6, Sat 10-2

Fairbanks Library
7122 North Gessner, Houston, TX
713-466-4438
Hours: Mon 1-9, Tue-Thu 10-6, Fri 1-6, Sat 10-5

Galena Park Library
1500 Keene Street, Galena Park, TX
713-450-0982
Hours: Mon, Wed & Thu 9-6, Tue 12-8, Fri 12-6, Sat 9-1

High Meadows Library
4500 Aldine Mail Route, Houston, TX
281-590-1456
Hours: Mon 1-8, Tue & Wed 10-6, Thu 10-8, Fri 1-6, Sat 10-5

Jacinto City Library
921 Akron, Jacinto City, TX
713-673-3237
Hours: Mon 1-6, Tue & Wed 10-6, Thu 10-8, Fri 1-6, Sat 10-2

Katherine Tyra @ Bear Creek Library
16719 Clay Road, Houston, TX
281-550-0885
Hours: Mon 1-8, Tue & Thu 10-6, Wed 10-8, Fri 1-6, Sat 10-5, Sun 1-5

Katy Library
5414 Franz Road, Katy, TX
281-391-3509
Hours: Mon & Tue 10-7, Wed 1-8, Thu 10-6, Fri 1-6, Sat 10-5

Kingwood Library
4102 Rustic Woods Drive, Kingwood, TX
281-360-6804
Hours: Mon 1-9, Tue & Thu 10-6, Wed 10-9, Fri 1-6, Sat 10-5

La Porte Library
600 South Broadway, La Porte, TX
281-471-4022
Hours: Mon 1-9, Tue & Thu 10 –7, Wed 10-9, Fri 1-6, Sat 10-5

Maud Smith Parks Library
1815 Westgreen Boulevard, Katy, TX
281-492-8592
Hours: Mon 1-9, Tue & Thu 10-9, Wed 10-6, Fri 1-6, Sat 10-5

North Channel Library
15741 Wallisville Road, Houston, TX
281-457-1631
Hours: Mon 1-9, Tue & Thu 10-6, Wed 10-9, Fri 1-6, Sat 10-5, Sun 1-5

Northwest Library
11355 Regency Green Drive, Cypress, TX
281-890-2665
Hours: Mon 1-8, Tue & Thu 10-6, Wed 10-8, Fri 1-6, Sat 10-5

Octavia Fields library
1503 South Houston, Humble, TX
281-446-3377
Hours: Mon 1-7, Tue & Thu 10-9, Wed 10-7, Fri 1-6, Sat 10-5

Parker Williams Library
10851 Scarsdale Boulevard, Suite #510, Houston, TX
281-484-2036
Hours: Mon 1-9, Tue & Wed 10-9, Thu 10-6, Fri 1-6, Sat 10-5

South Houston Library
607 Avenue A, South Houston, TX
713-941-2385
Hours: Mon 1-8, Tue-Thu 10-6, Fri 1-6, Sat 10-5

Spring Branch Memorial Library
930 Corbindale, Houston, TX
713-464-1633
Hours: Mon 1-9, Tue 10-9, Wed & Thu 10-6, Fri 1-6, Sat 10-5

Stratford Library
509 Stratford, Highland, TX
281-426-3521
Hours: Mon 12-8, Tue-Thu 9-6, Fri 1-6, Sat 9-1

Tomball College and Community Library
30555 Tomball Parkway, Tomball, TX
832-559-4200
Hours: Mon-Thu 8-9:30, Fri 8-6, Sat 10-5

West University Library
6108 Auden, Houston, TX
713-668-8273
Hours: Mon 10-8, Tue-Thu 10-6, Fri 1-6, Sat 10-5

Programs:

Infant Storytime: Ages birth- 18 months/ Features Mother Goose rhymes, movement, fingerplays, and songs.

Toddler Storytime: Ages 18 months- 3 years/ Features stories, finger plays, songs, and movement.

Preschool Storytime: Ages 3 years- 6 years/ Features stories, songs, finger plays, and occasional crafts.

Bi-Lingual Storytime: Ages 3 years- 6 years/ Kids have fun learning simple Spanish words and phrases.

School Age Storytime: Ages 5 years- 8 years/ Features stories, riddles, tongue twisters, poems, music, and occasional crafts.

Bedtime Storytime: An evening story for all ages

Craft Programs: Ages 6 years and older/ All necessary materials are provided.

Movie Time: All ages

After School Programs: Ages 8 years- 12 years/ Activities include computers, crafts, games, and book clubs.

Summer Reading Program

FORT BEND COUNTY LIBRARIES

www.fortbend.lib.tx.us

Locations:

Albert George Branch Library
9230 Gene Street, Needville, TX
979-793-4270
Hours: Mon 12-8, Tue 10-8, Wed & Thu 10-6, Fri 12-5, Sat 9-1

Bob Lutts Fulshear/Simonton Branch Library
8100 FM 359 South, Fulshear, TX
281-346-1432
Hours: Mon 12-8, Tue & Wed 10-6, Thu 10-8, Fri 12-5, Sat 10-

Cinco Ranch Branch Library
2620 Commercial Center Blvd., Katy, TX
281-395-1311
Hours: Mon 12-9, Tue & Thu 10-9, Wed 10-6, Fri 12-5, Sat 10-5

First Colony Branch Library
2121 Austin Parkway, Sugar Land, TX
281-265-4444
Hours: Mon 12-9, Tue-Thu 10-9, Fri 12-5, Sat 9-5

George Memorial Library
1001 Golfview Drive, Richmond, TX
281-342-4455
Hours: Mon-Thu 9-9, Fri & Sat 9-5, Sun 1-5

Mamie George Branch Library
320 Dulles Avenue, Stafford, TX
281-491-8086
Hours: Mon 12-8, Tue-Thu 10-6, Fri 12-5

Missouri City Branch Library
1530 Texas Parkway, Missouri City, TX
281-499-4100
Hours: Mon 12-9, Tue & Wed 9-9, Thu 9-6, Fri 12-5, Sat 9-5

Sugar Land Branch Library
550 Eldridge, Sugar Land, TX
281-277-8934
Hours: Mon 12-9, Tue & Thu 10-9, Wed 10-6, Fri 12-5, Sat 10-5

Programs:

Mother Goose Time: Storytime for ages 1 month- 12 months

Toddler Time: Storytime for ages 1 year- 3 years

Sotrytime: Ages 3-6 years

After School Break: For all school age children/ Activities include reading, crafts, and movies.

Summer Reading Program

GALVESTON COUNTY LIBRARIES

www.rosenberg-library.org

Locations:

Friendswood Public Library
416 Friendswood Drive, Friendswood, TX
281-482-7135
Hours: Mon-Wed 10-9, Thu 12-9, Fri & Sat 10-6

Genevieve Miller Library
8005 Barry Street, Hitchcock, TX
409-986-7814
Hours: Mon 6-8, Tue & Wed 10-5, Thu 10-8, Fri 9-5, Sat 10-1

Helen Hall Library
100 West Walker, League City, TX
281-554-1111
Hours: Mon-Thu 10-9, Fri & Sat 10-6, Sun 1-5

LaMarque Public Library
1011 Bayou Road, LaMarque, TX
409-938-9270
Hours: Tue & Thu 10-7, Wed 10-6, Fri & Sat 9-4

Mae S. Bruce Library
13302 6th Street, Santa Fe, TX
409-925-5540
Hours: Mon-Wed 10-6, Thu 12-8, Fri 10-5:30, Sat 10-1:30

Moore Memorial Library
1701 9th Avenue North, Texas City, TX
409-643-5979
Hours: Mon-Wed 9-9, Thu & Fri 9-6, Sat 10-4

Rosenberg Library
2310 Sealy Ave, Galveston, TX
409-763-8854
Hours: Mon-Thu 9-9, Fri & Sat 9-6

Programs:

Lapsit Storytime: Ages birth- 18 months

Toddler Storytime: Ages 18 months- 3 years

Preschool Storytime: Ages 3- 6 years

Bilingual Storytime: Ages 3- 6 years

Summer Reading Program

MONTGOMERY COUNTY LIBRARIES

www.countylibrary.org

Locations:

Central Library
104 I-45 North, Conroe, TX
936-539-7814
Hours: Mon-Thu 9-9, Fri & Sat 9-5

George & Cynthia Woods Mitchell Library
8215 Ashlane Way, The Woodlands, TX
281-364-4298
Hours: Mon-Thu 9-9, Fri & Sat 9-5

Malcolm Purvis Library
510 Melton Street, Magnolia, TX
281-259-8324
Hours: Mon 9-8, Tue-Thu 9-6, Fri & Sat 10-4

R.B. Tullis Library
21130 U.S. Highway 59 #K, New Caney, TX
281-577-8968
Hours: Mon-Wed 9-6, Thu 10-8, Fri 9-5, Sat 10-5

R.F. Meador Library
709 West Montgomery, Willis, TX
936-856-4411
Hours: Mon-Wed 9-6, Thu 9-8, Fri & Sat 9-5

South Regional Library
2101 Lake Robbins Drive, The Woodlands, TX
281-298-9110
Hours: Mon-Thu 9-9, Fri & Sat 9-5

West Branch Library
19380 Highway 105 West Suite #507, Montgomery, TX
936-788-8314
Hours: Mon, Wed, & Thu 10-6, Tue 10-8, Fri 10-5, Sat 10-4

Programs:

Infant Storytime: Ages birth- 18 months

Toddler Storytime: Ages 18 months- 3 years/ books, flannel board stories, finger plays, and songs.

Preschooler Storytime: Ages 3 years- 6 years

Children's Storytime: Ages 6 years- 12 years

Summer Reading Program

HOUSTON PUBLIC LIBRARIES

www.hpl.lib.tx.us

Acres Homes Branch Library
8501 West Montgomery, Houston TX
832-393-1700
Hours: Mon 12-8, Tues & Wed 10-6, Thu and Fri 12-6, Sat 10-6

Bracewell Branch Library
10115 Kleckley, Houston, TX
832-393-2580
Hours: Mon & Thu 12-8, Tue & Sat 10-6, Wed & Fri 12-6

Carnegie Branch Library
1050 Quitman, Houston, TX
832-393-1720
Hours: Mon & Thu 12-8, Tue & Sat 10-6, Wed & Fri 12-6

Central Library
500 McKinny, Houston, TX
832-393-1313
Hours: Mon-Thu 9-9, Fri & Sat 9-6

Collier Regional Branch Library
6200 Pinemont, Houston, TX
832-393-1740
Hours: Mon & Wed 10-8, Tue & Thu 12-8, Fri 12-6, Sat 10-6

Dixon Branch Library
8002 Hirsch, Houston, TX
832-393-1760
Hours: Mon 12-8, Tue & Wed 10-6 Thu- Sat 12-6

Fifth Ward Branch Library
4014 Market, Houston, TX
832-393-1770
Hours: Mon 12-8, Tue & Wed 10-6, Thu & Fri 12-6, Sat 12-6

Flores Branch Library
110 North Milby, Houston, TX
832-393-1780
Hours: Mon 12-8, Tue-Sat 10-6

Frank Branch Library
6440 West Bellfort, Houston, TX
832-393-2410
Hours: Mon & Thu 12-8, Tue & Fri 12-6, Wed & Sat 10-6

Freed-Montrose Branch Library
4100 Montrose, Houston, TX
832-393-1800
Hours: Mon & Thu 12-8, Tue 10-6, Wed, Fri & Sat 12-6

Heights Branch Library
1302 Heights Boulevard, Houston, TX
832-393-1810
Hours: Mon 12-8, Tues & Wed 10-6, Thu-Sat 12-6

Henington-Alief Regional Branch Library
7979 South Kirkwood, Houston, TX
832-393-1820
Hours: Mon 10-8, Tue 12-8, Fri 12-6, Sat 10-6

Hillendahl Branch Library
2436 Gessner Road, Houston, TX
832-393-1940
Hours: Mon & Thu 12-8, Tue 10-6, Wed, Fri & Sat 12-6

Johnson Branch Library
3517 Reed Rd, Houston, TX
832-393-2550
Hours: Mon 12-8, Tue, Wed & Sat 10-6, Thu & Fri 12-6

Jungman Branch Library
5830 Westheimer, Houston, TX
832-393-1860
Hours: Mon & Thu 12-8, Tue & Sat 10-6, Wed & Fri 12-6

Kendall Branch Library
14330 Memorial Drive, Houston, TX
832-393-1880
Hours: Mon & Thu 12-8, Tue & Fri 12-6, Wed & Sat 10-6

Lakewood Branch Library
8815 Feland, Houston, TX
832-393-2530
Hours: Mon 12-8, Tues & Wed 10-6, Thu- Sat 12-6

Looscan Branch Library
2510 Willowick, Houston, TX
832-393-1900
Hours: Mon 12-8, Tue & Wed 10-6, Thu-Sat 12-6

Mancuso Branch Library
6767 Bellfort, Houston, TX
832-393-1920
Hours: Mon 12-8, Tue & Wed 10-6, Thu- Sat 12-6

Mccrane-Kashmere Gardens Branch Library
5411 Pardee Street, Houston, TX
832-393-2450
Hours: Mon & Thu 12-8, Tue 10-8, Wed & Sat 10-6, Fri 12-6

McGovern-Stella Link Branch Library
7405 Stella Link, Houston, TX
832-393-2630
Hours: Mon & Thu 12-8, Tue, Wed, & Sat 10-6, Fri 12-6

Melcher Branch Library
7200 Keller, Houston, TX
832-393-2480
Hours: Mon 12-8, Tue & Wed 10-6, Thu & Fri 12-6

Meyer Branch Library
5005 West Bellfort, Houston, TX
832-393-1840
Hours: Mon & Thu 12-8, Tue 10-6, Wed, Fri & Sat 12-6

Moody Branch Library
9525 Irvington, Houston, TX
832-393-1950
Hours: Mon & Thu 12-8, Tue & Sat 10-6, Wed & Fri 12-6

Oak Forest Branch Library
1349 West 43rd Street, Houston, TX
832-393-1960
Hours: Mon & Thu 12-8, Tue & Wed 10-6, Wed, Fri & Sat 12-6

Park Place Regional Branch Library
8145 Park Place, Houston, TX
832-393-1970
Hours: Mon & Wed 10-8, Tue & Thu 12-8, Fri 12-6, Sat 10-6

Pleasantville Branch Library
1520 Gellhorn, Houston, TX
832-393-2330
Hours: Mon 12-8, Tue & Wed 10-6, Thu 12-6, Fri & Sat 1-6

Ring Branch Library
8835 Long Point, Houston, TX
832-393-2000
Hours: Mon 12-8, Tue, Wed & Sat 10-6, Thu & Fri 12-6

Robinson-Westchase Branch Library
3223 Wilcrest, Houston, TX
832-393-2011
Hours: Mon & Thu 12-8, Tue 10-6, Wed, Fri, & Sat 12-6

Scenic Woods Regional Branch Library
10677 Homestead Road, Houston, TX
832-393-2030
Hours: Mon & Wed 10-8, Tue & Thu 12-8, Fri 12-6, Sat 10-6, Sun 1-5

Smith Branch Library
3624 Scott Street
832-393-2050
Hours: Mon 12-8, Tue, Ed & Sat 10-6, Thu & Fri 12-6

Stanaker Branch Library
611 S/Sgt Macario Garcia, Houston, TX
832-393-2080
Hours: Mon & Thu 12-8, Tue & Fri 12-6, Wed & sat 10-6

Stimley-Blue Ridge Branch Library
7007 W. Fuqua, Houston, TX
832-393-2370
Hours: Mon 12-8, Tue & Wed 10-6, Thu- Sat 12-6

Tuttle Branch Library
702 Kress, Houston, TX
832-393-2100
Hours: Mon & Thu 12-8, Tue & Fri 12-6, Wed & Sat 10-6

Vinson Branch Library
3100 West Fuqua, Houston, TX
832-393-2120
Hours: Currently closed for renovations

Walter Branch Library
7660 Clarewood, Houston, TX
832-393-2500
Hours: Mon 12-8, Tues & Wed 10-6, Thu- Sat 12-6

Young Branch Library
5260 Griggs Road, Houston, TX
832-393-2140
Hours: Mon 12-8, Tue & Wed 10-6, Thu-Sat 12-6

Programs:

Babytime: Ages 6 months- 18 months and their caregiver/ Features stories, songs, finger plays, and toy time. This program is set up for one-on-one interaction between baby and caregiver.

Toddlertime: Ages 19 months and up/This is an informal playgroup with stories, songs, finger plays, and interactive activities.

Spanish Storytime: Bilingual stories

Arts and Crafts

Playgroups: Ages 6 months- 4 years

Summer Reading Program

Reading Programs

Read With a Child

Parents are their child's first teacher. Research shows that parents who read to their children contribute to healthy brain development and lay the foundation for learning to read. Reading to children helps them to develop a larger vocabulary, a longer attention span, and better listening skills.

Here are some simple things you can do to create a strong reader:

- Be fun and creative
- Ask questions as you read
- Relate stories to your child's life
- Re-read your child's favorite books
- Run your finger along the words as you read
- Let your child turn the pages
- Select stories that use repeated phrases
- Subscribe to a children's magazine
- Get a library card
- Ask your librarian for a recommended book list
- Fill your home with books
- Be a reading role model
- Tell stories to your child

Studies have shown that children who are read to on a consistent basis begin to develop both communication and thinking skills at a much younger age than children that aren't read to on a consistent basis. In addition, those skills continue to progress and develop much more rapidly in children that are read to consistently. This progression of skills will continue as long as you spend quality time reading with them.

Rhymers are Readers

Rhymers will be readers: It's that simple. Experts in literacy and child development have discovered that if children know eight nursery rhymes by heart, by the time they are four years old, they're usually among the best readers by the age of eight.

The importance of getting songs and rhymes into children's heads can't be overestimated. This sounds easy enough to achieve, but it's surprising and depressing to discover how many children come to school these days without even the most basic rhymes in their heads.

(Fox, Mem, Reading Magic Why Reading Aloud to our Children will Change their Lives Forever, Orlando: Harcourt, 2001).

Reading is Fundamental

www.rif.org

Parents can find articles and topics on motivating kids to read, guidelines for choosing good books, suggestions on school involvement and reading aloud with your child.

You can also search books by age group and content, get ideas for family activities, and explore other reading and literacy links.

Story Time in Houston and Surrounding Areas

(Schedules and Times Subject to Change)

NORTH

Barnes & Noble Booksellers/Champions
5303 FM 1960 West, Houston, TX
281-631-0681
Events: Tue & Thu 10:00am- Storytime for preschoolers

Barnes & Noble Booksellers
1201 Lake Woodlands Drive, The Woodlands, TX
281-465-8744
Events: Mon & Thu 11:00am- Storytime for preschoolers
2nd Sat of every month- American Girls Book Club for ages 8-12 (times vary)

Borders Books Music Movies & Cafe
9595 Six Pines Drive, The Woodlands, TX
832-585-0051
Events: Fri 11:00am- Storytime for preschoolers

NORTHWEST

Barnes & Noble Booksellers/Copperfield
7026 North Highway 6, Houston, TX
281-861-6842
Events: Thu 10:30am & Sat 12:00pm- Storytime for preschoolers

Barnes & Noble Booksellers/Town & Country
12850 Memorial Drive, Houston, TX
713-465-5616
Events: Tue & Thu 11:00am- Storytime for preschoolers

Barnes & Noble Booksellers/Vanderbilt Square
3003 West Holcombe Boulevard, Houston, TX
713-349-0050
Events: Tue & Wed 10:30am- Storytime for preschoolers

Barnes & Noble Booksellers
7626 Westheimer, Houston, TX
713-783-6016
Events: Sat 11:00am- Storytime for all ages

NORTHEAST

Barnes & Noble Booksellers/Deerbrook Mall
20131 Highway 59 North, Humble, TX
281-540-3060
Events: Wed 11:00am- Storytime for preschoolers
3rd Tue of every month at 7:00pm- American Girls Book Club for ages 8-12
3rd Fri of every month at 7:00pm- Pajama Rama Storytime. Kids wear their pajamas, listen to a story, sing songs, and eat cookies.

SOUTHWEST

Barnes & Noble Booksellers
2545 Town Center Boulevard, Sugar Land, TX
281-265-4620
Events: Sun 3:00pm- Storytime for preschoolers

Borders Books Music Movies & Cafe
12788 Fountain Lake Circle, Stafford, TX
281-240-6666
Events: Sat 3:00pm- Storytime for all ages

Borders Books Music Movies & Cafe
3025 Kirby, Houston, TX
713-524-0200
Wed 11:00am- Storytime for preschoolers

Borders Books Music Movies & Café
570 Meyerland Plaza, Houston, TX
713-661-2888
Events: Wed 11:00am- Storytime for preschoolers

SOUTHEAST

Barnes & Noble Booksellers/Clear Lake
1029 West Bay Area Boulevard, Webster, TX
281-554-8224
Events: Wed 11:00am & Sat 2:00pm- Storytime for preschoolers

Barnes & Noble Booksellers
5656 Fairmont Parkway, Pasadena, TX
281-991-8011
Events: 3rd Sat of every month at 11:00am- Storytime for all ages and a costume character for children to meet.

Book Bargains

By shopping online you can often find new and gently used books for up to 80% off. We've tried it and the deals are amazing!

www.half.com

www.overstock.com

www.amazon.com

www.barnes&noble.com

Children's Book of the Month Club
www.cbomc.com
Another great way to build your at home library! By signing up for the Children's Book of the Month Club, you get to choose 8 selections for $2.00. You're commitment is to buy 4 more books over the next 2 years. They frequently have great sales and clearance. Sign up online or email any inquires to customerservice@cbomc.com.

Top Picks

(Sorted by age group)

Here is a list of one hundred books selected by the National Education Association as great reading for children and young adults.

Books for All Ages

- The Giving Tree *by Shel Silverstein*
- Where the Sidewalk Ends: the Poems and Drawings of Shel Silverstein *by Shel Silverstein*
- Little Women *by Louisa May Alcott*

- The Wizard of Oz *by L. Frank Baum*
- Heidi *by Johanna Spyri*

Books for Preschoolers

- The Very Hungry caterpillar *by Eric Carle*
- Goodnight Moon *by Margaret Wise Brown*
- Brown Bear, Brown Bear, What do you see? *By Bill Martin, Jr.*
- The Rainbow Fish *by Marcus Pfister*
- Corduroy *by Don Freeman*
- The Snowy Day *by Ezra Jack Keats*
- The Runaway Bunny *by Margaret Wise*
- Guess How Much I Love You *by Sam McBratney*

Books for Children Ages 4-8

- Polar Express *by Chris Van Allsburg*
- Green Eggs and Ham *by Dr. Seuss*
- The Cat in the Hat *by Dr. Seuss*
- Where the Wild Things Are *by Maurice Sendak*
- Love you Forever *by Robert N. Munsch*
- Alexander and the Terrible, Horrible, No Good, Very Bad Day *by Judith Viorst*
- The Mitten *by Jan Brett*
- Stellaluna *by Janell Cannon*
- Oh, The Places You'll Go *by Dr. Seuss*
- Strega Nona *by Tomie de Paola*
- The Velveteen Rabbit *by Margery Williams*
- How the Grinch Stole Christmas *by Dr. Seuss*
- The True Story of the Three Little Pigs *by Jon Scieszka*
- Chicka Chicka Boom Boom *by John Archambault*
- The Complete Tales of Winnie the Pooh *by A. A. Milne*
- If You Give a Mouse a Cookie *by Laura Joffe Numeroff*
- The Lorax *by Dr. Seuss*
- Amazing Grace *by Mary Hoffman*
- Jumanji *by Chris Van Allsburg*
- Math Curse *by Jon Scieszka*
- Are you My Mother? *By Philip D. Eastman*
- The Napping House *by Audrey Wood*
- Sylvester and the Magic Pebble *by William Steig*
- The Tale of Peter Rabbit *by Beatrix Potter*
- Horton Hatches the Egg *by Dr. Seuss*
- Basil of Baker Street *by Eve Titus*
- The Little Engine That Could *by Watty Piper*

- Curious George *by Hans Augusto Rey*
- Wilfrid Gordon McDonald Partridge *by Mem Fox*
- Arthur series *by Marc Tolon Brown*
- Lilly's Purple Plastic Purse *by Kevin Henkes*
- The Little House *by Virginia Lee Burton*
- Amelia Bedilia *by Peggy Parish*
- The Art Lesson *by Tomie de Paola*
- Caps for Sale *by Esphyr Slobodkina*
- Clifford, the Big Red Dog *by Norman Bridwell*
- The Paper Bag Princess *by Robert N. Munsch*

Books for Children Ages 9-12

- Charlotte's Web *by E.B. White*
- Hatchet *by Gary Paulsen*
- The Lion, the Witch, and the Wardrobe *by C.S. Lewis*
- Bridge to Terabithia *by Katherine Paterson*
- Charlie and the Chocolate Factory *by Ronald Dahl*
- A Wrinkle in Time *by Madeline L'Engle*
- Shiloh *by Phyllis Reynolds Naylor*
- Little House on the Prairie *by Laura Ingalls Wilder*
- The Secret Garden *by Frances Hodgson Burnett*
- The Box Car Children *by Gertrude Chandler Warner*
- Sarah, Plain, and Tall *by Patricia MacLachlan*
- The Indian in the Cupboard *by Lynne Reid Banks*
- Island of the Blue Dolphins *by Scott O'Dell*
- Maniac Magee *by Jerry Spinelli*
- The BFG *by Ronald Dahl*
- The Giver *by Lois Lowry*
- James and the Giant Peach: A Children's Story *by Ronald Dahl*
- Little House in the Big Woods *by Laura Ingalls Wilder*
- Roll of Thunder Hear My Cry *by Mildred D. Taylor*
- Number the Stars *by Lois Lowry*
- Mrs. Frisby and the Rats of Nimh *by Robert C. O'Brien*
- The Best Christmas Pageant Ever *by Barbara Robinson*
- Matilda *by Ronald Dahl*
- Tales of the Fourth Grade Nothing *by Judy Blume*
- Ramona Quimby, Age 8 *by Beverly Cleary*
- The Trumpet of the Swan *by E. B. White*
- The Chronicals of Narnia *by C. S. Lewis*
- The Phantom Tollbooth *by Norton Juster*

- Tuck Everlasting *by Natalie Babbitt*
- Anne of Green Gables *by Lucy Maud Montgomery*
- The Great Green Hopkins *by Katherine Paterson*
- Little House books *by Laura Ingalls Wilder- Laura Ingalls Wilder Webquest*
- Sideways Stories from Wayside School *by Louis Sachar*
- Harriet the Spy *by Louise Fitzhugh*
- A Light in the Attic *by Shel Silverstein*
- Mr. Poppers Penguins *by Richard Atwater*
- My Father's Dragon *by Ruth Stiles Gannett*
- Stuart Little *by E. B. White*
- Walk Two Moons *by Sharon Creech*
- The Witch of the Blackbird Pond *by Elizabeth George Speare*
- The Watsons Go to Birmingham-1963 *by Christopher Paul Curtis*

Books for Young Adults

- Where the Red Fern Grows *by Wilson Rawls*
- The Hobbit *by J.R. R. Tolkien*
- Summer of the Monkeys *by Wilson Rawls*
- The Cay *by Theodore Taylor*
- The Sign of the Beaver *by Elizabeth George Speare*

Books About Books

Best Books For Kids Who (They Think) Hate to Read: 125 Books That Will Turn Any Child into a Lifelong Reader
By Laura Backes

Great Books for Boys: More than 600 Books for Boys Ages 2 to 14
By Kathleen Odean

Great Books for Girls: More than 600 Books for Girls Ages 3-14
By Kathleen Odean

Children's Magazines

General Interest for Ages 2 to 12

Cricket, the Magazine for Children, P.O. Box 52961, Boulder, CO 80322-2961.

Highlights for Children, 2300 West Fifth Avenue, Columbus, OH 43272-0002.

Story Magazines for Ages 4 to 9

Chickadee, Young Naturalist Foundation, P.O. Box 11314, Des Moines, IA 50340.

Ladybug, Cricket County Lane, P. O. Box 50284, Boulder, CO 80321-0284.

Sesame Street Magazine, Children's Television Workshop, One Lincoln Plaza, New York, NY 10023.

Science, Nature, Sports, Math and History for Ages 7 to 12

Cobblestone: The History Magazine for Young People, Cobblestone Publishing, Inc., 30 Grove Street, Peterborough, NH 03458.

DynaMath, Scholastic, Inc., 730 Broadway, New York, NY 10003.

National Geographic World, National Geographic Society, 17th and M Streets NW, Washington, DC 20036.

Online Literacy Information

Want to find more about reading and literacy? Explore some of these websites:

Read to Achieve
www.nba.com

International Reading Association
www.reading.org

Comic Book Project
www.edpath.org/home.html

Ready to Learn
www.pbs.org

International Reading Association
www.reading.org/focus/adolescent_books.html

Chapter

Media in the Home

Chapter 9

Media in The Home

Today, more than ever, there is a need for parents to be involved in their children's media choices. Making educated, well-informed decisions is the key for parents and their children.

What is your Family Watching?

Did you know?

- American children, ages 2-17, watch television on average almost 25 hours per week or 3 ? hours a day. Almost one in five watch more than 35 hours of TV each week (Gentile & Walsh, 2002).
- Television is the top after school activity chosen by children ages 6 – 17 (Center for Media Education, 1997).
- 28% of children's television shows contain four or more acts of violence (Woodward, 1999).
- 44% of children and teens report watching different programs when their parents are not around (Strasburger & Donnerstein, 1999).
- Beginning in 2000, all new television sets contain a V-Chip that parents can program to filter out objectionable programs.
- During the 1998/1999 television season the prime time evening hours were the most popular time slot for children ages 2 – 11 (Barron's, 1999).
- Young children who see media violence have a greater chance of exhibiting violent and aggressive behavior later in life than children who have not seen violent media (Congressional Public Health Summit, 2000).
- Violence (homicide, suicide, and trauma) is a leading cause of death for children, adolescents and young adults; more prevalent than disease, cancer or congenital disorders (American Academy of Pediatrics, 2001).

Media's Effect on Body Image

The popular media have increasingly held up a thinner and thinner body image as the ideal for women. The ideal man is also presented as trim, but muscular. These images give our children unfair expectations of what they are supposed to live up to.

In a survey of 9 & 10 year old girls, 40% have tried to lose weight according to an ongoing study funded by the National Heart, Lung and Blood Institute (USA Today, 1996).

One author reports that at age 13, 53% of American girls are "unhappy with their bodies." This grows to 78% by the time girls reach 17 (Brumberg, 1997).

In a study on fifth graders, 10-year-old girls and boys told researchers they were dissatisfied with their own bodies after watching a music video by Britney Spears or a clip from the TV show "Friends" (Mundell, 2002).

You can find more information on these and other topics at **www.mediafamily.org**.

Some Solutions and Suggestions

To prevent impulse watching, use the TV guide before turning on the set.

Videotape TV shows for your child so they have a backup when there is nothing appropriate on the television for them to watch.

Keep television sets out of children's bedrooms.

Two hours of quality television programming per day is the maximum recommended by the American Academy of Pediatrics.

Use the V-Chip in your TV to screen objectionable programs.

Know what your children are watching. Go online and review some of the popular programs.

Be aware of Kid-Friendly TV ratings and warnings.

Educate yourself and your family about media choices.

Make informed decisions regarding the media you will allow in your home.

Turn off the TV! Pick one of our activities from this book and go have some fun.

Helpful Websites

National Institute on Media and the Family

www.mediafamily.org

The National Institute on Media and the Family is a national resource for research, education and information about the impact of media on children and families. Based in Minneapolis, Minnesota, the National Institute on Media and the Family was created to provide information about media products and their likely impact on children to parents and other adults so they can make informed choices. Home of Kid Wise TV ratings.

TVTurnoff Network

www.tvturnoff.org

Come discuss it, learn more about it, and see how others have turned it off. TVTurnoff Network helps children and adults watch less television and promotes healthier lives and communities.

Parents Television Council

www.parentstv.org

The Parents Television Council (PTC) was established in 1995, offering private sector solutions to restore television to it roots as an independent and socially responsible entertainment medium. This website includes top ten best and worst shows to watch with your family, TV ratings, family guides, articles, and more.

Computer Safety

The Internet, initially the domain of adult users, has rapidly become a place where people of all ages surf for fun and information. Children increasingly have easy access to the Internet through school, the library and home computers. The world of information is at a child's fingertips for school projects, homework, interest areas, hobbies and play. Read on to find out how to protect your child and screen the content that is coming through your computer and into your house.

Did you know...

- "In fiscal year 1998, the FBI opened up roughly 700 cases dealing with online pedophilia, most of them for posting child pornography, and about a quarter dealing with online predators trying to get children under 18 to meet with them. By 2000 that figure had quadrupled to 2,856 cases." Source – *"The Web's Dark Secret" Newsweek, 3/19/01.*

- Based on interviews with a nationally representative sample of 1,501 youth ages 10 to 17 who use the Internet regularly, approximately one in five received a sexual solicitation or approach over the Internet in the last year. One in thirty-three received an aggressive sexual solicitation- a solicitor who asked them to meet them somewhere; called them on the telephone; sent them regular mail, money or gifts. One in four had an unwanted exposure to pictures of naked people or people having sex in the last year. Source – *"Report Statistical Highlights." From the National Center for Missing and Exploited Children, Crimes Against Children Research Center and Office of Juvenile Justice and Delinquency Prevention. 6/00*

- The most popular celebrities searched for were Britney Spears, Pamela Anderson, Backstreet Boys, Jennifer Lopez and Eminem. Pokemon was the popular specific toy or game searched. Playboy was the most popular media property. Source – *"Alexa Research Finds 'Sex' Popular on the Web..."Business Wire. 2/14/2001*

- According to NetValue, children spent 64.9 percent more time on pornography sites than they did on game sites in September 2000. Over one quarter (27.5%) of children age 17 and under visited an adult web site, which represents 3 million unique underage visitors. Of these minors, 21.2 percent were 14 or younger and 40.2 percent were female. Source – *"The NetValue Report on Minors Online..." Business Wire. (Taken from study by NetValue, Internet activity measurement service) December 19, 2000.*

- Pornographers disguise their sites (i.e. stealth sites) with common brand names, including Disney, Barbie, ESPN, etc. to entrap children. They also purchase common websites when they expire before the original user has a chance to renew them.

If you are wondering what you can do to protect your children and combat pornography in you home there are a few simple steps you can take:

Keep track of what your kids are viewing on the Internet. If you are not sure how to pull up a "history" on your computer, it's easy. Simply:

- Click on History (which is on your toolbar at the top). It may just be an icon, so scroll over the icons individually and a name will appear for that icon.
- On the left you'll see a list of the last few days, and under that the names of the sites visited.
- A really clever child (and most are) might delete the history. If the history is cleared, that in itself may be a warning sign that something is wrong.

For basic protection, you can easily restrict the types of sites the browsers will allow. In Internet Explorer, click on:

- Tools/Internet Options/Content
- The first paragraph is "Content Advisor", click "Settings"
- You'll be asked to enter a password so that only you can change the parameters
- You can then set the level of language, nudity, sex, and violence

There is more help out there through different websites and Internet filters. A site with great links is **www.webroot.com**; it's a site for software to protect businesses and homes. It also has a great section about children. Click on their ChildSafe box, and it will guide you through some great tips and products. Also visit **www.crayoncrawler.com**, which gives you a browser that you can download that acts as a sifter for all sorts of common problems.

Some other sites to check: **www.cybersitter.com**, **www.cyberpatrol.com**, **www.safesurf.com**, and **www.netnanny.com**.

The most important thing is to get to know your kids and your computer! Discuss these topics with them, educate them about the dangers of pornography, and keep your computer in an open place in your home. Don't write yourself off as a parent who does not know much about computers. If you don't know much about how to work your computer, learn. Your children shouldn't expect that they can slide by undetected because their parents are "techno-dummies".

Read on for more helpful information regarding the Internet and computers in your home.

Some Tips for Parents

These tips for safeguarding your child's Internet use are from the *U.S. Department of Education: Parents Guide to the Internet.*

Interacting with Others on the Internet:

Just as we tell our children to be wary of strangers they meet, we need to tell them to be wary of strangers on the Internet. Most people behave reasonably and decently online, but some are rude, mean, and even criminal. Teach your children that they should:

- Never give out personal information (including their name, home address, phone number, age, race, family income, school name or location, or friends' names) or use a credit card online without your permission.
- Never share their password, even with friends.
- Never arrange a face-to-face meeting with someone they meet online unless you approve of the meeting and go with them to a public place.
- Never respond to messages that make them feel confused or uncomfortable. They should ignore the sender, end the communication, and tell you or another trusted adult right away.
- Never use bad language or send mean messages online.
- Also, make sure your children know that people they meet online are not always who they say they are and that online information is not necessarily private.

Limiting Children to Appropriate Content on the Internet

Even without trying, your children come across materials on the Internet that are obscene, pornographic, violent, hate-filled, racist, or offensive in other ways. One type of material – child pornography – is illegal. You should report it to the Center for Missing and Exploited Children by calling 1-800-THE LOST (843-5678) or going to www.missingkids.org. While other offensive material is not illegal, there are steps you can take to keep it away from your children and out of your home.

Make sure your children understand what you consider appropriate for them. What kinds of sites are they welcome to visit? What areas are off limits? How much time can they spend, and when? How much money, if any, can they spend? Set out clear, reasonable rules and consequences for breaking them.

Make online exploration a family activity. Put the computer in the living room or family room. This arrangement involves everyone and helps you monitor what your children are doing.

Pay attention to games your older child might download or copy. Some are violent or contain sexual content.

Look into software or online services that filter out offensive materials and sites. Options include stand-alone software that can be installed on your computer, and devices that label or filter content directly on the web. In addition, many Internet Service Providers and commercial online services offer site blocking, restrictions on incoming e-mail, and children's accounts that access specific services. Often, these controls are available at no additional cost. Be aware, however, children are often smart enough to get around these restrictions. Nothing can replace your supervision and involvement.

Find out what the Internet use policy is at your local library and school.

Other Ideas

Use Internet blocking or filtering software.

Provide education, talk to your child about safety on the World Wide Web.

Establish family rules about Internet use

Make it a rule that your children not give out family information without the parents' consent.

Consider making a family contract for online safety and posting it next to your computer.

Sources:

Kids Online Project. Outgrowth of the Internet Online Summit: Focus on Children held in Washington D.C., December 1997.

National Center for Missing and Exploited Children, (at www.missingkids.org) *Child Safety on the Information Highway*. Consumer Reports. June, 1997 and September, 1997.

Family Contract for Online Safety

(from **safekids.com**)

Kids' Pledge

1. I will not give out personal information such as my address, telephone number, parents' work address/telephone number, or the name and location of my school without my parents' permission.
2. I will tell my parents right away if I come across any information that makes me feel uncomfortable.
3. I will never agree to get together with someone I "meet" online without first checking with my parents. If my parents agree to the meeting, I will be sure that it is in a public place and bring my mother or father along.
4. I will never send a person my picture or anything else without first checking with my parents.
5. I will not respond to any messages that are mean or in any way make me feel uncomfortable. It is not my fault if I get a message like that. If I do I will tell my parents right away so they can contact the service provider.
6. I will talk with my parents so that we can set up rules for going online. We will decide upon the time of day that I can be online, the length of time I can be online, and appropriate areas for me to visit. I will not access other areas or break these rules without their permission.
7. I will not give out my Internet password to anyone (even my best friends) other than my parents.
8. I will be a good online citizen and not do anything that hurts other people or is against the law.

Child sign here

I will help my child follow this agreement and will allow reasonable use of the Internet as long as these rules and other family rules are followed.

Parent (s) sign here

For Teens

Backyard Jungle

www.backyardjungle.org

Backyard Jungle is a participatory multimedia site where kids learn about ecology and new ways to explore their natural surroundings.

Don't Buy It

www.dontbuyit.org

Don't Buy It challenges kids to question advertising, evaluate media, and become smart consumers.

It's My Life

www.pbskids.org/itsmylife

It's My Life invites kids to share their feelings about the social, emotional, and physical issues that affect them.

The Plastic Fork Diaries

www.plasticforkdiaries.org

Teens explore their relationship to food: nutrition, athletic performance, cultural significance, and the vanishing family meal.

General Websites

Cyberkids

www.cyberkids.com

The Cyberkids Launchpad provides interesting spots on the Web to explore. Immerse yourself in art, computers, music, science, nature, museums, entertainment, and all kinds of other activities.

Haring Kids.com

www.haringkids.com

Kids under 14: fun interactive activities to inspire a love of learning and art, online books, authorized art shows.

Headbone

www.headbone.com

This site allows kids to do everything from write and edit to design and maintain the pages. There are interactive virtual communities, head to head games, fun columns, hidden messages and more.

Kids Domain

www.kidsdomain.com

Great family resource. Reviews on books, toys, games and movies. Ideas for holiday fun, crafts, travel and more.

Kidlink

www.kidlink.org

Join Kidlink's moderated global dialogs, e-mail, chats, and interactive projects. Available in several languages.

KidsCom

www.kidscom.com

An Educational and Entertaining Electronic Playground for kids ages 4 to 15 that emphasize the creativity of youngsters. In English, German, French and Spanish.

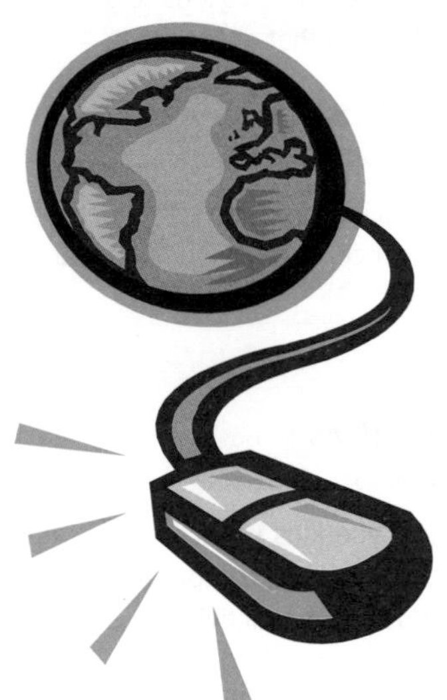

Nick Jr.

www.nickjr.com

This site is great for younger children. Use the Quick Search to find what you are looking for quicker. The Quick Search is organized by: Age-by-Age Activities, Activity Finder, Nick Jr. Shows, and Message Board.

Noggin

www.noggin.com

Lots of activities for kids including Sesame Street games.

PBS Kids

www.pbskids.org

This is the hangout for all of the favorite PBS stars: Arthur, Theodore Tugboat, Mister Rogers and more. Each TV site offers activities, games, and coloring pages.

Planet Oz Kids

www.planetozkids.com

Oban the Knowledge Keeper and his fellow storytellers will take you through the world of myths and legends. This site presents common themes found in stories from various cultures of the world and invites you to learn about the myths and legends of your country and other cultures.

Sesame Workshop
www.sesameworkshop.org

Fun for both parents and kids, find your favorite characters and activities and even an interactive Elmo!

The Case.com for Kids
www.TheCase.com/kids

Who doesn't love a good mystery? At TheCase.com you can create your own mysteries, read scary stories, and try out magic tricks.

World Kids Network
www.worldkids.net

This site is dedicated to the advancement of children's education. It's motto – "Be anyone, do anything, or find almost anything". You can do anything from join clubs, play games, do homework, visit museums, or even be a volunteer for the World Kids Network (WKN).

Helpful Websites

Connect For Kids
www.connectforkids.org

This nonprofit site provides news and information on issues affecting kids and families, over 1,500 helpful links to national and local resources, and two e-mail newsletters.

GetNetwise
www.getnetwise.org

GetNetWise is a public service brought to you by a wide range of Internet industry corporations and public interest organizations. The GetNetWise coalition wants Internet users to be only "one click away" from the resources they need to make informed decisions about their family's use of the Internet.

Yahooligans! Parents Guide
www.yahooligans.com

Search under "Parents Guide". Provides tips and guidelines for safe surfing with your family, monitoring tools, educational information and more.

Kid Friendly Websites

The World Wide Web (WWW) is a wonderful resource for children. It can be compared to a gigantic library containing information on almost every topic imaginable. We scoured the web for the best sites for kids and families. We hope that you find this list fun and helpful.

Online Resources

American Library Association's Great Web Sites for Kids

www.ala.org/greatsites

One of the best resources for kid friendly websites and helpful information. A committee selects sites based on specific criteria:

- Authorship/Sponsorship: Who put up the site?
- Purpose: Every site has a reason for being there – what is it?
- Design and Stability: A great site has personality and strength of character.
- Content: A great site shares meaningful and useful content that educates, informs, and entertains.
- Read more about their criteria and browse through some of their recommended sites.

Berit's Best Sites for Children

www.beritsbest.com

This is a directory of safe sites for children up to the age of 12. Sites are rated and listed by subject.

Fact Monster from Information Please

www.factmonster.com

This is a great site for kids needing help with a report or project. You can search this site by keyword or by subject category.

Virtual Reference Shelf

www.loc.gov//rr/askalib/virtualref.html

Great for reports and general information. Over 30 links from Arts and Music, History, Quotes, Almanacs and more.

Yahooligans
www.yahooligans.com

Presented by the popular website Yahoo!, Yahooligans! is a web guide for kids. Children can use the search engine to find information or they can click on the many categories geared for kids. There are also parent and teacher guides to help adults utilize this web guide for kids.

Dictionaries
www.dictionary.com

www.onelook.com

www.webster.com (go to the kids section!)

Encyclopedias
www.britannica.com

www.encyclopedia.com

Thesaurus
www.bartleby.com

www.thesaurus.com

Government

The White House for Kids
www.whitehousekids.gov
The White House, its history, moments of the Presidency, kids and pets in the White House.

www.afterschool.gov
Kids and teens now have access to government information appropriate to their age group, from the Federal Government. Useful information such as college opportunities and funding, information on substance abuse, health, math, fun stuff, and lots more.

www.kids.gov
Links to federal kid's sites along with some of the best kid's sites from other organizations all grouped by subject. Explore, learn and have fun.

50States.com: States and Capitals

www.50states.com

This is an amazing site. It is perfect for elementary school kids, up to high school. It gives you information on state capitals, state birds, governors, congressional representatives, and much much more!

Language Arts

Ask Jeeves For Kids

www.ajkids.com

Jeeves uses a unique search tool that allows kids to ask questions on almost any subject while providing fast, easy, and safe ways to find answers.

Education Place

www.eduplace.com/kids

This site has all kinds of mind games. One is an online version of MAD LIBS. In Wacky Web Tales, the user is asked to produce words to create a funny story.

English Zone

www.english-zone.com

This website provides over thirty interactive exercises in grammar, vocabulary, idioms and spelling. The exercises are divided into three levels: easy, intermediate, and advanced. Students are able to click onto the answers and check their work when they are done.

Fun Brain

www.funbrain.com

Find games for any subject. This website can make studying fun for any child! Kids can choose the level of difficulty they wish to play.

Math / Money

A+ Math

www.aplusmath.com

This is a helpful site for elementary and middle school students working on their basic skills. Flash cards are generated quickly and are provided for many topics.

Ask Dr. Math
forum.Swarthmore.edu/dr.math

Have a question about a math problem? Ask Dr. Math! Simply submit questions to Dr. Math by filling out his Web form or by sending him an e-mail for help, and you will receive an answer to your question via e-mail.

Bank High School
www.bankhs.com

Bank High School is tuned to the more sophisticated user with Flash 6 a requirement. Learn how to manage money, how banks can be of assistance, how stocks and bonds boost savings, what credit is, how to finance a car, and much more.

Bank Jr.
www.bankjr.com

This web site, powered by Zion's Bank, teaches elementary and grades 6+ all about money, ask the Money Kid and get answers on the web site, learn about the history of money, money basics, money math, money in your life, and more. Take a quiz in each section. Parents should become involved too.

H.I.P. Pocket Change
www.usmint.gov/kids

Want to start a coin collection? Here's the place to start, including a tour of the U.S. Mint, adventures & games. Teachers have lesson plans, a guide and a library for resources.

Kids Bank.Com
www.kidsbank.com

This is a great site for the beginner saver. This site allows kids to learn about saving, and then discover why a bank is the best way to do it.

Young Investor
www.younginvestor.com

Young Investor introduces the fundamentals of money and investing in a colorful way that might grab the attention of the youthful set. Sign up on your first visit and the Young Investor pages tailor their content to your age group.

Reading

ALA - American Library Association
www.ala.org/alsc

The American Library Association collected and reviewed this list of sites.

Create Your Own Newspaper – CRAYON
www.crayon.net

CRAYON automates the process of constructing a personalized, Web-based newspaper for free! To use this site, simply click on Create Your Free Newspaper, enter your e-mail address, and choose a password.

Scholastic Newszone
www.scholastic.com

Scholastic Newszone is the homepage for all the editions of Scholastic News Online. The homepage is updated daily with the day's news, sports, special events and polls.

Seussvile
www.seussville.com

The Cat in the Hat, Sam-I-Am, Horton Hears a Who!, and the rest of the Seuss characters welcome you to Seussville. Check out Dr. Seuss's playground in cyberspace. You can play games, chat with the Cat in the Hat, win prizes, and find out about new Dr. Seuss books, CD-ROMs and much more.

Sports Illustrated for Kids
www.sikids.com

Sports Illustrated for Kids has interactive activities and games as well as stories on today's latest sports heroes. Check out the day's scores, stats, and standings at the Stat Center. Good articles included from the printed magazine version.

The Internet Public Library: Story Hour
www.ipl.org/youth/storyhour

Offered by the Internet Public Library. Here students can hear and/or read stories by clicking on the picture icon or the site. Some stories offer audio narration with the text.

Time for Kids
www.timeforkids.com

This companion to the Time for Kids magazine connects youth with up to the minute news and current events. The site also includes a dictionary, measurement conversion table, country information and games. Full text articles are available in English and Spanish.

Science/Social Studies

Discovery School
school.discovery.com

Explore natural phenomena, go back in time, or examine a variety of exciting themes at the Discovery Channel School Online.

National Geographic For Kids
www.nationalgeographic.com/kids

From the famous National Geographic is a website with articles, games and quizzes for kids. This site provides an accessible menu at every page. Nice photographs and world information available.

NASA Kids
www.nasa.gov

For students K-8. This site has sections on Space and Beyond, Rockets and Airplanes, Projects and Games, and Pioneers and Astronauts. This site is full of child friendly information such as space, space suits, living in space, sundials, weather, the water cycle, careers, and astronomy.

Planet Pals
www.planetpals.com

A website dedicated to preserving the planet. Kids can do searches, read articles, or talk about saving the planet Earth. A wonderful environmental site.

Ranger Rick
www.nwf.org/kids

Offered by the National Wildlife Federation, this website has activities dealing with the endangered animals. It gives ideas for kids in specific age groups.

Sounds of the World's Animals
www.georgetown.edu/cball/animals/animals.html

This site has a simple menu. Choose sounds listed by the animal or by the language. Also included for young readers is *Spelling the Sounds of the World's Animals.*

SpaceKids
www.spacekids.com

Space and science news stories written for young users, a space Q&A section hosted by a team of science teachers, interactive Shockwave games, and a photo gallery. Lots of entertainment for kids of all ages.

StarChild
starchild.gsfc.nasa.gov/docs/StarChild/StarChild.html

This is a learning center for young astronomers put together by a special team at NASA. This site covers everything you'd want to know about the universe and includes many high quality photographic images.

The Wild Ones
www.thewildones.org

This site offers an exciting opportunity for children to preserve endangered species. Each section at this site is designed to improve survival aspects for endangered species.

The Wonderful World of Insects
www.earthlife.net/insects

A glossary is provided. Information on classification of the insect orders is excellent. Kids – follow the link to The Bug Club.

Who is Dr. Universe?
www.wsu.edu/DrUniverse

There isn't a single question you can't ask Dr. Universe! She'll answer your question herself or go to Washington State University's research team for advice. She goes to libraries, field sites, or virtually anywhere to get your question answered.

Writing

Kid Authors
www.kidauthors.com

Kid Authors is a creative place for kids to share their stories and poems for other people to read. Stories are posted by genre (mystery, fairy tales, etc.) and writers can fill out an easy online form.

Penpal Box
www.ks-connection.org

Children wishing to write to other children can find a pen pal by going to this website. This site is safe for use and permission from parents is a must.

Stuart Stories
www.stuartstories.com

This site can be used for online reading and writing practice. They can access the site, choose the activities they want, and do a writing activity. Appropriate for children ages 3 to 15.

Telling Tales
www.tellingtales.com

This site has excellent activities to help children with their writing. "Stuff to Do" is the page containing diverse writing exercises. There are story starters, a "Mad Lib" page, files for characters and plots, and skeletons (outlines) that help provide a start for writing ideas.

Chapter 10

At Home Fun

Chapter 10

At Home Fun

The next time your kids are whining for something to do, or you just want to get them away from the TV, try some of these fun and easy at home activities. Kick back and have fun with your kids! These ideas are also great for playgroups.

Play Clay Recipe

Every child loves clay! They love it so much; the store bought stuff seems to disappear fast (sometimes in their tummies). A batch of this moldable mush will keep them busy and building. Store it in airtight containers to make it last for a few weeks. And don't worry if they eat it, it's made from the goodness of your own kitchen!

Ingredients

- 1 cup all purpose flour
- ? cup salt
- ? teaspoon cream of tartar
- 1 cup water
- 1 teaspoon vegetable oil
- Food Coloring

Mix the flour, salt, cream of tartar, water, and oil in a saucepan. Cook over medium heat until it holds together (keep mixing or it will stick to the bottom of the pan). When the clay is cool enough to touch, knead it on a floured surface, divide it into smaller balls, and add a different shade of food coloring to each ball.

Foil Figures

Use aluminum foil to mold a masterpiece. Kids can create their own statues, people, or creatures out of aluminum foil. These fun figures can strike any pose your child likes!

What Can I do with Butcher Paper?

What can't you do with white butcher paper? Roll the paper out as far as the eye can see and let your kids loose. They can create an imaginary world full of landscapes, houses, and roadways for their favorite toy figures. Have them trace their feet and hands and turn them into monster prints. Have a group of kids create a mural and hang it on your back fence. The ideas are endless.

Crayon Rubbings

Kids can collect simple items from the backyard: leaves, flowers, pine needles, small rocks, bits of wood, or old screen. Lay the items under some lightweight paper and rub gently with a flat crayon until the picture appears. Hint: Tape the paper down when possible for an easier etching!

Paint to Music

Get your kids' bodies and imaginations moving. Grab your paints and set your kids free. Try different moods of music and have them paint what they hear. Is it happy or sad? Fast or slow? Are the lines long or short? Is one song a certain color? Change the music up and see what they produce! Try jazz, blues, salsa or classical music. You might want to take this activity outside to manage the mess! To make a cleaner indoor variation use crayons, markers, or colored pencils on a big sheet of butcher paper.

Blind Fold Drawings

This fun drawing game is a great thing to try with kids and adults. Brainstorm some basic objects with your kids. Write the items or characters down on small pieces of paper and put them in a bowl. Each person can draw a piece of paper out of the bowl, tie up their blindfold, and draw away. Set a timer. When the timer goes off, see if the kids can guess what the others have drawn!

Homemade Mock Chalk

This tough counterpart is great for use on concrete.

Mix two parts plaster of Paris with one part warm water. Add powdered tempera paint to get the desired color. For each stick line a toilet paper tube with waxed paper, seal one end with tape, and pour in the mixture. Tap the tube to release bubbles. Let harden. Voila, this chalk will last for years.

Chalk Painting

Create a watercolor masterpiece on your driveway by drawing with chalk before or during a light rainstorm. Big, basic images work the best! Your child's art will rank up there with Monet when the storm subsides.

Rose-Colored Windows

On a gray day or in the middle of the winter, satisfy your longing for flowers and springtime by trying this fun activity. Use washable paints to create a flower garden on your window. Use paintbrushes and fingers to create stems, leaves, and different flower blossoms. This will add a splash of color and fun to a gray day.

(FamilyFun)

Ice Cube Painting

Freeze colored water in ice cube trays; children can paint with the ice cubes. This slippery art project will provide plenty of fun and color any day of the week. Freeze a popsicle stick in each section to provide a little more control for younger children. Coffee filters work well to paint on with this medium because they absorb the water well.

Finger Paint

Ingredients

- 2 tablespoons sugar
- 1/3 cup cornstarch
- 2 cups cold water
- 1/2 cup clear dishwashing liquid
- Food coloring (for vibrant colors, use food coloring paste)

Mix the sugar and cornstarch in a small pan, then slowly add the water. Cook over low heat stirring until the mixture becomes a smooth, almost clear gel (about 5 minutes). When the mixture is cool, stir in the dishwashing liquid. Scoop equal amounts into several containers and stir in the food coloring.

Make Tiny Bubbles

For a slew of miniature bubbles, tape together a bunch of plastic drinking straws. Dip one end in the bubble solution, hold the other about one inch from your mouth (do not put your lips on the straws) and blow. Learn how to blow all kinds of bubbles at **www.bubblemania.com.**

(FamilyFun)

Homemade Bubble Wands

You can use straws and strings to weave together some of the best bubble wands in existence. Here are a few other ideas from FamilyFun Magazine:

Miniature Paper Clip Wand

How to make it: Bend a paper clip into a bubble wand shape.
Dipping container: Cap from a small jar.
What you'll get: A single baby bubble.

Flyswatter Bubblette Wand

How to make it: Grab a clean flyswatter.
Dipping container: Frisbee turned upside down.
What you'll get: Cumulus cloud-like masses of mini bubbles.

Classic Coat Hanger Wand

How to make it: Bend hanger into a circle and handle. Wrap the circle with string.
Dipping Container: Upside down trash can lid.
What you'll get: A looong bubble!

Giant Hula Wand

How to make it: Dig out your hula-hoop.
Dipping container: Kiddie pool.
What you'll get: Say aloha to the biggest bubbles ever!

Bubble Recipe

Ingredients

- 3 cups water
- 1/3 cup light corn syrup
- 1 cup dishwashing liquid
- Add food coloring for colored bubbles, if desired

Mix all ingredients together and what have you got? Our favorite bubble recipe! Store your bubble blend in a covered container. Great tip: The best time to blow bubbles is when the air is calm and muggy, such as after a rain shower. Bubbles last longer when it's humid.

Here are some other recipes to try out to find the perfect mega-bubble mixture:

Recipe 1

- Dawn Ultra or Joy Ultra - 1 part
- Distilled Water - 15 parts
- Glycerin or White Karo Syrup - 1/4 part

Recipe 2

- Joy - 2/3 cup
- Water - one gallon
- Glycerin - three tablespoons

Recipe 3

- Regular Dawn or Joy - 1 part
- Distilled Water - 10 parts
- Glycerin or White Karo Syrup - 1/4 parts

Recipe 4

- Ultra Ivory Blue - 1 cup
- Water - 12 cups
- Glycerin - 1 Tablespoon

Play Four Square

Remember playing four square at recess? You can create this fun game in your driveway in a bounce! Draw a four square court on your driveway with chalk, grab a good ol' red playground ball and let the games begin. See if you can remember all of the variations for your kids (Giants, baby bounce, double bounce, etc.) Or, try having players call out the name of a country, a state, an animal, a movie star, or another category. A player is out if they repeat something that's already been said.

Materials

- Red playground ball
- Chalk
- Four Players
- Classic 4-square

Play Ball!

Pack a Costume Suitcase

To encourage hours of magic, masquerade, and make-believe, pack old suitcases with dress-ups and disguises. Store the suitcases under your child's bed. We recommend scouring your closets, attic, dollar stores, and local thrift stores for any of the following items:

- Fancy old dresses, scarves and purses
- Hats- top, straw, witch, police, fireman, or cowboy hat; fedoras; Easter bonnets; baseball caps; chef's toques; football helmet; hockey mask
- Feather boa
- A piece of sheer, velvet, or heavy fabric with a dress clip—an instant cape!
- Shoes of all kinds—cowboy boots, Chinese slippers, high heels
- Bathrobe or a kimono
- Wigs and fake fur for beards and sideburns
- Bandanas
- Costume jewelry and plastic bead necklaces
- Eyewear—nonprescription glasses, shades, and goggles
- Lipstick and eye shadow

- A black eye pencil for whiskers and mustaches
- Plastic Fangs
- Wands
- Crown or tiara
- Angel Wings, Devil Horns
- Tutu
- Masks
- Dad's old ties
- Sports jerseys
- Scrubs and a stethoscope
- Old swimsuits, fins, snorkel and mask
- Umbrellas

Act Out Stories from Books

The story line of almost any book can be acted out. Some that work best are nursery rhymes, songs, or simple books. Props are not necessary, but you can bust out your costume suitcase and the kids are set. Have them make animal noises or sing songs. Let them alternate roles or change the ending of the story.

Tailor the Toilet Paper

Buy the cheap stuff when it's on sale. Offer each child a roll and let them wrap away. Play "Wrap the Mummy," or use the toilet paper to "mend wounds," create casts, or head wraps. Let them stuff their clothes with toilet paper and have a rolling race across the lawn. Did you ever think toilet paper could be so fun?

Camp-Out Indoors

Create a wilderness retreat in your own living room. Drape your table in an old sheet to create a tent, or grab a real one of your own. Grab your canteen and some sleeping bags. Roast marshmallows over the stove, make smores, and eat hot dogs. Grab a flashlight and turn off all of the lights. Tell ghost stories! We recommend:

You might even want to set out a bunch of your favorite stuffed animals to make it an extra wild night!

Pet Rocks

Scout around your yard or be on the lookout during a nature hike for rocks that would make great faces. Look for rocks that have face-like features. Stick pebbles, plastic googly eyes, and pom-poms in place with regular glue or a glue gun. Add detail to your rocks with fun fur, sparkles, acrylic paint, yarn, or anything you can find around the house. Be creative!

Become a Master Builder

Cardboard boxes of all shapes and sizes are good starters for any building project. Children can tape them together and paint on them. In no time, ordinary boxes become houses, buildings, fire trucks, or forts. Start by collecting cardboard boxes in various shapes and sizes. Tape the boxes shut with packing tape, or leave them open depending on what the master builder has in mind. Using markers, crayons, or tempura paint your kids can decorate the boxes with windows, columns, drapes and mailboxes. You can even add tissue paper flowers, bushes, or paper flags. If you don't have plain brown boxes, wrap yours with butcher paper or turn them inside out and tape them back together.

Shining Stars

With this handy stargazing device, your kids won't have to wait until nighttime to view their favorite constellations. Instead they can cast their own stellar images on a wall or ceiling in a darkened room.

Materials

- Marker
- Large paper cup
- Pushpin or thumbtack
- Flashlight

Draw a constellation (such as the Northern Cross, or the Big or Little Dipper) on the bottom of a large paper cup. Then use the pushpin to make a small hole in the center of each star. Turn of the lights and hold the cup so that the bottom is pointing toward a wall. Shine the flashlight into the open end of the cup, angling it a bit to diffuse the rays, and enjoy a starry view.

(FamilyFun)

Spin Art

Dig out your old record player or go to your local thrift store to find a cheap used one. Poke a hole in the center of a paper plate, set it on the record player as if it were a record. Have your kids hold the tips of one or more markers (crayons or colored pencils work too) on the plate and turn the player on. Repeat on the other side of the paper plate.

Create a Rain Stick

Your child can make a rain stick of his own from a cardboard mailing tube and dry rice or beans. Here's how:

Materials

- 1/2 pound of finishing nails
- Hammer
- Cardboard mailing tube
- 1-2 cups of small beans or rice
- Tape
- Acrylic Paint
- Paintbrushes

Randomly hammer nails into the sides of the cardboard mailing tube. Ideally the nails should be almost as long as the tube is wide. With one end of the tube securely capped (tape if necessary), pour the beans or rice into the cylinder. Then place a hand over its open end and tilt the tube to test the sound. You can pour out some of the filler or add more until you achieve the sound you like. (If you want a slower-sounding fall, hammer in more nails.) Cap the open end and tape.

Now decorate the outside of the rain stick with acrylic paint. Once the paint dries completely, tilt the stick, close your eyes, and listen to the rainfall.

(FamilyFun)

Wind Bags

Throw your grocery bag to the wind with this kite-flying feat. First, tie together the handles of a plastic shopping bag with the end of a ball of string. Staple a few 2-foot lengths of ribbon to the bottom of the bag for kite tails. Now find a windy spot outdoors and start running. As the bag fills with air, slowly let out the string and the kite should begin to soar and dive.

(FamilyFun)

Paper Bag Puppets

You can make enough puppets for your own puppet show in a matter of minutes!

Materials

- Colored Markers/Paint
- Plain brown lunch size paper bag
- Scrap pieces of fabric
- Stapler
- Yarn, String, Raffia, or Fun Fur

Draw or paint a face on the paper bag. Add hair from yarn, or clothes from pieces of scrap fabric. Have your kids put on a puppet show together. When you're done, store them up and pull them out another day.

Self Portrait Plates

This activity can work for kids of any age. This mask-making project is a real crowd pleaser. The kids can cut out pictures from magazines and paste them together in a Picasso-like self-portrait. Or they can get extra creative and give their piece two different eyes and two different ears, crazy hair, or wild expressions. Use something sturdy like a paper plate or poster board as the backbone for this project. You will need something that will absorb all of that glue!

Set out magazines, markers, crayons, construction paper, yarn, fun fur, glue sticks, scissors, and other decorating supplies. Use the supplies set out to create hair, eyes, lips, noses, freckles, and other features. These fun masks are great for parties and groups!

Rainbow Stew

Mix 1/3 cup sugar, one cup cornstarch, and four cups of cold water. Cook until thick and divide into three bowls. Add a generous amount of red, blue, and yellow food coloring so that each bowl contains a separate color. In a heavy-duty sealable bag, place about three tablespoons of each color they've requested. Roll the bag to push the air out and then seal and tape closed with a bit of duct tape.

Now knead, squish, and squash, the balls of color into every possible color combination.

Juice Box Boat Races

Turn your empty juice box into a boat in a matter of minutes. All you need is an empty juice box, a couple of extra straws, and some sail décor!

Cut a rectangular sail from the scrap plastic or paper. Let your kids personalize their sales with markers, glitter, stickers, or crayons. Punch a hole at each end and thread the straw through. With the scissors or the tip of a knife, cut a small "X" in the center of the empty juice box, insert the straw, and sail. Float your boat in the wading pool and blow through another straw to send it sailing. Have "yacht races" for popsicle prizes, or have them see what tricks they can maneuver with their little juice boat.

Make a Family Quilt

This project will require a little more time for the parent but will become a treasured keepsake in years to come. Have everyone in the family pick out their favorite fabrics and cut them into 8-inch squares. Emphasize that they should choose a fabric that represents their own personality in some way. Create a patchwork quilt out of the colorful scraps that they have selected.

More Great Resources

FamilyFun Boredom Busters
Edited by Deanna F. Cook

Find 365 creative, inventive, and expertly chosen projects that will ensure there is always something fun to do every single day of the year. Features bright, full color photographs.

The Little Hands Big Fun Craft Book
Creative Fun for 2-6 Year Olds
By Judy Press

Make a hearts and flowers necklace, a handprint family tree, a noodle nametag, or a tooth fairy pouch. Over 70 fun arts and crafts projects encourage creativity.

FamilyFun Crafts

Edited by Deanna F. Cook

The perfect resource for busy families in search of creative and exciting ways to turn free time into fun family time, Disney's FamilyFun Crafts nurture a child's creativity through painting, drawing, paper crafts, kitchen crafts, nature crafts, homemade toys, and much more. Color illustrations.

You can find any of these books online and in bookstores. If you're looking for a great deal try **www.half.com**, or buy "used" **from www.amazon.com**.

Chapter 11

In The Garden

Chapter 11

In the Garden

As winter ends, we look forward to spring, which bring rebirth in nature. Soon the days will be longer, school will be out, and families will spend more time outside. If you're looking for a fun outdoor activity that allows the whole family to participate, consider a family garden! From selecting your vegetables and flowers, preparing the earth and planting, to finally harvesting, gardening can be a wonderful way to involve your children in a healthy hobby you can also enjoy.

Life Lessons of Gardening

Along with the fun of getting dirty, gardening helps children learn valuable lessons about patience as they wait for vegetables to grow, responsibility as they see how necessary their care is to the garden, and even loss when flowers die at the end of a season. "They learn about nurturing a life and what it takes to keep something alive," says Amy Gifford, an education associate for the National Gardening Association.

The garden can teach us and our children profound lessons about life and the world around us. Here are just a few of the many benefits of gardening with your family:

Science
It teaches them about the lifecycle and the wonders of nature, not to mention earth science and the effects we have on our environment. Kids also get a first-hand account into the miracle of life trapped inside a single seed - something to be discovered and cherished.

Life 101

Gardening offers a great opportunity to connect with nature on a deeper level - by touching it, caring for it, and watching it grow. Gardening teaches the rhythms of the seasons and the life cycle. The garden is life's lessons in action- there is no telling or listening - only doing and waiting. If they don't water the plants, they'll die. If they don't tend the weeds, they'll take over. Though the lessons seem small, they are the first steps toward larger ideas and responsibilities.

Relaxation

Gardening has also been shown to reduce stress - no matter what your age. The quiet, calming effect of gardening can soothe the stressed out or overstimulated child. Even better, the garden appeals to all five of our senses - we can see, touch, smell, hear, and even "taste" our garden. The healing effects of gardening are well documented, and are even being used in programs to help children of abuse and/or broken homes to rebuild their self-esteem.

Family Time

Gardening is also a great time to connect with your kids. Talk together, or work quietly along side each other. You never know - you may rediscover your child in the backyard pumpkin patch!

Other benefits of gardening for children include:

- Improvement in fine and gross motor skills
- Improved social skills
- Enhanced self-esteem
- Enhanced sensory perception and creativity

Garden Tips

Gardening can be made easy and fun for children of all abilities by keeping in mind a few things:

- Caring for their own section of the garden can give children a great feeling of accomplishment as they watch their own plants grow and change.
- Let kids have their own spot. If they want to toss 10 seeds in one hole, let them and they will see what happens. Allow them to learn from their own experiences.
- Have drinks and snacks available.
- Provide small or child-sized tools for better grip.
- Use larger seeds for easier handling; place smaller seeds into a spice jar and sprinkle for easier planting.
- Allow for frequent rest breaks.
- Plant plants that grow quickly and easily.
- Modify the garden using raised beds, containers, or trellises, to make gardening easier for a child with special needs.
- Don't forget the sunscreen and hats!

Create Your Own Grass Man

Paint a silly face on a medium size terra cotta pot. Place some gravel at the bottom of the pot, fill it with soil, and sprinkle a handful of grass seeds on the surface. Keep it damp and in a light place. In a few weeks, the grassy hair will grow. But if you don't take control, it will grow and grow and grow. Give it a trim and create your own grassy hairstyle.

Magic In A Pot

Place some pebbles at the bottom of a bucket or a 9-inch planting pot. Fill the pot to the brim with potting compost. Sprinkle about 20 seeds on the top, cover them with a bit of compost, and water them. Leave the pot in a warm, light place. After a couple of weeks, seedlings will begin to show.

When you have good growth from your seedlings, you can put the pot outside. Place little plastic figures or tiny gnomes among the little plants.

Seed Starter Ideas

Flowers

Fill an empty egg carton with compost. Push one seed into each cup so that it is covered by the soil. Water to make the soil damp. Shoots should appear after about a week or two. When the shoots are strong enough, transfer them into the garden.

Vegetables

Use empty yogurt containers (from a six pack of yogurt). Fill with compost and plant your vegetable seeds. Tape a picture of what you have planted to the side of the container. When the plant is big enough, transfer it to the garden.

Catnip Sock Toy

Catnip is simply irresistible to cats. Fill a bag or a sock with catnip and watch your kitty go crazy! Create a face on a colorful sock with buttons and beads, and fill the sock with catnip. Add rice or dried peas to make it heavier. Tie a knot and let your cat loose on it.

Picture Pots

Give your plants a personality by decorating their pots. Paint bugs, flowers, polka dots, zebra stripes, or create a spooky castle.

To paint pebbles and pots, use acrylic or poster paint. To make sure they are shiny and waterproof, mix the paints with PVA glue. Use one part PVA glue to every two parts paint.

Ping Pong Ball Plant Labels

Plant curious Ping Pong labels all over your garden. Simply make a hole in a Ping Pong ball and stick it on top of a plant cane. Use waterproof pens or markers to decorate them and write the name of the plant.

Air Plants

This plant needs no soil, barely needs water, and doesn't even like too much sunlight! This is an air plant. They can perch on rocks, trees, and even telephone wires! They hardly demand any attention but will certainly attract it.

Pop the air plant in a vase or perch it on a surface. Give it a good, allover spray with cool purified water, about once a week. Sit back and watch it grow!

Grow A Sweet Potato

The perfect indoor gardening project, this sweet potato vine is quick and easy to grow.

Materials

- Sweet potato that has begun to sprout
- 2 toothpicks
- Glass jar
- Terra-cotta pot and potting soil

Pierce the middle of the sweet potato with toothpicks, one on each side, and suspend over the jar. Fill the jar almost to the top with lukewarm water and set it on a bright windowsill. Be sure that the root end of the potato, called the pointier, faces downward. In 7-14 days, you'll see whiskery rootlets growing under the water. In a week or two, you should see tiny red sprouts at the top, which will soon open into red-veined green leaves.

When growth is about 6-8 inches high transplant the potato to a flowerpot. Fill the pot about a third of the way with soil, put in the tuber and add soil up to the growth. Cover the tuber completely to discourage rotting. Water often to keep the soil lightly moist.

(FamilyFun)

Community Gardens

Edith L. Moore Nature Sanctuary

440 Wilchester Blvd.
Houston, TX

www.houstonaudubon.org
Hours: Open 7 days a week from 7:00am to 7:00pm
Price: FREE

This park runs along a creek and has a restored log cabin that offers a variety of educational programs. Bird watching is the most popular past time here and you can print off a bird checklist from the website.

Hermann Park

6001 Fannin St.
Houston, TX
One of the largest parks in the Houston area, it is home to the Houston Zoo, The Miller Outdoor Theatre, Museum of Natural Science, and the Japanese Garden. Other areas of the park include a water playground, picnic pavilions and FREE unlicensed fishing for kids 12 and under. This is a great place to spend the day!

Houston Arboretum and Nature Center

4501 Woodway
Houston, TX
713-681-8433
www.houstonarboretum.org
Hours: Open 7 days a week from 8:30am to 6:00pm
Price: FREE

Walk more than 5 miles of trails and experience nature in the middle of Houston.

Jesse H. Jones Park and Nature Center

20634 Kenswick Dr.
Humble, TX
281-446-8588
www.hcp4.net
Hours: Park is open 7 days a week: March through October from 8:00am-7:00pm
December and January from 8:00am-5:00pm
November and February from 8:00am-6:00pm
Nature Center is open daily all year round from 8:00am to 4:30pm
Price: FREE

Mercer Arboretum
2306 Aldine Westfield Rd.
Humble, TX
281-443-8731
www.hcp4.net
Hours: Open Monday through Saturday 8:00am to 7:00pm and Sunday 10:00am to 7:00pm
Price: FREE

You might think this is just a place for plant lovers but anyone can appreciate this beautiful botanical garden. See rare species of plants like the carnivorous insect eating plants. See the butterfly nursery and the hundreds of fish in the Koi ponds. Don't forget your camera and bug spray!

Nature Discovery Center
7112 Newcastle
Bellaire, TX 77401
713-667-6550
www.naturediscoverycenter.org
You do not want to miss a chance to visit this place. It is in Russ Pitman Park in the middle of Bellaire. The center has a hands-on approach designed to spark an interest in children for nature and science. They have a discovery room with boxes, fashioned after those in the Smithsonian, where kids can explore a crystal cave, or reconstruct a turtle skeleton. Kids are also delighted when they get to see the baby chicks, frogs, snakes, and other animals here.

Hours: Open Tuesday through Sunday 12:00pm-5:30pm
Price: FREE

Great Gardening Books

The Gardening Book
DK Publishing

Colorful photographs and step by step instructions show you how to create over 50 projects from a miniature garden that fits into the palm of your hand to grass people with heads you can groom. This Book is perfect for budding gardeners who want to get growing.

Kid's Gardening
by Kevin Raftery, Kim Gilbert, and Jim M'Guinness

Now young readers will know from whence those carrots came. This full-color extravaganza contains nearly a hundred pages of wipe-clean card-stock, hundreds of illustrations, dozens of growing activities, plus 15 varieties of vegetable, flower, and herb seeds.

National Gardening Association Guide to Kids' Gardening
National Gardening Association

This is the official youth gardening guide of the 250,000 member National Gardening Association. It combines more than 70 gardening project ideas with practical how-to advice on starting and maintaining a youth garden. Included with the purchase of each book is a free six-month membership in the National Gardening Association.

Roots, Shoots, Buckets & Boots: Gardening Together With Children Sunflower Houses: Inspiration from the Garden-A Book for Children and Their Grown-Ups
by Sharon Lovejoy

The pictures and illustrations alone are enough reason to buy these books. The author keeps a young child's attention span in mind and emphasizes the small wonders a garden brings.

The projects are not only kid-friendly, but also give a child reason to stick it out from planting to harvest. These books go one step further in skillfully weaving in science, folklore, and practical gardening information.

Helpful Websites

www.kidsgardening.com

The National Gardening Association is a nonprofit organization established in 1972 to help people through gardening. This site is one of the best resources we have found. It includes helpful gardening tips, activities, books, and more. It is both an excellent educational and family resource.

www.gardens4kids.com

Their themed garden plans have been specially created so that children and adults of all ages and abilities can use them to plant a beautiful and inspiring theme-based garden! All garden plans are designed by a master gardener to encourage a unique opportunity for children and adults. This allows them to have an appreciation for the wonders of our natural world within a garden.

Chapter 12

Parties and Gatherings

Chapter 12

Parties and Gatherings

Whether you are planning a theme party at your home or looking to move the party elsewhere, we think you'll find some of these local party resources helpful. Rent a "bounce house" or have a bowling bash. You'll find lots of ideas for the perfect party.

Entertainers

All entertainers in this section make your child's party easier by coming to you. They will come to your house or location of your choice. Keep in mind that traveling fees may apply. Be sure to call before booking your party.

A Bash Entertainment

713-977-5022

A Bash Entertainment provides costume-characters including Disney and cartoon characters, as well as, clowns. Each character comes to the party with their own special music, games for the children to play, and a picture of themselves for the kids to color. During the party, the character will pose for a picture with the children.

Price: $95-$160

A Better Party

281-351-0038

www.abetterparty.net

Full service party agency including: clowns, costume characters, balloons, face painting, music, tea parties, and even a petting zoo.

Price: Varies depending on needs, please call.

All Houston Clowns & Performers

281-360-7140

www.houstonclowns.com

A party agency featuring "award winning" clowns, magicians, balloon artists and DJ's. Clowns perform on stilts and unicycles.

Price: Varies depending on needs, please call.

Angelic Tea Parties At Your Door

281-350-1848

www.angelicteapartys.com

Party includes personalized invitations mailed for you, real china, personalized place cards, tables and chairs, dress-up clothes, music, and vanity tables. It is a "Victorian princess tea-party" at your home. During the party the girls will dress up and have a beauty session at a vanity table, followed by a fashion show and tea party. For a great party favor, each girl will get to decorate and take home her own vanity mirror.

Price: $325 for 8 girls, $400 for 8-12 girls. Setup and cleanup are included.

Baloonatics

281-980-8200

www.kidspartyrental.com

This place has everything you need for a fantastic birthday party. They have clowns, seasonal characters, magicians, superheroes, balloon sculpting, face painting, and inflatable activities.

Price: Varies depending on needs, please call.

Bannor Birthday

713-694-4457

If your children love acting, they will love Bannor Birthday! The owner is a drama teacher and a storyteller. She is great with all ages. For younger children, she tells stories, brings crafts, and sings songs. For an older crowd, she brings the theater to the party with costumes and wigs. She directs the children and teaches them how to act.

Price: $75 for 30 min. show & $100 for 1 hour show.

Big Top Clowns

281-350-4432
www.bigtopclowns.com

Big Top Clowns have many different clowns to choose from. Their clowns can perform comedy and magic, balloon twisting, face painting, and storytelling.

Price: Birthday packages starting at $85.

Caricatures by Tom

713-291-2468

Houston artist Tom Rye will come to your party location and create humorous caricatures of the guests. He brings his easel and materials and will have the drawing completed in minutes. Children have fun watching him draw. It makes a wonderful party favor.

Price: $150 per hour. Tom can draw 8-12 people per hour.

Carranza Puppets

281-890-5210

Your child will have the choice of two, 30-minute, hand puppet shows: "The Three Little Pigs" or "The True Story of Little Red Riding Hood." A 2-foot-tall string puppet, a Jack-in-the-box and Mr. Clown will also be amongst the guests at the party as part of the birthday package. They will come to your home or indoor location of your choice.

Price: $185.00

Cherie Kay

281-807-7878
www.cheriekay.com

Birthday party packages can include: magic performed by your child, magic performed using doves and rabbits, comedy, storytelling, games, balloon art twisting, and more.

Prices: $175-$300. Cherie will customize your party and price to meet your desires and children's age level.

Comedy Magic Shows by Alan Anderson

713-952-2526

www.alananderson.com

Alan Anderson 's magic shows are different than must magicians. He appears regularly at The Children's Museum of Houston and several restaurants in the area. His shows are a mixture of magic, comedy, and audience participation. His shows are 45 minutes and the birthday child becomes the Official Magician's Assistant and helps him throughout the show.

Prices: Vary depending on date, location, and number of people in party.

Funtastic Fun Times & Parties

281-361-9090

Twinkles and Sparkles the Clown, Bootsy and Oopsey the Clown, themed parties, face painting, crafts, balloon twisting and hands-on games.

Price: Birthday packages starting at $150.

Houston Clown Fun

713-266-6438

www.houstonclownfun.com

Clowns, characters, balloon art, face painting, story telling, and much more!

Price: Vary depending on needs, please call.

Incredible Characters

281-484-1300

www.incrediblecharacters.com

Costume characters, princesses, superheroes, magicians, clowns, and jugglers.

Price: Varies depending on needs, please call.

Leialoha's Hula Company (Let's Hula)

281-353-1032

www.letshula.com

Entertainers include Hawaiian hula dancers and fire-knife dancers. There are 4 shows available to choose from and range from 30-60 minutes. The birthday child will receive a flower lei and a special Polynesian gift.

Prices: $225-$500 depending on type of show and length of show selected.

Let's Have a Party

281-242-1344
www.letshaveapartynow.com

Costume characters, clowns, face painters, magicians, princess parties, DJs, and moonwalks.

Prices: Vary depending on needs, please call

Mad Science

713-663-7623
www.madscience.org/houston

Birthday children and guests will have fun wearing a lab coat and becoming a Mad Scientist for the day. Party is 45-60 minutes long and is recommended for children ages 5-12. It is suited for any group size and is held at your location. Party may include objects floating in air, fireworks, a plasma ball lit by energy, water lit with an eerie green glow or making super stretchy putty. All party guests will get to make their own gooey-green slime.

Mad Science also does school workshops, after school programs, summer camps and other special events. Call for details.

Prices: $145.00 for up to 15 children. Ad-ons $20.00 - $25.00

Muffie the Clown

281-355-6935

Muffie the Clown is an adorable clown specializing in children's magic shows, face painting, and balloon sculpting.

Price: 1 hour magic show with balloons- $150, 1 ? hour magic show with balloons and face painting-$225.

Party Fire Department

713-560-3883

www.partyfiredepartment.com

Party includes a tour of the fire truck and equipment, a short course on fire safety, the opportunity to try in the yellow fire fighter coats and helmets, and best of all a ride around your neighborhood in the fire truck.

Prices: $300 if located inside the 610 Loop, $350 if located between the 610 Loop and Beltway 8, and $400 if located between Beltway 8 and Grand Parkway.

Professor Chrome Dome

281-488-3422

www.profchromedome.com

Ed Sheinberg is a family entertainer who uses his magic to make children laugh and to educate them. He loves involving the kids by letting them help perform the magic tricks. Professor Chrome Dome offers 2 fun shows. First a 1-hour stage show featuring magic, illusions and mind reading. The two-in-one show features a 20-minute stage show and a 40-minute class teaching them how to perform their own magic tricks.

Price: $200 for the two-in-one show & $225 for the stage show

Ted Schwank

281-579-7770

www.schwankmagic.com

Ted Schwank is a nationally recognized magician and entertainer. He has appeared with Bob Hope and Disney. He is a master magician and juggler. He brings live birds and rabbits and lets your children become magicians.

Prices: Silver Package is $300, Gold Package is $350, and the Platinum Package is $395.

Texas Snakes & More

713-934-7668

www.texassnakes.net

Mr. Clint the Snake Man will make your birthday party fun and educational. He brings 8-10 non-aggressive and non-venomous snakes for children to touch and hold, while teaching them fun facts about snakes. He usually brings a three-toed box turtle or a bearded dragon (lizard) as well. Each party includes up to a 1-hour snake show (time is adjusted to fit the appropriate age of the child). The birthday child will receive a snake poster, a junior snake handler certificate, and a wooden cobra snake.

Price: $125 for up to 12 kids and $150 for up to 25 kids.

The Cookie Art Cart

281-447-5026
www.thecookieartcart.com

Let your birthday child be a chef for the day. This company will bring all the supplies needed to create yummy cookies. You just provide the location and the table. They provide the cookie dough, cookie cutters, frosting, decorating utensils, aprons, and even the oven. The birthday child will select the cookie cutters to use during the party, and assist in rolling and cutting out cookies. All guests will get to wear a chef's hat and learn to make, bake, and decorate their cookies. At the end of the party, the kids will enjoy eating an 8- inch, round, decorated cookie cake provided by The Cookie Art Cart. Parties usually last 90 minutes. Each child will get to take home 2 neatly packaged cookies.

Price: $200 for 10 children and $275 for 15 children.

Party Facilities

Adventure Bay

13602 Beechnut, Houston, TX
281-498-SWIM
www.adventurebay.com

Parties include all day admission for 10 guests and 2 hours at a reserved party pavilion. The birthday child receives free admission into the park.

Price: Splash package-$12.99 per person, Castaway package- $15.99 per person and includes a choice of a splash meal or inner tube for each child, Paradise package-$18.99 per person and includes both a splash meal and an inner tube for each child.

Aerodrome Ice Skating

8200 Willow Place North, Houston, TX
281-84-SKATE
www.aerodromes.com

Price includes skating admission and skate rental, 1-hour in private decorated party room, party host, all paper products, balloons, a choice of 2 slices of pizza or a hot-dog and chips, and 2 glasses of soda. A minimum of 6 guests is required.

Price: $7 per person.

See advertiser index on pg 445

AMC Theatres

www.amctheatres.com

There are 11 Houston locations with 3 all inclusive birthday party packages to choose from. Please check their website to find a location near you.

Price: Please check their website for details. Each location may differ in what they have to offer.

AMF Bowling Centers

www.amf.com

There are several AMF Bowling Centers in and around Houston. Each facility offers birthday party packages. Most locations offer a choice of hot dogs or pizza, unlimited drinks, shoe rental and 1 hour of bowling. Please view their website online to find a location near you and call to find out pricing information.

Price: Range from $11-$15 for a minimum of 8 children.

Bananas Play, Party n' More

10706 Grant Road, Houston, TX

281-460-6642

www.funbananas.vze.com

An exciting indoor play and party center. Kid programs are available in tumbling, kindermusik, arts and crafts, piano, and Spanish. Parties include 2 party professionals, themed tablecloths, napkins, plates, confetti, a filled piñata, and party favors to take home. Parties are 2 hours and include a choice of 2 activities.

Price: $218.00

Build-A-Bear Workshop

Locations: Baybrook Mall, Deerbrook Mall, First Colony Mall, Memorial City Mall, The Galleria, & The Woodlands Mall

1-877-789-2327

www.buildabear.com

Each guest will make a one-of-a kind stuffed animal to bring home. Party includes a party leader, party favors, printable invitations and thank-you cards. The guest of honor will receive a goody bag filled with an autograph bear, picture frame and party photo, and a Build-A-Bear Workshop birthday song CD.

Price: Start at $10 per child. You set the price depending on the animal and optional outfits and accessories selected. Accessories cost $2-$15.

Celebration Station
180 W. Rankin Road, Houston, TX
281-872-7778
6167 Southwest Freeway, Houston, TX
713-981-7888
www.celebrationstation.com

Price: The basic package is $9.99 per child and includes all day use of the clubhouse, 16 game tokens, 90 minutes at a reserved party table, a party host or hostess, 2 slices of pizza, unlimited soft drinks, ice cream, invitations, party hats and balloons. The Birthday child will also receive a special gift and 100 redemption points. The deluxe package is $13.99 and includes the basic package plus one ride of their choice (miniature golf, go-karts or bumper boats.) The ultimate party package is $19.99 per person and includes everything included in the basic package plus all day use of the go-karts, bumper boats, and clubhouse. A minimum of 6 guests is required for each party.

Chuck -E- Cheese
www.chuckecheese.com

Price includes 20 tokens, 90 minutes at a decorated table, 2 slices of pizza per child, unlimited soft drinks, and birthday cake, along with a hostess to serve the guests. The birthday child will receive a souvenir cup, a special balloon, a bag of cotton candy, and a birthday crown. During the party, the children will receive a personal visit from Chuck-E-Cheese himself. Don't forget the special birthday show performed by Chuck-E-Cheese and friends!

Price: $9.99 per child, minimum of 5 children.

There are 8 locations in Houston, please check the website for specific addresses and phone numbers.

Cinemark Theatres

www.cinemark.com

Birthday Party packages include a movie of your choice, use of the party room, a hostess to serve pizza and drinks, balloons, and paper goods. During the movie, each child will receive a drink and popcorn. Party guests are to arrive 2 hours before the movie showtime.

There are 9 Cinemark locations in and around the Houston area. Please check their website for specific addresses and phone numbers, as well as birthday party prices.

Cute Kids Sassy Kids

10801 Spring Cypress Road, Spring, TX

832-717-4611

www.cutekids-sassykids.com

Their specialty is themed parties, with 8 different themes available. Costumes are included and range from ballerina tutus to cowgirl attire. Parties are 1 ? to 2 hours and include activities, cake and food for both the adults and children.

Price: $300-$350 for up to 12 girls. Prices vary depending upon the theme selected.

Fun in Swimming (FINS)

7827 Spring Cypress, Spring, TX

281-320-8821

www.funinswimming.com

Party includes use of the swimming pool, certified lifeguards, use of the viewing room for party refreshments and gifts, and game activities upon request.

Price: Start at $95 for 1 ? hours and vary depending on the number and age of the swimmers. $35 non-refundable deposit fee to reserve date and time (applicable towards party fee).

Gatti Town

1475 FM 1960 Bypass, Humble, TX
281-446-PRTY
www.humblegattitown.com

At Gatti Town, you will find a huge pizza buffet, a carousel, bumper-cars, an indoor rock-wall, and over 100 high-tech video games.

Price: $12 per guest for the Bronze package which includes: reserved seating for 1-? hours, buffet and drinks, a $5 dollar game card for each guest and a $10 card for the birthday child, 2 attractions per guest, a party hostess, and a free spin on the birthday wheel. $15 per guest for the Silver package and includes everything in the bronze package, but a $10 game card for each guest and a $15 card for the birthday child. $20 per guest for the Gold package and includes everything in the silver package plus 3 attractions per guest, birthday cake and candles, party invitations and thank-you cards, and a goodie bag for each guest.

Glamagirlz

Katy Mills Mall, Katy, TX
281-644-4002
www.glamagirlz.com

Glamagirlz is a retail store inside of Katy Mills Mall, but is also a place for girls to get pampered with a make over party. Makeovers include a fun hairstyle with glitter, makeup application and nail painting. There are 3 party themes to choose from: Princess Party, Diva Party, or a Pop Superstar Party.

Price: $20 per girl and includes a makeover, music, games and a themed accessory for each girl to take home. The birthday girl will receive a glamagirlz tee shirt for her friends to autograph. $18 per girl for a makeover only.

Gymboree Play and Music (4 locations)

1990 Post Oak Boulevard, Houston, TX
713-953-0444
14623 Memorial, Suite B, Houston, TX
713-953-0444
17776 Tomball Parkway #35A, Houston, TX
713-953-0444
3340 FM 1092, Suite 120, Missouri City, TX
713-953-0444
www.gymboree.com

Gymboree Play and Music is for children newborn to 5 years old. Parties are 1 ? hours and include use of the gymboree room and equipment, an expert teacher to lead in age appropriate songs, activities and games.

Price: $180.00. Currently enrolled members receive a $20 discount.

Hit-Away Indoor Sports Facility

10920 FM 2920, Tomball, TX
281-HIT-AWAY
www.hit-away.com

Activities at this facility include automated batting cages, hitting lanes, basketball and volleyball court, a moonwalk and slide, a soft-style playground, and video games.

The All Star birthday package includes a private party room, pizza, soft drinks, use of the basketball court, moonwalk, playground and slide.

Price: $12.95 per child for 10-20 kids and $11.95 per child for 21-40 kids.

Houston Gymnastics Academy

5804 South Rice Avenue, Houston, TX
713-668-6001
www.houstongymnastics.com

The birthday party starts with a musical warm-up and children will be split into groups, depending on the number of guests (must have a minimum of 10 guests). Guests will then rotate to the 4 stations set up in the gym (trampolines, obstacle courses, etc). Next, they will enjoy cake and refreshments. Parties are 1 hour and 10 minutes and the level of difficulty will be set to the age and ability of the children. Participants must be in gym attire.

Price: Plan A $13.00 per child for members and $15.00 per child for nonmembers and includes birthday balloons and an open gym pass. Plan B is $14.00 per child for members and $16.00 per child for nonmembers and includes a balloon for each child, an open gym pass, paper goods, apple juice or fruit punch, and creative invitations mailed out to each guest.

Houston Scuba Academy

12505 Hillcroft, Houston, TX
713-721-7788
www.houstonscubaacademy.com

Price includes 1? hours in the pool, use of masks and snorkels, 2 certified supervisors, snorkeling games, underwater photos, and 30 minutes in classroom for cake and presents.

Price: $150 for up to 15 kids.

Houston Zoo
1513 N. MacGregor, Houston, TX
713-533-6500
www.houstonzoo.org

Party includes all day admission to the zoo for up to 25 guests, use of the pavilion for 2 hours, birthday cake, punch, and table decorations.

Price: $350 for general public and $320 for Houston Zoo members. Reservations must be made 2 weeks in advance.

Jumpin' Jak's
3403 FM 1960 W, Houston, TX
281-537-8833
www.jumpinjaks.qpg.com

Party includes play area, custom invitations, a cake, decorations, and plates, all in the theme of your choice. They will provide 2 hostesses to serve your party with food and drinks for the children as well as adults. Each child will receive a picture of themselves, goody bag, play pass, and a balloon. Birthday child gets a t-shirt, a play-for-free membership card, and duplicates of all the pictures.
Price: The Congo Play area - $195 for 1.5 hours for 12 kids or $229 for 1hour 45 min for
16 kids. Goldrush Pass Play area - $295 for 2 hours for up to 20 kids.
Rocket City - $285 for up to 18 kids
23 Cranberry Lane - $259 for up to 14 kids
*Additional children for any party is $5.00 per child *
Weekdays are open to the general public. Kids "pay your age" max is $4.00.

See advertiser index on pg 445

JW Tumbles
6777 Woodlands Parkway, The Woodlands, TX
281-298-7755
www.jwtumbles.com

JW Tumbles is a children's gym for infants up to children 9 years of age. The gym is equipped with slides, swings, and obstacle courses.

Price: $225 for members and $250 for nonmembers and includes a 2 hour party and 2 tumbler trainers to assist the children and clean up after the party. Parties are for birthday child and up to 19 guests.

Kids Town
9440 Louetta Road, Suite #10, Spring, TX
281-370-2700
www.kidstown-champions.com

Kids Town is an indoor play and party center. Choose from 7 indoor party rooms, all with different themes. Parties are 1 ? - 2 hours, depending on the part selected. Price includes themed invitations, private playtime, a private decorated party room, a party hostess and paper goods.

Price: Big Town Party Room- $210 for up to 25 kids, Kids Town Party Room- $185 for up to 16 kids, Princess Tea Room- $165 for up to 12 kids, Dazzling Diva Room- $15 per child for up to 15 girls, Barbie Party Room-$150 for up to 12 kids, Tiny Town Room- $165 for up to 12 kids, and Moonwalk Party Room $165 for up to 12 kids.

A $100 deposit is required to reserve party.

Indoor playrooms are open, to the public, weekdays for $3 per child.

Laser Quest
13711 Westheimer Road, Houston, TX
281-596-9999
6560 FM 1960 West, Spring, TX
281-397-6612
100 West Bay Area Boulevard, Webster, TX
281-316-3794
www.laserquest.com

Price includes two 20-minute laser quest missions per person, 45 minutes in a private party room, a complimentary pass for the birthday child and a 2-for-1 pass for all guests (redeemable at a future date). Must have a minimum of 6 players to book party and can have a maximum of 32 players.

Price: $13 per person

Mad Potter Studios

4882 Beechnut, Houston, TX
713-664-8808
1963-A West Gray, Houston, TX
713-807-8900
1341 South Voss Road, Houston, TX
713-278-7300
4787 Sweetwater, Sugar Land, TX
281-313-0555
www.themadpotter.com

Paint-your-own-pottery parties include an instructor, paint and supplies, idea books, glazing and firing, a food table and balloons. Parties are for 8 or more painters.

Price: $5 per person for 1-hour (recommended for ages 3-8), $8 per person for 1 ? hours (ages 9-14), $10 per person for 2-hours (ages 15 and up), $5 for each additional hour.

Main Event

19441 Interstate 45 North, The Woodlands, TX
281-355-5511
www.maineventusa.net

Price: The Big Blast package is $89.95 and includes 1-hour of bowling and shoe rental for 8 kids, a private party room, party supplies, and one selection from the party menu (hamburgers, hot dogs or pizza). The Power Up package is $99.95 and includes 1 game of laser-tag for 10 kids, a $3 game card, private party room, party supplies, and one selection from the party menu. The Extreme Event Package is $149.95 and includes 1 game of laser-tag and 1-hour of bowling for 10 guests, a private party room, party supplies, and one selection from the party menu.

Moody Gardens

Galveston, TX
1-800-582-4673
www.moodygardens.org

Price includes 24 invitations, a decorated party area, birthday cake and fruit punch, all paper goods, and admission to one Moody Gardens attraction. There are two themes to choose from, wild things and beach bash. Parties are 2 hours for children ages 1-12 and will accommodate up to 24 guests. Party times are either 10:00am or 2:00pm.

Price: Mon-Fri $200, Sat & Sun $225. Members discount: Mon-Fri $175, Sat & Sun $191.25. Children under the age of 1 are free

Mountasia
17190 Highway 249, Houston, TX
281-894-9791
2600 Eastex Freeway, Kingwood, TX
281-359-4653
www.mountasia.com

Price: The basic package is $9.95 (+ tax) per child and includes 10 tokens, 2 slices of pizza, unlimited soft drinks, 1 hour of table time, a party host, cups, plates, napkins, and balloons. All guests receive a free round of golf for a future visit. The birthday child also receives a special gift. The deluxe package is $13.95 per child and includes everything in the basic package plus a choice of two attractions; mini golf, bumper boats, or go-karts. The ultimate package is $17.95 per child and it adds a 3 hour unlimited use to mini golf, bumper boats and go-karts, to the basic package.

Oil Ranch
#1 Oil Ranch Road, Hockley, TX
281-859-1616
www.oilranch.com

Activities include pony rides, milking cows, train rides, hay rides, swimming, fishing, miniature golf, volleyball and horseshoes. There is also a dairy barn, baby animal farm, Indian Village, swings and playgrounds.

Price: $7.99 per person for guests 2 years old and up (under 2 years is free). Group rates for 10 or more: $5 per person on weekdays and $7 per person on weekends.
See advertiser index on pg 445

Old MacDonalds Farm
3203 FM 1960 East, Humble, TX
281-446-4001
www.eieio.com

Activities include 12 petting zoos, train rides, a giant mountain of sand, pony rides, a duck pond, a swimming pool, a hay barn, Indian village, picnic grounds, covered gazebos, and concession stands.

Price: $5.75 a person (+ tax). Children under 18 months are free. All activities are included.

Pump It Up

10910 West Sam Houston Parkway N, Suite 100, Houston, TX
281-469-4205
923 South Mason Road, Katy TX
281-829-5711
23810 highway 59 North, Kingwood, TX
281-359-5515
536 Sawdust Road, Spring, TX
281-465-4747
www.pumpitupparty.com

A large indoor play area filled with inflatable play structures.

Price: $150-$230. Prices vary depending on group size, time, and day of the week. Higher price allows longer time spent in the party area, more guests, and is on the weekends. All party packages include: 30 min in fully-decorated party room, great music, full-color invitations, paper plates, cups, napkins and forks.

See advertiser index on pg 445

Rocket Town

528 West Bay Area Boulevard, Webster, TX
281-554-6446
www.countdowncreations.com/rocket-town

Rocket Town is a space memorabilia and souvenir store located near NASA Space Center. Inside is home of the Birthday Blast-off. Children will have the opportunity to dress up in an astronaut suit and explore space in the Rocket Town Mission Control and Destiny Lab. After learning about space, the children will be entertained by the Mad Science Show and get to make their own green slime to take home.

Price: $195 for up to 15 children. Add-on packages also available.

Rosie Posie
123 D. Main Street, Spring, TX
713-208-5777
www.rosieposiepartyroom.com

Rosie Posie is located inside one of Old Town Spring's cottage homes. The party room has 4 decorated children's tables, 2 adult tables, and a cake and gift table. They use antique plates, and china teacups and teapots. There is a dress up area with lace dresses, floppy hats, shoes and jewelry for the girls to dress up in. The hostess will serve heart-shaped peanut butter and jelly sandwiches and strawberry tart cookies. The hostess will also teach the girls proper tea etiquette. Each girl will receive a fun party bag and the birthday girl will receive a beaded charm bracelet inside of a rose.

Price: $200 for up to 8 guests for 2 hours. $5 for adults if they want to be catered to, otherwise no charge.

Sam Houston Equestrian Center @ Hermann Park Stables
13551 Lew Briggs Road, Houston, TX
713-433-PONY (7669)
www.hermannparkstables.com

The Sam Houston Equestrian Center is an indoor air-conditioned party room and horse stable. Birthday parties are one-hour divided into two 30-min sessions. The first 30 minutes, children will ride the horses and the last 30 minutes will be spent playing games and learning horsemanship. The children will also have the opportunity to feed the horses carrots. Participants must be in "riding attire" and bring a bicycle helmet.

Price: $250 for 10 riders. A $50 non-refundable fee is required to hold the date.

Snip-its
The Woodlands Mall, The Woodlands, TX
281-419-4222
www.snipits.com

Glamour Party includes dress-up clothes, all the supplies to have your child's hair styled, nails painted, and makeup done. Also includes a party organizer, birthday cake, juice, party-favors, and a special gift for the birthday girl. You will also receive a disposable camera to take all the glamour shot pictures you want.

Price: $50 deposit and $24 per child (up to 8 guests).
See advertiser index on pg 445

Splashtown Waterpark

21300 I-45 North, Spring, TX
281-355-3300
www.sixflags.com/parks/splashtown

Price includes an all day admission pass to the park, 45 minutes in a birthday bungalow, pizza, soft drinks, cake and ice cream.

Price: $18.99 +tax per person, minimum of 8 guests. Must book party at least 1 week in advance with a $25 non-refundable deposit.

Tank's Paintball

14820 Katy-Hockley Road, Katy, TX
713-862-5555
www.tankspaintball.com

Parties include all your paintball equipment, 200 paintballs per person, referees, and 2 hours of playing time on one of the 9 indoor and outdoor fields.

Price: $200 for 10 guests.

Texas Rock Gym

9716 Old Katy Road, Houston, TX
713-973-ROCK
201 Hobbs Road, Suite A1, League City, TX
281-338-ROCK
www.texasrockgym.com

Parties last for 3 hours and include the harnesses and one mandatory safety course for the group. Party guests will also have their private area including tables and chairs for food and drinks. A minimum of 10 climbers must be present.

Price: Vary depending on the day of the week and number of climbers in the group. A $50 deposit is needed to reserve the party's date and time.
See advertiser index on pg 445

The Children's Museum of Houston

1500 Binz, Houston, TX
713-522-5747
www.cmhouston.org

Price includes 20 invitations for you to send to your guests, a special guided birthday tour for up to 20 children, free admission for an unlimited number of adult escorts, and an exclusive party room with tables, chairs and tablecloths. The birthday child will receive a Children's Museum t-shirt and a multi-colored balloon bouquet.

Price: $225.00. A $50 deposit is required, $25 is non-refundable. In order to host a birthday party, you must be a member of the Children's Museum. One adult for every 5 children is required (no charge for adults). Paper goods, refreshments and cake are not provided, but you may bring your own.

The Little Gym

14090-B Memorial Drive, Houston, TX
281-558-9500
16642 Champion Forest Drive, Spring, TX
281-370-3031
3571 Highway 6 South, Sugar Land, TX
281-277-5470
www.thelittlegym.com

Party includes private use of the entire gym for 1-hour with an instructor who teaches music, movements and games. Invitations and clean up are also included. Parties are for children 1-12 years of age.

Price: Memorial location $209 (members) $229 (non-members), Spring location $185 ($75 non-refundable fee to hold reservation and $110 the day of the party), Sugar Land location $205 (members) $225 (non-members)

See advertiser index on pg 445

The Putting Edge

7620 Katy Freeway (in the Marqe Entertainment Center), Houston, TX
713-263-7051
www.putting-edge.com

The Putting Edge is an 18-hole, indoor, glow-in-the-dark miniature golf center. Parties are 1 hour and 45 minutes for a minimum of 10 guests.

Price: $10.95 per person for the silver package and includes invitations, golf, and a party room. $14.95 per person for the gold package and includes everything in the silver package plus a party host, 2 slices of pizza and soft drinks for each guest. $19.95 per person for the platinum package and includes everything in the gold package plus a glow-in-the dark gift for the birthday child and guests. A $50 non-refundable fee is required to reserve the date of the party.

The Sports House

9606 Hillcroft, Houston, TX

713-9-SPORTS

20740 Gulf Freeway, Webster, TX

713-977-6787

www.thesportshouse.net

The Sports House is an indoor sports facility with 10 training fields, 5 batting cages, a volleyball court, basketball court and 3 pitching mounds. Birthday parties are 1 ? hour and include playing all the sports offered in the gym, a relay race in the fielded tunnel, time in the batting cage, and 15-20 minutes in the party room. A minimum of 10 children is required to attend the party and children must be at least 5 years old, turning 6.

Price: $15 per person for the blue ribbon party package and includes invitations, a personal party hostess, set up and clean up, paper goods, unlimited drinks, a customized birthday cake, thank you cards and a tee shirt for the birthday child. $20 per child for the gold party package and includes everything in the blue ribbon package plus a goodie bag and 2 slices of pizza per guest. A $50 deposit is required to reserve the party.

The Story Book Cottage

5814 1st Street, Katy, TX
281-574-5707
www.thestorybookcottage.com

The Story Book Cottage offers elegant tea parties for the birthday girl and up to 10 guests. Choose from 2 different party packages; The Birthday Delight Dress-up Tea Party and the Elegant Dress-up Tea Party. Parties are by reservation only.

Price: $175 for the Birthday Delight Dress-up Tea Party and includes each girl having her finger nails painted, a fashion parade, story time, a Polaroid taken of each girl, making a picture frame for the Polaroid, cupcakes to decorate, lemonade or kool-aid in antique tea cups, a ribbon Halo for each guest and a mini porcelain tea-set for the birthday girl. $290 for the Elegant Dress-up Tea Party and includes a special dress for the birthday girl to wear, beaded gowns for the birthday guests, tiaras, hats, bracelets, and boas to wear, magic fairy dust for each guest, finger nails painted, a fashion parade, story time, a personal Polaroid, personalized party invitations, a table decorated with flowers, glass plates, and teacups. Finger sandwiches, blue berry muffins, fruit and birthday cake will be served for lunch. Each guest, including the birthday girl, will receive his or her own mini tea set to take home.

Velocity Games

8492 Highway 6 North, Houston, TX
281-858-LOUD
510 South Mason Road, Katy, TX
281-391-3278
www.velocitygamesonline.com

Parties include party invitations, your own party host, a private area with big screen TVs and couches, and over 200 of the hottest video games for all ages to choose from. All birthday guests will receive a free one-hour card.

Price: $150 (Monday-Thursday) for up to 15 guests for 2 hours, $200 (Friday-Sunday) for up to 15 guests for 2 hours, and $300 (Any Day) for up to 20 guests for 2 hours.

Rentals and Party Services

Affordable Moonwalks Etc

281-879-0179
www.affordablemoonwalks.us

Specializes in inflatable moonwalks and wet or dry slides. Rentals are for 4 or 8 hours and include delivery, set-up and take down. The company's guarantee is "clean and on time or it's free!" Serving all Greater Houston areas.

Price: Moonwalks starting at $80, slides starting at $216.50.

Astounding Party Rentals

281-353-9990
www.kidsandgames.com

Moonwalks, rock walls, obstacle courses, concession machines, petting zoo, clowns, and tables and chairs.

Price: Moonwalks starting at $85 for 4 hours, $135 for 6 hours, and $185 for 8 hours. Rock wall & obstacle courses starting at $650.

Awesome Moonwalks & Party Rentals

832-814-6902
www.awesomemoonwalks.com

Specializes in moonwalks, but also does face painting and balloon twisting. Serving Southwest Houston.

Price: Moonwalks starting at $99 for 4 hours and $125 for 8 hours.

Chocolate Academy

713-683-3866
www.chocolateacademy.com

A party for all chocolate lovers! The Chocolate Academy presents a chocolate party where everyone makes and decorates their own chocolate. Call or online and order the chocolate party in a box kit. This kit comes with real milk chocolate, "chocolatier" hats for all the birthday guests, chocolate molds, invitations and envelopes, thank-you cards and envelopes, "I love chocolate" stickers to place on the hats, "created by" stickers, party favor bags to take the chocolate home in, birthday balloons and ribbon, a tablecloth, "honorary chocolatier" certificates, and step-by-step instructions to making the chocolate.

Price: $89 for 10 children

Cullen Amusements

281-955-1422

www.cullenamusements.com

Moonwalks, slides, inflatable games, concession machines, and tables and chairs. Has been serving the Houston area since 1985.

Price: Moonwalks are $119 for 4 hour rentals and $139 for 8 hours.

Fiesta Moonwalk

713-334-3322

www.fiestamoonwalk.com

Specialize in moonwalks. Several selections to choose from.

Price: All moonwalks are $100. Wet & Dry Slides are $185.

Foam Rox

713-461-0899

www.foamrox.com

Foam Rox will come to your location and fill your yard with foam. Their foam machines put out over 25,000cu/ft of foam per hour. Recommended for children ages 4 and up.

Price: $249 for 1st hour and $125 for every hour after. The 20x20 ft inflatable foam pit (optional) is $75 for the whole day.

Fort Bend Moonwalks

281-208-0815

www.fortbendmoonwalks.com

Moon walks, wet and dry slides, concession stands, and carnival rides. They have been serving Southwest Houston for 5 years.

Price: All moonwalks are $95 for the day. Delivery and set up are included. $175 for slip & slides and $225 for waterslides.

Houston Party Rental

281-353-2254

www.houstonparty.com

Moonwalks, wet and dry slides, games, and concession machines. They have been serving Houston for 14 years. Their kind staff will handle all of the party planning, including delivery, set-up and clean up.

Price: Moonwalks starting at $120.

Jump A-Lot
281-827-8246
www.jumpaway.com

Moonwalks, concession machines, tables and chairs, etc. Ask about free delivery and Sunday specials.

Price: Moonwalks are $75 for 4 hours and $90 for 7 hours. Price includes delivery, setup, and pickup.

Jumpin Jax Inflatables
281-550-8088
www.jumpin-jax-inflatables.com

Moonwalks, wet and dry slides, concession machines, tables and chairs. Jumpin Jax provides service to all of Houston.

Price: Moonwalks starting at $85 for 4 hours and $95 for 6 hours.

Jumpy Things
832-928-7515
www.jumpythingshouston.com

Moonwalks, toddler table and chairs. Serving Houston for 18 years.

Price: Moonwalks starting at $95 for 8-hour rentals. Price includes delivery, setup and pick up.

Life of the Party
832-434-5341
Specialize in moonwalks, character moonwalks, and waterslides. Delivery, set-up and clean up is included.

Price: Moonwalks starting at $90 a day, character moonwalks starting at $100 a day, waterslides starting at $175 a day.

Moon Leaps
281-352-2520
www.moonleapsmoonwalk.com

Moonwalks, wet and dry slides, interactive games, concession machines, and tables and chairs. Serving the Greater North Houston Area. Free delivery, set-up and pick-up.

Price: Weekly moonwalk rentals starting at $85 (Monday-Friday).

Party Toys by Deb

832-250-1547

www.partytoysbydeb.com

Children will love having this custom train come to your next party! The train is comfortable, has a covered top and seatbelts. Children have the opportunity to have a picture sitting on the train and wearing an engineer hat.

Price: $175 per hour for the first 2 hours and $150 per hour after 2 hours. Traveling fees may apply.

Space Walk of Houston

10101 Gulf Freeway, Houston, TX

713-910-JUMP (5867)

www.herecomesfun.com

Moonwalks, wet and dry slides, and obstacle courses. Servicing all Houston areas. They will deliver or for no additional charge, you can do a customer pick-up, which enables you to keep the equipment longer.

Price: Moonwalks are $130 for all day rentals plus delivery and $85 for customer pick-up.

Texas Moonwalks & Party Rentals

713-502-2625

www.texasmoonwalks.com

Over 30 moonwalks, inflatable obstacle courses, water slides, concession machines, and tables and chairs. Serving all of the Greater Houston area.

Price: Moonwalks starting at $95 for 4 hours and $120 for all-day rentals. Waterslides starting at $195 for 4 hours and $245 for all-day rentals.

Tumble Bus of Texas

281-630-9678

www.tumblebusoftexas.com

Tumble bus is a full-sized school bus emptied out and turned into a gym on wheels. The bus is filled with rings, balance beam, mini trampoline, monkey bars, vaults, wedge-mats and more. Price includes 1-hour of fun-filled activities, instruction and supervision on equipment. Each child gets a goodie bag and the birthday child gets a special gift.

Price: $200 for the 1st hour and $100 for each additional hour, for up to 15 kids. Parties can only be held on Friday evenings and all day Saturday and Sunday.

Chapter 13

Seasonal Events

Chapter 13

Seasonal Events

No matter what time of year it is, you can always find something exciting going on in Houston. We have compiled a list of traditional annual events that you'll definitely want to check out. From the Houston Livestock Show and Rodeo, to the Houston Hot Sauce Festival there's bound to be something for everyone. We've also included some fun ideas for building family traditions in your own home. Grab your family and explore something new and exciting this month, you'll be glad you did!

Winter

(December, January, February)

Campfire Christmas- December
George Ranch Historical Park, Richmond, TX
281-343-0218

www.georgeranch.org

Enjoy wagon rides around the ranch and eating tasty holiday food around a live campfire.

Christmas Boat Lane Parade- December
Clear Lake
281-488-7676

www.clearlakearea.com

More than 200 boats decorate their decks with light and other Holiday displays. They sail around the lake and up to Galveston Bay. The beautiful boats light up the Clear Lake channel and can be seen from the shore as well as the waterfront restaurants.

Christmas Candlelight Tours- December
Sam Houston Park/Downtown Houston
713-655-1912

www.heritagesociety.org/candlelight.html

Candles and 19th-century decorations brighten the 7 historical structures at Sam Houston Park. Carolers and choirs sing as you walk through the park and admire the lighting.

Dickens on the Strand-December
The Galveston Island Strand
409-765-7834

www.dickensonthestrand.com

A scene straight out of the Dickens novel! Free entertainment including parades, over 100 costumed vendors, strolling carolers, musicians and bagpipers. Food and crafts are also available. This event takes place the first weekend in December.

First Night- December
Cynthia Woods Mitchell Pavilion, The Woodlands, TX
281-450-9503

www.firstnight-thewoodlands.org

Held on New Years Eve with more than 50 musical performers and lots of dancing.

Mayor's Official Downtown Houston Holiday Celebration-December
Hermann Park/Downtown Houston
713-437-6482

Join the mayor as he kicks off the holiday season in Hermann Square; with an upbeat outdoor show filled with fireworks, music and entertainment. People love watching the lighting of the huge Christmas tree outside of city hall.

Nutcracker Saturdays- December

Moody Gardens/Galveston Island

800-582-4673

www.moodygardens.org

Nutcracker Saturdays are held every Saturday in December. There are local choirs, storytelling, dancers, arts and crafts for the whole family to enjoy.

Theatre District Ice Plaza- December

Fish Plaza (in front of Wortham Center)

713-250-3670

Skate day or night, December to early January, at this outdoor ice-skating rink. What a rare holiday treat for Houston!

The Sounds of Texas Music Series- January

Crieghton Theatre, Conroe, TX

936-441-7469

www.thesoundsoftexas.com

A unique concert series that attracts music lovers from all over the United States. The series starts in January and goes through June.

Frontier Days in Old Town Spring- February

Old Town Spring, Spring, TX

281-353-9310

www.oldtownspringtx.com

Activities include a cowboy camp with Civil War reenactments, an Indian Village, arts, crafts, food and drinks, rides and a chili cook-off.

Houston Livestock Show and Rodeo Parade- February

Downtown Houston

832-667-1000

www.hlsr.com

Thousands of trail riders come to Houston from hundreds of miles away, to kick off Houston's Livestock Show and Rodeo. This is an annual tribute to Texas and our traditions. Marching bands and western-themed floats fill the downtown streets.

Mardi Gras! Galveston- February
The Galveston Island Strand
888-425-4753

www.mardigrasgalveston.com

Each year more than ? a million people gather in the streets of Galveston Island to take part in largest Mardi Gras in Texas. The celebration lasts for 12 days and 11 nights with non-stop entertainment. There are parades, live music, food, masked balls, and fun costumes.

Spring

(March, April, May)

Bluebonnet Festival- March
Chapel Hill
888-273-6426

This festival celebrates the new season of bluebonnets. Activities include face painting, hayrides, pony rides, train rides, a petting zoo, and games for the kids. Adults enjoy the music, dancing, and food. Don't forget to take pictures of the kids sitting in fields of bluebonnets!

Houston Livestock Show and Rodeo- March
Reliant Park, Houston, TX
713-791-9000

www.hlsr.com

The world's largest 3 week rodeo featuring a barbeque cook off, professional rodeo competitions, a petting zoo, an outdoor carnival, shopping, all kinds of food, livestock exhibits, and concerts from some of the biggest names in music.

Montgomery County Fair & Rodeo- March
Montgomery County Fair Grounds, Conroe, TX
936-760-3631

10 days of rodeo fun! Families will enjoy the live music, games, barbeque cook-off, and mush more.

River Oaks Garden Club's Azalea Trail-March

The Gardens at Bayou Bend/ River Oaks

713-523-2483

www.riveroaksgardenclub.org

Tour the gardens at Bayou Bend and surrounding River Oaks landscaping to see the beautiful azaleas in bloom.

Grand Kids Festival- April

Grand 1894 Opera House/Galveston Island

409-765-1894

A festival celebrating family and folk arts. Held the 2nd weekend in April with live entertainment, unique booths offering "hands-on" activities for children and children's arts and crafts.

Houston Children's' Festival- April

Downtown Houston

www.houstonschildrensfest.com

Named as "Houston's Official Family Celebration." Activities and entertainment appeal to the whole family. Most activities inside the festival are free and include 10 family adventure areas, 6 stages of entertainment and over 350 games, activities, music, crafts, and exhibits. Children under 3 are free.

Houston International Festival- April

Downtown Houston

713-654-8808

www.ifest.org

Experience live music, art and food from all over the world. Each year, a different country is selected and more than 20 blocks of downtown Houston are filled with activities and food pertaining to that country.

Japan Festival- April

Hermann Park/Downtown Houston

713-963-0121

www.jashouston.org

Held at the beautiful Japanese Gardens in Herman Park, to celebrate Japanese culture. Activities include a traditional tea ceremony, Japanese food and games, musical performances, and demonstrations of martial arts, origami, and Ikeban flower design.

Sam Houston Folk Festival- April
Sam Houston Memorial Park, Huntsville, TX
936-294-1832

A festival celebrating the life of General Sam Houston. Activities include museum tours, arts and crafts, folk dancers, live music, ethnic food, historical re-enactments, a petting zoo and storytellers.

Texas Crawfish and Music Festival- April
Old Town Spring, Spring, TX
1-800-OLD-TOWN

www.texascrawfishfestival.com

The largest crawfish festival outside of Louisiana. Activities include three stages of musical entertainment, a large family area with carnival and train rides, petting zoo, clowns, face painters and more. Don't forget about the terrific food and crawfish! The festival is held last two weeks in April.

World Fest- April
AMC Meyer Park, Houston, TX
713-965-9955

www.worldfest.org

World Fest is for all movie buffs. It is Houston's own International Film Festivals and the world's largest international film and video competition. Dozens of featured short and documentary films, TV commercials and music videos are screened.

Cinco de Mayo Celebration- May
The Miller Outdoor Theatre/Hermann Park
713-284-8352

www.milleroutdoortheatre.com

A celebration of Mexican nationals and their heritage. Festivities include a parade downtown and a festival with mariachi bands, dancers and food.

Everyones Art Car Parade-May
Downtown Houston
713-926-6368

www.orangeshow.org

Hundreds of car artists from across the country use their creativity and imagination to decorate their car. Cars are decorated with fruit, flowers, or anything fun and unique. It is a fun parade featuring art on wheels.

Ice Cream Festival-May
Downtown Brenham, TX
888-273-6426

www.brenhamtexas.com

Everyone in Texas loves Blue Bell Ice Cream! Enter the ice cream eating contest and you can eat all the ice cream you can handle. Or just enjoy the live bands, balloons, clowns, train rides, and pony rides. Festival is held the first Saturday in May.

K-9 Fun Run- May
Sam Houston Park/Downtown Houston
www.houstonhumane.org

Dogs and their owners enjoy this "fun run' to help raise money for the Houston Humane Society.

Pasandena Strawberry Festival- May
Pasadena Fairgrounds, Pasadena, TX
281-991-9500

www.strawberryfest.org

Live entertainment, arts and crafts, children's games, carnival rides, good food, a barbeque cook-off, and, of course, lots of strawberries. There are strawberry cooking, eating and growing contests. A crowd favorite is the "World's Largest Strawberry Shortcake." Proceeds go to scholarships to local students and books for college libraries. Children under 5 are free.

Rock-the-Dock- May
Kemah Boardwalk
877-285-3624

www.kemahboardwalk.com

Free concerts every Thursday night at 6:30 pm, May through September.

Texas Crab Festival- May
Crystal Beach, Galveston, TX
800-786-3863

www.galveston.com

Activities include tug-of-war, sandcastle competitions, a treasure hunt in the sand, live music, volleyball tournaments, and of course crab races and a crab cook-off.

Summer

(June, July, August)

AIA Sandcastle Competition- June
Galveston Island/East Beach
409-672-EAST

The largest sandcastle competition in Texas. Over 60 teams create incredible sand-castles. Held the first Saturday in June.

Fireworks Friday- June
Kemah Boardwalk
877-285-3624

www.kemahboardwalk.com

Every Friday night at 9:30pm, enjoy free firework shows.

Funfest- June
Texas City, TX
888-860-1408

Live music, arts and crafts, carnival rides, a car cruise, barbeque cook-off, catfish fry, children's activities, and more.

Galveston Caribbean Carnival Festival-June
Galveston Island
409-763-5326

www.galveston.com

Live entertainment, food, music, arts and crafts, limbo competition, costume contest and parade.

Galveston Summer Band Concerts- June
Galveston Island
888-425-4753

www.galveston.com

Every Tuesday evening enjoy free music by the Galveston Beach Band, family entertainment, and a flag parade for children. Concerts begin in June and go through August.

George Ranch Juneteenth Celebration- June
George Ranch Historical Park, Richmond, TX
281-343-0218

Celebrating the day Texas slaves learned of the signing of the Emancipation Proclamation. A re-enactment of this historical moment is performed. Activities also include, gospel music, tours, and food.

Juneteenth Celebration- June
Miller Outdoor Theatre/Hermann Park
713-284-8352

A month-long celebration of African-American heritage including parades, blues, gospel and jazz performances.

Sailboat Racing- June
Clear Lake
281-334-4252

Professional and amateur sailors get together for a free, friendly sailboat race on the waters of Clear Lake. Held every Wednesday evening June to October.

Sizzilin' Summer Saturdays- June
Splashtown Water Park, Spring, TX
281-355-3300

www.sixflags.com/parks/splashtown

Saturdays from 12:00pm-5:00 pm, at the wave pool deck, enjoy music, games, contests and prizes. This event starts in June and goes through July.

Annual 4th of July Fireworks Spectacular- July
Clear Lake
281-488-7676

Celebrate the 4th of July watching this spectacular firework show over beautiful Clear Lake.

Fourth of July at Miller Outdoor Theatre- July
Hermann Park/ Downtown Houston
713-284-8350

www.milleroutdoortheatre.com

Fireworks accompanied by a dramatic 16-cannon salute, performed by the Houston Symphony.

Kids Week- July
Lone Star Flight Museum, Galveston, TX
409-740-7722

Kids rule the entire 2nd week in July! Activities include, color contests, airplane flying contest and learning all about airplanes. Kids 13 years and younger are free.

Power of Freedom Festival- July
Eleanor Tinsley Park at Buffalo Bayou
713-522-9123

www.festivalsofhouston.com

Live entertainment, food, games, and a spectacular firework show.

Red, Hot and Blue Festival and Fireworks Extravaganza- July
Cynthia Woods Mitchell Pavilion, The Woodlands, TX
281-363-2447

A festive celebration taking place over several days; including a food, music, games, a Houston Symphony performance, parade, and fireworks show.

Ringling Bros. And Barnum and Bailey Circus- July
Reliant Stadium, Houston, TX
www.feldinc.com

More than 120 renowned circus acts gathered in 3 rings. Fun for crowds of any age!

Ballunar Liftoff Festival- August
NASA Space Center
281-488-7676

www.ballunarfestival.com

Over 100 hot air balloons fill up the sky and participate in airborne competitions and an evening balloon glow. There are exciting skydiving and hang gliding expeditions as well as arts and craft booths and food from local restaurants.

Blessing of the Fleet- August

Kemah Boardwalk

877-285-3624

www.kemah.net

At the beginning of shrimp season, Priests come out to Kemah to bless all the boats. Activities include a boat parade, music, games, food and a carnival.

Houston International Jazz Festival- August

Downtown Houston

713-839-7000

www.jazzeducation.org

Jazz musicians from around the world come to celebrate the birth of jazz with outdoor performances.

Houston Shakespeare Festival- August

Miller Outdoor Theatre/Hermann Park

713-284-8352

www.milleroutdoortheatre.com

A tribute to the great playwright, William Shakespeare. Enjoy free performances throughout the whole month with productions of 2 plays by the University of Houston Theatre department.

Fall

(September, October, November)

Fiesta Italiana- September

Houston Farm & Ranch Club, Houston, TX

713-524-4222

www.houstonitalianfestival.com

Celebrating the heritage and culture of Italy. Enjoy great music and food, including the grape stomp and a pasta-eating contest.

Fiestas Patrias- September

Downtown Houston

713-926-2636

Hispanics representing Mexico and several Central America countries gather to celebrate their independence from Spain. Activities include a fantastic parade, street dancing and outdoor festivals.

Houston Hot Sauce Festival- September

Houston Farm & Ranch Club, Houston, TX

281-558-3518

www.houstonhotsauce.com

Stage entertainment, free kids activities, amateur salsa competition, arts and crafts, and of course food. Sample hot sauce, salsa, jams, spices, chips and dips, and other fiery hot food.

Kite Fest- September

Galveston Island

888-425-4753

www.galveston.com

Learn to fly a kite or just sit back, enjoy the nice weather and constant breeze and watch the kites go by. There are kite demonstrations and different kites from all over the world.

The Great Tastes of Houston- September

Downtown Houston

713-522-9723

The mayor's official fall celebration. Come try samples of menu items from Houston's best restaurants.

Bayou City Art Festival- October

Hermann Square/ Downtown Houston

713-521-0133

www.bayoucityartfestival.com

Several block of downtown are filled with paintings, sculptures, jewelry and music.

Boo-on-the-Boardwalk- October

Kemah Boardwalk

877-285-3624

www.kemahboardwalk.com

The whole month of October families will enjoy events ,such as, the haunted house, pumpkin decorating, hayrides, magic shows and live spooky music.

Fright Fest-October
Six Flags Astro World, Houston, TX
713-799-1234

www.sixflags.com

Every Friday, Saturday and Sunday evening Astro World turns into a haunted house full of people dressed in scary costumes. Most rides are open.

Ghostly Gardens- October
Moody Gardens, Galveston Island
800-582-4673

www.moodygardens.org

Spooky activities including trick-or-treating, creepy-crafts and a costume contest.

Greek Festival- October
3511 Yoakum Boulevard, Houston, TX
713-526-5377

www.agoc.org/greekfestival

Activities include lively Greek music, folk dancers in authentic costumes, Greek food, cathedral tours, and kids Athenian playground and activities.

Halloween Boo-Bash- October
Traders Village, Houston, TX
281-890-5500

www.tradersvillage.com

Trick-or-treating, carnival games, puppet shows, magic shows, and live music. A free "spoktacular" for kids. Parking is $2.

Texas Renaissance Festival- October

FM 1774, Magnolia, TX
281-356-2178

www.texrenfest.com

Take a trip back to the 16th century at the largest renaissance festival in the world! This festival covers over 50 acres with 21 stages providing over 200 daily performances; including magic shows, juggling, and jousting. There are over 300 arts and crafts shops, 60 food and beverage shops, knights, castles and over 3,000 costumed characters.

Wings Over Houston Air Show- October

Ellington Field
713-266-4492

www.wingsoverhouston.com

The 3rd largest air show in the US, featuring flight demonstration and aerobatic acts. The crowd favorite is the explosive re-enactment of the attack on Pearl Harbor. Kids love the food and kiddie carnival.

Annual Children's Festival- November

Cynthia Woods Mitchell Pavilion, The Woodlands, TX
281-363-3300

www.woodlandsceneter.org

A festival just for kids. A huge children's playground with games, music, food, and educational activities.

Home for the Holidays- November

Old Town Spring, Spring, TX
281-651-9955

www.oldtownspring.com

The whole town of Old Town Spring will be decorated with bows and lights. Starting the last weekend of November and going through Christmas Eve, carolers, choirs and other performers will entertain you as shop and walk the streets.

International Quilt Festival- November

George R Brown Convention Center/Downtown Houston
713-781-6864

www.quilts.com

More than 1,000 quilts on display, demonstrations and mini-classes, more than 800 booths of quilting supplies and quilts.

Lighting of the Doves- November

The Woodlands Town Center, The Woodlands, TX

281-419-5630

www.town-canter.com

Activities include special dance and music performances to kickoff the opening of The Ice Rink. Families can skate through the middle of January.

Nutcracker Market- November

Reliant Park, Houston, TX

713-535-3231

www.nutcrackermarket.com

This event is for those who love to shop until they drop! The Reliant Park is transformed into a shopping extravaganza with every holiday decoration imaginable, home décor, toys, clothing, jewelry, food, and much more. Proceeds go to the Houston Ballet Guild.

Thanksgiving Day Parade- November

Downtown Houston

713-654-8808

This is a huge downtown parade with floats, marching bands, costumed characters, and an early visit from Santa Claus.

Uptown Tree Lighting Ceremony- November

Post Oak Boulevard

713-621-2011

www.uptown-houston.com

Half-a-million holiday lights simultaneously light up 80 Christmas trees that line Post Oak Boulevard. Choirs and bands sing and fireworks light up the sky. The lighted trees are displayed all season long.

Family Traditions

Family traditions and rituals have multiple benefits. Comfort and security are among the biggest. Whether you attend a festival or event every year together as a family, or you have a special ritual or tradition in your home, the benefits will be visible.

Traditions impact a sense of identity, provide security and comfort, help to navigate change, teach values, pass on ethnic and religious heritage. They also teach practical skills, problem solving, and generate wonderful memories! Here is a listing of resources that will help you start and keep traditions in your own family:

- Little Things Long Remembered- Making Your Children Feel Special Every Day- *By Susan Newman*
- The Book of New Family Traditions- How to Create Rituals for Holidays and Everyday- *By Meg Cox*
- New Traditions- Redefining Celebrations for Today's Family- *By Susan Abel Lieberman*
- Mrs. Sharp's Traditions- Reviving Victorian Family Celebrations of Comfort and Joy- *By Sarah Ban Breathnach*

Chapter 14

Volunteer Opportunities

Chapter 14

Volunteer Opportunities

A great way to build values into your family is to volunteer together. Read on to find valuable information about volunteering in Houston and the surrounding areas.

Did you know. . .

- Youth who volunteer are more likely to do well in school, graduate, vote, and be philanthropic. –UCLA, 1991
- Young people who volunteer just one hour or more a week are 50% less likely to abuse
- drugs and engage in at-risk behavior. – America's Promise 2001
- 89% of households give to charities each year.
- 44% of American adults volunteer.
- 83.9 million American adults volunteer each year. That's equivalent to over 9 million full-time employees at a value of $239 billion!

A new study shows that people who begin volunteering as students are:

- Twice as likely to volunteer as adults
- More likely to give generously to charitable causes
- More likely to teach their own children to volunteer

Courtesy of **www.independentsector.org**

What To Expect When Volunteering

Volunteering is different for every person. No two people will have the same volunteer experience. However there are a few things that will be similar, especially when you are first beginning. Here is a short list of what you should know and what you might expect.

1. Be prepared to work.
2. Be prepared to wait.
3. Be prepared to fill out forms.
4. Wear reasonable clothes.

5. Remember you only get out what you put in.

The Rights of a Volunteer

- Volunteerism itself is a basic right.
- Volunteers have a right to know what is expected of them.
- Volunteers have the right to good training.
- Volunteers have the right to be treated with respect.
- Volunteers have a right to set goals for themselves.
- Volunteers have a right to feel good about their service.

Volunteer Houston

3033 Chimney Rock Suite 460, Houston, TX
713-965-0031
www.volunteerhouston.org

Hop online and check out all the great places to volunteer in Houston. Find monthly calendars and opportunities for individuals, families, groups, children, and youth. Need more information? Give them a call and they can answer your questions and direct you to where you need to be. Or call and listen to their prerecorded message on how to request volunteer services and/or receive information on volunteer opportunities. Volunteer services are dedicated to providing easy access to volunteer opportunities.

www.volunteermatch.org

This website is an amazing resource for anyone who wants to get involved in their community. Enter your zip code or city and hit "search." This will tell you the name of the organization needing volunteers, the location, date, time, and the age group recommended. There are hundreds of volunteer opportunities in Houston and surrounding areas!

The following are Quick Lists of service opportunities provided online through Volunteer Houston and Volunteermatch.org:

Family Volunteering

www.pointsoflight.org & www.1-800-volunteer.org

Serving together as a family is possible more often than you think. Check out these opportunities to enrich your time together as a family through volunteering.

Group Volunteering

Rally your family, friends, church group, club, or business and take on a service opportunity. Group volunteering builds teamwork and makes an instant, positive impact in morale.

Youth Volunteering
We are never too young to start volunteering. You will find volunteer opportunities tailored specifically for youth.

Children's Health and Well-being
Children are the future of Houston! Volunteers are needed to help children who are sick, handicapped, need after-school tutoring, etc.

Services Benefiting Elderly Persons
There are many opportunities to help the elderly in Houston. You can deliver meals and help out at local nursing homes.

Special Events
Many programs plan annual fund- raisers, auctions, walk-a-thons, races, or other large-scale service projects. This list is the key to learning how to help with these events.

Holiday Volunteer Opportunities
There are many service opportunities available during the Holidays, especially during November and December. Although family volunteering is a wonderful holiday tradition, we ask you to keep in mind that need knows no season. Children need mentors in March, empty shelves need donations in June, and lonely neighbors need care in September. If you don't find the volunteer opportunity you're looking for during the holidays, consider making your family's contribution during another season of service.

Ideas for Self-Starters
Volunteering doesn't always have to be done through or with an organization. Open your eyes and you will see thousands of service opportunities around you! Only your imagination limits the possibilities. This list gives you several suggestions of volunteer projects you can do completely on your own.

Make A Donation
Even if your time is limited, you can still help! You can make a donation by sending money or donating items such as clothes, shoes, toys, etc.

Volunteer Centers

Volunteer Bay Area
1300 A Bay Area Boulevard, Houston, TX
281-282-6034

Volunteer Houston/Central
Volunteer Houston Office
3033 Chimney Rock Suite 460, Houston, TX
713-965-0031

Other Places To Volunteer

Boys and Girls Clubs of Greater Houston
1520 A-Airline Drive, Houston, TX
713-868-3426
www.bgc@bgclubs-houston.org

Several volunteer opportunities for children ages 7-17 years old.

Libraries
Most libraries welcome offers of help from the community. At some libraries, youth may volunteer in the summer for children's reading programs. Please contact your local library for other opportunities.
(See Chapter 9 for library phone numbers)

Northwest Assistance Ministries (NAM)
15555 Kuykendahl Road, Houston, TX
281-885-4555
www.namonline.org

NAM has an ongoing need for volunteers. Opportunities range from answering phones to stocking the food pantry shelves. We are sure there is something for everyone.

The Houston Zoo
1513 North MacGregor, Houston, TX
713-533-6500
www.houstonzoo.org

The Teen Volunteer Program (Zoo Crew) is a ten-week program for teens in the summer, starting the first week in June to the middle of August.

United Way of the Texas Gulf Coast
713-685-2300
www.uwtgc.org

The United Way of America is a nation-wide agency that provides several services. For volunteer information, call and ask for volunteer office.

Chapter 15

Memories and Keepsakes

Chapter 15

Memories and Keepsakes

We've given you plenty of ideas on how to make memories with your family, now the trick is to preserve them! We have included a list of scrapbook stores and some of their most popular classes to get you organized and preserving those stacks of pictures. We've even found someone who will make your scrapbook for you! What more could you ask for?

Scrapbooking Supplies

NORTH

Lone Star Scrapbook Company
27842 I-45 North, Spring, TX
281-296-2296
www.lonestarscrapbook.com

This store has a great selection of paper and stickers. A favorite class offered is the Introduction to Scrapbooking class. This class is held every Monday and is free of charge. They offer late-night crops on Wednesdays from 6pm-9pm and Fridays from 6pm-12am. Both classes are free for members. Non-members pay $2/hour on Wednesday night and $10/night on Friday. Check online for their full selection of classes.

Memories
7676 FM 1960 West, Houston, TX
281-890-0789
www.memories.com

Memories is a nation-wide scrapbook chain with stores in 9 other states. They carry everything you need to make a memorable scrapbook. One of the most popular classes is Moonlight Madness. This crop class is $5 and is held every Friday night from 6-11 pm. To see other classes offered, check their class calendars online.

Picture Perfect Plus
17425 Stuebner Airline, Spring, TX
281-251-8605
www.pictureperfectplus.com

Schedules change every month. Popular ongoing classes are Mother and Daughter Night, held the 3rd Saturday from 6-10pm, and their Friday night crops held every Friday night from 7pm-12am. Fee for this class is $7. Join their Cuttin' Up Club for an annual fee of $25; meetings are held the 2nd Tuesday night of each month. They also offer a summer camp for kids, teaching them the how to start a scrapbook and different scrapbooking techniques. Check out their website to see monthly class calendars.

Scrapabilities
4901 FM 2920, Spring, TX
281-528-6563
www.scrapabilities.net

Scrapabilities specializes in offering their customers the best scrapbooking instruction. They offer classes for beginners, the advanced and everything in between. Classes are held every Tuesday from 7-9pm and are available to everyone. Their Frequent Buyer Program is $7.50 per year and enables you to receive 5% off all purchases, $2 off any class and unlimited use of their die cut machines.

NORTHWEST

Maridawn's Scrapbook Store

870 South Mason Road Suite 130, Katy, TX
281-392-3033
www.maridawn.com

This store is fully stocked with all your scrapbook supplies and accessories. It also has a work area equipped with die cut machines, paper cutters, punches, and other supplies to make cropping convenient. Best of all, you can come and crop any hour that the store is open.

Memory Depot

7083-A highway 6 North, Houston, TX
281-550-2395
www.memorydepotonline.com

Memory Depot is a new scrapbook store in Houston. The store originated in Austin, Texas and was selected, by Better Homes and Gardem, as one of the top ten stores in North America. You will find everything you need for your scrapbooking and rubber-stamping needs. The classes offered are always new and exciting. You can join them the last Friday of every month for Midnight Madness from 6pm-midnight. Check their website for classes scheduales and other events/

NORTHEAST

A Little Crafty

4003 Rustic Woods Drive Suite J, Kingwood, TX
281-360-5530
At this store you will find the latest supplies for your scrapbooking and stamping needs. They offer many classes demonstrating the newest scraping techniques. Crop nights are every other Friday from 7pm-12am.

SOUTHWEST

Photos Forever

4061 Bellaire Boulevard, Houston, TX
713-662-0200
www.photosforever.biz

At Photos Forever not only will you find all your scrapbooking needs, they also sell unique purses, belts and all kinds of fun things for women. Every Friday night from 6-11pm is a free crop class. Participants bring a potluck snack to share while they scrapbook. What a fun way to meet new friends!

Scrapbook Generations

13745 Southwest Freeway, Sugar Land, TX
281-265-7272
www.scrapbookgenerations.com

This store is family-owned and operated. The friendly staff is there to help you preserve your memories. They have a large selection of tools and supplies as well as classes for beginners to the experienced scrapers.

Scrap It All

1032 Studewood Street, Houston, TX
713-866-4031
www.scrapitall.com

Scrap It All is located in the Houston Heights. They offer several fun scrapbooking classes during the day and some nights as well. They have "open crop nights" where anyone can come and use their crop room to scrapbook. They have a great selection of scrapbooking supplies form all the leading scrapbook manufacturers. You can even schedule a private crop party for you and your friends. Call or go online for details.

The Scrapbook Shoppe

3016 1st Street, Rosenberg, TX
281-239-8845
www.scrapbook-shoppe.com

Not only do they carry a large selection of scrapbooking tools, they have custom scrapbooks for Terry, Lamar, and Foster High School. They also carry paper with the local the high school's name and mascot on it.

The Scrapbook Village

3424 FM 1092 Suite 270, Missouri, TX
281-208-5251
www.thescrapbookvillage.com

This store offers the service of giving your scrapbook a more professional look by "Embossing Your Albums." For a yearly fee of $25, or a fee of $2 and hour, you will have access to all the scissors, stamps, punches, die-cut machines, and paper cutters. They even offer private crop parties and birthday parties.

SOUTHEAST

Beyond Scraps

2530 Garden Road #B2, Pearland, TX
281-412-7555
www.beyondscraps.com

Beyond Scaps offers many different classes. Every Friday from 6pm-12am come and crop for only $5. Or pay an annual fee of $25 and you will receive unlimited use of the crop room. If you want to keep the kids busy this summer, enroll them in their Kids Summer Camp. Kids will create pages using pictures from their previous year at school and receive a camp shirt and their own 12x12 album.

Just 4 Fun Scrapbooking

2540 East Broadway Suite C, Pearland, TX
281-412-7338
www.just4funscrapbooking.com

Great selection for your entire scrapbook needs. One-third of the store is filled with paper, stencils, pens, and punches. Another third of the store is stocked with stickers and embellishments. The remaining third, you will find scrapbooks, die-cuts, and a large cropping area. Here you will find the entire Mrs. Grossman's line of albums and stickers. They are also a distributor for Club Scrap paper.

Novel Approach

607 South Friendswood Drive #15, Friendswood, TX
281-992-3137
www.novelapproachonline.com

Novel Approach has a wonderful selection of scrapbooks, rubber stamps and paper. Best of all, they offer some of the most fun and creative scrapbook classes we have ever seen! For example, join their NYOBC (not your ordinary book club) to learn and share your scrapbook ideas or to learn new and exciting techniques. Monthly meetings are held the 3rd Saturday of the month. They also have a Breakfast Club held one Saturday a month from 8-11am. For $37.50, you will receive a kit with all the supplies needed to complete an album and a donut breakfast with coffee and juice. Hop online to see more of their fun scrapbooking activities.

The Scrapbooking Place

4116 Center Street, Deer Park, TX
281-479-8088
www.scrapbookingplace.com

The Scrapbook Place offers a large selection of paper, stickers, embellishments, bazzill cardstock, and albums. You will find top quality supplies and products at low prices. Join them every Friday night from 7pm-12am for crop night. Cost for this class is $10. Check out their website for calendars of the different classes offered and to receive printable coupons.

Other Resources

Close to My Heart

www.closetomyheart.com

If you love rubber stamping, hop online and check out their collection of rubber stamps and other scrapbooking accessories. Or call 888-655-6552 to locate a demonstrator in your area.

Crafters Story Box

www.craftersstorybox.com

This online store has thousands of products up to 50% off. They carry all the supplies for your scrapbooking needs. You can select from many different albums, paper, stickers, rubber stamps, punches, die-cuts, templates, etc. They even have a clearance center where products are marked down to very low prices. Fast worldwide shipping is available.

Creative Memories

www.creativememories.com

To find a consultant in your area visit their website. With their line of scrapbooking, your consultant will help you complete albums and discover how to add meaning to your photos.

Heart of Texas Scrapbook Club (HOTS Club)

www.scrapbookclub.tripod.com

The HOTS Club is for all Texans who love to scrapbook! This website provides a way for all scrappers to share and learn new information and scrapbook ideas. It also informs you of local cropping retreats and events. Best of all, membership is free!

Keepsakes By Kelli – Custom Memory Albums

www.kbk-custommemoryalbums.com

If your photographs are in piles, drawers, or boxes and you can't imagine trying to fit them all into a scrapbook; you might want to contact Kelli. Using your pictures and memorabilia, she will create a customized album that you will be proud to display and share. Visit her website for pricing and details.

Pages of Your Past

951-788-2201

www.pagesofyourpast.com

If you are too busy to sit down and scrapbook or you feel like you are not creative enough to put a scrapbook together, Pages of Your Past will do the work for you. They will create layouts and all you do is attach the pictures on the page. It is that easy! Samples of their pages can be viewed online. Visit the website for pricing and details.

Stampin' Up

www.stampinup.com

This company has an awesome selection of stamps to order by mail or online. Whether you want to purchase a catalog, host a workshop or become a demonstrator yourself, check out this website for all the information. To find a demonstrator in your area, fill out the required fields on their site and they will match you up with the names of the demonstrators nearest you.

We R Memory Keepers

1-877-PICK-WE-R

www.weareonthenet.com

This company sells original books and albums. They also sell page protectors and cute seasonal punch-outs. Order online or call for a catalog.

Great Photographers

These photographers have been recommended by Mama's like you. We selected these photographers because other parents have had great experiences having them photograph their children and families. We hope that you find someone you'll love to work with and more importantly someone who will provide you with those priceless portraits that you will treasure for years to come.

Alisa Murray Photographers
281-431-2883
www.alisamurray.com

At Alisa Murray Photographers they specialize in prenatal, newborn, and childhood portraits. Their prenatal portraits focus on your belly, making the womb a piece of art in and of itself. For those of you who want every moment of your child's life documented, Alisa Murray photographers will go to the hospital to take pre-labor, labor, delivery, and post- labor pictures. Visit their website for samples of their package plans.

Christine Meeker Photographers
126 Venice Street, Sugar Land, TX
281-565-4285
www.christinemeeker.com

Christine Meeker Photographers specialize in hand tinted black and white images. They created a new color style called white. This style is "clean, colorful, and fun." Because babies grow and change so much, especially their first year, you can get unlimited first year photography for $295. For those of you who like their work and do not live in Sugar Land, they do many outdoor photo events at places like Galveston Beach and The Woodlands. These events are held on select weekday mornings and weekends. View their website for more information.

Eden Studio
802 Lehman Street, Houston, TX
713-694-7303
www.lisajane.com

Lisa Jane is a children's photographer with 25 years experience. She has earned every award in professional photography and is a professional photographer for Kodak. Her work is known and honored world - wide. You may have seen her work on greeting cards, calendars, and stationary. She shoots at her studio, where she has created 3 fully landscaped acres. The peaceful gardens are full of flowers, butterflies, unicorns, enchanted castles, and fairies. Lisa Jane created a studio where your childhood dreams and imagination become a reality. She wanted to create an image that you and your child could look back on and be reminded of the "sweet innocence of childhood." View samples of her work online and you will be amazed at her unique and creative style!

Farrah Braniff Photographs

713-795-0455
www.farrahbraniff.com

Farrah Branniff specializes in creative, personal, and natural photography. She has 15 years of experience and strives to make each and every photograph unique and distinctive. She makes her pictures less about artificial scenery and props and more about the beauty and wonder of children. She will come to the location of your choice. The photo session fee is $150 and lasts 1-3 hours; until she captures the very best images. This allows plenty of time for your child to get comfortable and let their real personality shine through. Visit her website and check out the various specials and packages throughout the year.

Life Style Photography

281-444-9234
16300 Kuykendahl #410, Houston, TX
www.lifestylephotography.biz

Life Style Photography's goal is to make your experience in their studio an exciting and memorable one. Photographers Chuck and Carol have photographed children and families for 13 years. They shoot in their studio or in their Outdoor Portrait Garden. Each portrait can be in color, black and white, or sepia tone. They strive to capture each child's personality to create a unique portrait for you to treasure.

Studio One to One Photography

713-228-7121
www.S121.com

Studio One to One brings the style of a private photography studio to the retail environment. They use simple props and backgrounds, creating a more casual look. After the session is complete, you will be able to immediately view the proofs on video. Session fees are only $9.95 per child and they offer children value packs starting at $39.95. They are currently located in shopping malls in Houston and Dallas. They plan to enter other cities in Texas in the near feature. Visit one of their 6 Houston Studios: Baybrook Mall, First Colony Mall, Katy Mills Mall, Memorial City Mall, Willowbrook Mall, and The Woodlands Mall.

The Picture People

1-800-341-HOUR

www.picturepeople.com

At The Picture People, you can get everything from family portraits to playful children's portraits. Best of all, portraits are available the same day you come in. They strive to have portraits ready in about an hour. Customers can purchase mats and frames fully assembled and ready to be placed on the wall. You can also turn your favorite photo into an umbrella, jigsaw puzzle, magnet, key-chain, tie, and mouse pad. These specialty items will be delivered to your home within 2-3 weeks. They also offer custom greeting cards and envelopes. The Picture People have more than 300 studios operating in 34 different States. Visit one of their 5 Houston locations: Baybrook Mall, The Galleria, Memorial City Mall, The Woodlands Mall, and West Oaks Mall.

Treasured Moments

22620 Loop 494, Kingwood, TX

281-460-8172

www.kimriley.com

Kim Riley is the owner and photographer of Treasured Moments. She has been a photographer for 14 years. Every child has different personalities and expressions that make them unique and special. She tries to capture the expressions and feelings that reflect who they are. All portraits are shot on location. She will come to your home or any natural setting of your choice. Visit her online to view samples of her work.

Valerie Adame Photography

6920 Bayway Drive, Baytown, TX

281-424-1501

www.adamephoto.com

This studio specializes in personalized portraits. They understand that each person has a different preference of how they want the picture to look. Every opinion is important to them and they will strive to meet their client's specific needs and desires. At Valerie Adame Photography, they want your picture to be "your own," not "cookie-cutter." Individuality is very important to them. Visit them online and view their gallery of beautiful pictures.

Chapter 16

Feeding and Clothing the Crew

Chapter 16

Feeding and Clothing the Crew

Like everyone else, we've tried to figure out how to save money on groceries! We've come up with some great ideas, and even better…people to help.

Money Saving Grocery Tips

Pick the Right Store

Even though stores are becoming increasing diversified in what they sell, each has a core strength. Quickly learn the core strengths of the store near you. Basic grocery stores, for example, are excellent at providing product and price selection, frequent shopper programs, and double coupon days. However, their bulk store counterparts have their own niche of offering good pricing on high-volume, name brand, and non-perishables. National drugstore chains and superstores are best for health and beauty products.

Know Before You Go

Never make a trip to the store without making a list and checking your inventory. This act alone will save you tons of time and lots of money. It is also a good idea to quickly assemble any coupons you plan to use.

Eat First

Grocery store managers have learned over the years about the subtle influences of smells and locations. This includes the aroma of fresh baked bread, the site of a perfectly seasoned, slow-turning chicken; or maybe the intrigue of a new machine that is strategically placed on the end-cap of an isle. Everything seems to look good when our stomachs are crying out for food! Statistics show you spend about 17% more when shopping hungry!

Be Ad Savvy

Check the ads each week. They often come in the Sunday paper, by direct mail, but can also be picked up on Monday or Tuesday at the front of the store. Every grocery store marks a few of it's products way down, in the hopes of recouping the cost by having you stay and do all of your shopping there. This generally works, as people tend to not want to go to multiple locations to do their shopping. The key is to watch for the best buys, then plan to pick up those items on the way to wherever your going that day (dropping the kids off at school, on the way to work, etc.). Then do your normal shopping at the store you designate as the best overall.

Coupons and Rebates

It takes work to save money on groceries, but coupons and rebates are worth the time. The best way to use coupons is to first, find them and plan your menus for the week based on what you found. If you don't find a use for a particular coupon, don't be afraid to pass it on to someone else or discard it. The reduced price may be a good deal or the item could be appealing, but buying things that have no plan for consumption doesn't save you money. Be aware that many items listed in the weekly circulars are not always that good of a deal- the best coupons are usually on the first page or two.

Store Brands – Try it, You May Like It!

Generic is a good thing of the past. Besides the social stigma, most of the items tasted pretty bad. Grocery marketers found that this lead to, at best, a reluctant customer base. Thankfully, generic has evolved into store brands. These give you a more interesting label and a much better taste. While not all are as perfect, each requires some experimenting; many are worthy of our kitchen shelves. The biggest difference is in the price, where you will routinely notice 25-50% savings off the name-brand products.

Fight Against Impulse Buying

As we stated before, never go into a grocery store without a plan. Even if you are only picking up a few things, put them on a list and stick to it. You can even write down the dollar figure you want to stay within and spend within that number. Another important consideration is time. When possible, give yourself plenty of time to quickly scan and compare prices. However, don't give yourself so much time that you end up wandering the isles.

Comparison Shopping

Once or twice a year, take a few hours to visit stores and compare prices. Remember to compare apples to apples so that your assessment is accurate. Always compare the base price, not the sales price. One helpful thing to look for in comparison-shopping, is the unit price. This will show you what the product costs per ounce or pound and allows you to quickly compare two competing products or brands. Another consideration is the expiration or "use by" date found on most perishable products (milk, eggs, cottage cheese). Be sure the sale item isn't marked down because it's expiring in two days (unless you plan to consume it that quickly).

Beware of Gimmicks

Buying 10 bottles of catsup for $10 isn't the same value as 10 boxes of cereal for $10. Both sound like a deal, but they are not equal and some aren't even much of a deal at all. It's also important to understand the stores rules on buying multiple items. The sale may cleverly advertise but 10 for $10, but it usually doesn't mean you have to buy that quantity to get that deal. Check with the store's customer service first, but it is usually possible to buy 3 for $3 and 7 for $7.

The Moment of Purchase

Stores offer hundreds of thousands of individual items for sale and their prices change daily. Because of human error, it is very common for a price not to get changed accurately in the store's computer system. Allow yourself the ability to watch for these mistakes, or quickly scan the receipt when you get to the car. Once you leave the parking lot, you more than likely won't drive back to the store to dispute something- it's usually not worth the time.

Control the Experience

It isn't always possible to shop alone, but we have all seen this or maybe even been there ourselves: A mother with small children enters the store, the pleading and begging start almost immediately. Before long, mom has either left in frustration with only half the shopping done or the kids have persuaded her to buy $20 worth of items not on her list. On the other hand, it's good for children to learn good grocery store behavior and shopping techniques. Maybe only take one or two children at a time so you can better manage and control the experience.

Other Great Ideas

Try Meal Sharing

If you've got some good friends in the neighborhood or close by this idea might workout perfect for you.

Here's how it works: Each family takes a turn cooking for the other two families one night per week. The catering family shops, prepares and delivers the meal for a total of twelve people. Busy schedules are taken into account with the catering schedule changing on a weekly basis. The menus are all agreed upon in advance with likes and dislikes accounted for. The meals can be well balanced each including salad, bread and an entrée.

Groups who have tried this agreed that the additional one night per week was worth the two nights off. They were also encouraged by spending less on average than they did previously. It actually cost less for the three-day period, even though they spent more on their assigned nights. Watch out for sales at local grocery stores, you'll find that it is less expensive buying a larger volume of food.

Cook For A Month In Advance

The main idea: Cooking a month worth of meals and side dishes during one eight-hour session and then storing them in the freezer. You can end up with spending less than $150 a month on family dinners. You can also do a small cooking session for breakfast foods like waffles and muffins. Plan your once-a-month cooking around what's on sale. Let's say your going to make several chicken recipes; it helps to buy chicken on sale at $1.99 a pound instead of $4.99 a pound.

You might choose your recipes on Monday according to what sales come out in the weekend supermarket circulars, and then shop on Wednesday. Before your Friday or Saturday cooking marathon begins, you should do as much preparation work as possible. This includes chopping and grating vegetables and browning ground beef.

If you're just starting out, the idea of cooking a month's worth of food can be overwhelming. Try a mini-session to prepare food for the next week or two. Instead of making one tray of lasagna, make three and freeze two. When you take your cooking to the monthly level, try taking 15 recipes and doubling them so you'll only be eating the same meal twice.

Some Good Books for Freezer Cooking

Freezer Cooking Manual from 30-Day Gourmet: A Month of Meals Made Easy

Frozen Assets: How to Cook for a Day and Eat for a Month
www.dvo.com
Pay $14.95 and download 100 perfect freezer meal recipes.

Other Resources

Do you dread the question "What's for dinner tonight?" Would you like to eliminate the hassle of planning and preparing meals? Are you tired of putting the same old dinner together or picking up dinner at a drive-thru restaurant? Do you find your family eating out several times a week because you're too busy or tired to cook, or do you just not like to cook? If you answered yes to one, or all of these questions, we have found the perfect solution for you! Listed below are the seven locations in Houston where you can go and assemble one-month worth of delicious, nutritious, freezable meals. They do the planning and shopping for you, allowing you to spend less time in the kitchen and more time with your family. All you do is show up assemble the meals, take them home and put them in the freezer. Best of all, no clean up! The cleaning and dishes are done for you!

Overall food expenses can be dramatically lower. The savings come from lots of different places, and they really add up: (1) Less time spent grocery shopping and less junk food purchases. (2) No more throwing away spoiled ingredients that you never quite got around to cooking. (3) Fewer expensive drive-through and restaurant bills caused by pressed time and lack of desire to cook. (4) No grocery waste from needing to buy a minimum quantity of an ingredient, when you really just need a little bit for your recipe. (5) Time is money and your time is worth a lot. A few hours at one of these locations, can save you up to 22 hours of recipe selection, grocery shopping, food preparation, etc. Having more time to spend on something more valuable to you is worth a lot!

Dream Dinners

870 South Mason Road, Suite 104, Katy, TX
832-969-0690
www.dreamdinners.com
See advertiser index on pg 445

A Freezable Feast
9061 Gaylord Street, Houston, TX
713-973-1471
www.afreezablefeast.com

Frozen in Thyme
479 Bay Area Boulevard, Houston, TX
281-282-9927
www.frozeninthyme.com

Let's Do Dinner, Inc.
4606 FM 1960 West, Suite 175, Houston, TX
281-893-6857
www.letsdodinner.biz

Make It and Bake It
902 Main Street, Humble, TX
281-548-CHEF
www.makeitandbakeit.com

Village Table/Kingwood & Memorial
14092 Memorial Drive, Houston, TX
281-556-0660
www.villagetable.com

Village Table/West University
5330 Weslayan Street, Houston, TX
713-839-7333

The Grocery Game

www.thegrocerygame.com

Some of our own Houston Mama's have discovered a great way to save a bundle on groceries, by playing The Grocery Game. The company's founder, Teri Gault, always loved collecting coupons and saving her family money. This hobby of hers became a passion and before she knew it The Grocery Game was in the works. She created "Terri's List," which shows the best prices on hundreds of products compared to the manufacturers' coupons; giving you the best possible savings at your local grocery stores. The Grocery Game does all research and work for you, making it a fun and easy way to save hundreds of dollars each month on groceries. Here's what you do: Each week you will spend about 15 minutes cutting out coupons of products from the newspaper that your family will use. You then organize and file them by general categories. Every Monday you print out "Terri's List" off the website. After 12 weeks all your family's supplies are stockpiled at the lowest prices possible. Terri finds the sales, coupons, and secret sales of major stores in your area. The concept is pretty easy and Terri does all the work for you. Several Houston Mama's swear by it! Participating grocery stores in the Houston area include: HEB, Kroger, Randalls, and Albertsons.

Kids Eat Free

Taking the family out to eat can get expensive! We have found a way to save money and still enjoy going out to dinner.

Many major restaurant chains in Houston offer "Kids Eat Free" Programs or reduced price menus for children. Some of the restaurants offer a free kids meal when an adult meal is purchased. Most of the restaurants offer free birthday meals or a free birthday desert. We have also found that most "kids eat free" days are on Tuesdays or off-peak hours. The following restaurants are some of the places we have found that offer this program. Please remember to call ahead to confirm.

- Boston Market
- Burger King
- Champps
- Chick-Fil-A
- Chili's
- Ci-Ci's Pizza
- Cliff's Hamburgers
- Denny's
- Fazzolis
- The Golden Corral
- IHOP
- James Coney Island
- Jason's Deli
- Kettle Restaurant
- Lone Star Steak House
- Luby's
- Pizza Hut
- Roadhouse Grill
- Ryan's
- Shoneys
- Sweet Mesquite
- The Pasta House

Websites to Visit

The concept is the same for all of these websites. They provide printable coupons for big name brands, services, and restaurants. Browse around for products you routinely buy and your favorite places to eat, then print the coupon.

www.coolsavings.com

www.couponcart.com

www.eversave.com

www.hotcoupons.com

www.valpak.com

Clothing the Crew

Specialty Shops

Are you ever wondering why everyone else has really unique things that you just can't seem to find in the big name stores? It's because they shop in some of our locally owned stores. Take an afternoon and browse through some of these great hidden treasures.

NORTH

Animal Crackers Kidwear
471 Sawdust Road, The Woodlands, TX
281-362-9388
A complete selection of designer children's clothes, baby gifts, shoes and accessories can be found at Animal Crackers Kidwear.

Baby Town Spring
201 Midway, Spring, TX
281-528-9100
Baby Town Spring is located in Old Town Spring. They carry a large selection of christening gowns for girls and christening outfits for boys, as well as clothes for boys and girls, accessories and some gift sets.

Cute Kids-Sassy Kids

10801 Spring Cypress, Spring, TX

832-717-4611

People love to come to this store to buy socks and hair bows. They carry socks and bows that match almost any outfit. If you can't find a bow that matches the outfit you want, they will make a bow to match and have it ready when you are finished shopping. You can also find western clothes for girls. Their specialty Haven Line has adult and children's clothes that match one another.

Freckle Town

18502 Kuykendahl Road, Spring, TX

281-355-9949

Freckle Town carries boy's sizes newborn-size 7 and girl's sizes newborn-size 16. Books, gift items and Groovy Girl dolls can also be found here. The owner of this store also owns Apple Tree Kids, in Kingwood and Tea Cups & Tadpoles in The Woodlands. Be sure to check out the other stores as well.

Janie and Jack (2 locations)

1201 Lake Woodlands Drive, The Woodlands, TX

281-298-6747

5135 West Alabama, Houston, TX

713-599-1686

Janie and Jack is conveniently located just outside of the Woodlands Mall. They carry infant clothes for boys and girls in sizes newborn to size 4. You will also find shoes and accessories to match the outfits and silver heirloom keepsakes.

Pink Cowboys

1440 Lake Woodlands Drive, Suite I, The Woodlands, TX

281-419-0600

This store carries children's clothing and accessories for girls and boys. Girl's sizes are from infant to size 16 and boy's sizes are from infant to size 4. You will also find all the essential baby items, perfect for a baby shower gift. They carry beautiful hand-painted lamps and rocking chairs. Special deliveries can be made to the Woodlands and Conroe Hospital.

Teacups & Tadpoles

4775 W Panther Creek, The Woodlands, TX

281-681-0639

Teacups and Tadpoles carry specialty clothing, accessories, toys, and gifts. Boy's sizes start at newborn and go up to size 7 and girl's sizes are from newborn to size 16.

NORTHWEST

Giggles Children's Boutique

15442 FM 529, Houston, TX

832-593-9988.

At this store you will find a large selection of girls clothing, shoes, accessories, hair bows, hats, umbrellas, pajamas, and sunglasses. Girl's clothing sizes are from newborn to size 6. If you are a mother of multiples, a discount will be given. They do carry select boy items, but quantity is limited.

See advertiser index on pg 445

Rattle Tattle

6110 North Highway 6, Houston, TX

281-855-4288

Rattle Tattle offers specialty clothing including dance clothes and shoes, gymnastics wear and sportswear. They also carry christening outfits, special occasion and formal wear. Selection for boys is limited.

NORTHEAST

Apple Tree Kids

2714 W Lake Houston Parkway, Kingwood, TX

281-360-9250

They carry clothing from newborn sizes to size 16, as well as, shoes, accessories, beautiful christening gowns and gifts.

Buckles and Bows

1251 Kingwood Drive, Kingwood, TX

281-359-0034

This store carries quality baby gifts, cribs, bedding, and clothing for infants and toddlers.

SOUTHWEST

Bebe De France

1800 Post Oak Boulevard, Suite 160, Houston, TX

713-621-2224

Bebe De France carries clothes and shoes imported from France and Italy, giving your baby international style. Clothes are for boys and girls and come in sizes newborn to 8.

Doodles Baby Gifts & More
2504 Rice Village Boulevard, Houston, TX
713-528-2900
www.doodlesbaby.com
This store carries all your baby's essentials including nursery furniture, crib bedding, room décor, and strollers. One of our favorites is the beautiful "Moses baskets." They also carry a large quantity of toys, including one of the largest selections of Groovy Girls Dolls.

Haute Baby
1121 Uptown Park Boulevard, TX
713-355-1537
www.houstonhautebaby.com
Haute Baby offers the ultimate in baby chic! They carry both infant and toddler clothing for boys and girls, but mainly infant clothes. Their clothing sizes range from newborn to size 4T. They have their own Haute Baby signature collection, Uptown collection, and Christening outfits. You will also find custom crib bedding, nursery furniture, Paddy Gordon books, Jill Smith Designs, diaper bags, and specialty gifts. One of our personal favorites is the mommy & baby yoga wear. Baby registry is also available.

Jacadi
5085 Westheimer (Galleria Mall), TX
713-621-9522
www.jacadi.com
Jacadi has been creating children clothes for 25 years. Their stores and brand of clothing can be found in over forty countries. They are known for their high-quality, modern, refined products; consisting of clothes, shoes, and every other baby need. Every year, Jacadi creates 2 collections of clothes and shoes.

Oilily
5085 Westheimer, Houston, TX (Galleria Mall)
713-355-8303
www.oilily-world.com
Oilily's originated over forty years ago in The Netherlands. Their first American store opened in 1987 in Boston. Shortly after, stores were all over the UK, Japan, and Spain. Their line of clothes is known worldwide. Oilily's apparel is known for it's vivid colors and rich textures. They carry baby, toddler, and children clothes; including socks, shoes, and coats. You will also find unique and fun purses and backpacks.

Tulips & Tutus
238 West 19th Street, Houston, TX
713-861-0301
This quaint little boutique is located in The Heights, one of the oldest and most historic neighborhoods in Houston. In fact, 19th Street is famous for it's fun little shops. Tulips & Tutus is just one of many shops you will find along the street. They sell a wide variety of cute items, including children's clothing and accessories, candles, books, toys, and even adult pajamas with slippers to match. For the dog lovers, you will find many specialty dog products.

Resale & Consignment Shops

Consignment shops are a great place for moms who are looking for higher quality items, but don't want to spend the designer price. Because children, especially babies, outgrow their clothes so quickly; consignment shops are perfect! You will find gently used items, sometimes even brand new. Most shops will even pay you cash for your gently used clothes.

NORTH

Kid to Kid
6777 Woodlands Parkway, The Woodlands, TX
281-419-3339
See advertiser index on pg 445

Ladies-n-Kidz Rerunz
5032 Fm 2920, Spring, TX
281-353-4544

The Kids Barn
16064 Bridelwood, Conroe, TX
936-271-7444

NORTHWEST

Saturdays Child Resale Shop
829 South Mason Road, Katy, TX
281-578-9425

Young & Restless
2515 Ella Boulevard, Houston, TX
713-861-7647

SOUTHWEST

Children's Orchard
12572 Westheimer Road, Houston, TX
281-558-2229

Andrew's Corner
2508 Sunset Boulevard, Houston, TX
713-522-7355

Lil' Tykes Trading Post
3544 Highway 6, Sugarland, TX
281-325-0633

Second Childhood (2 locations)
2280 West Holcombe Boulevard, Houston, TX
713-666-3443

1922 Fountain View, Houston, TX (SW)
713-789-6456

A Kids Depot
16634 Sea Lark Road, Houston, TX
281-480-7873

Changes Kids
920 West Main Street, League City, TX
281-338-5164

Kidz Korner
3622 Fairmont Parkway, Pasadena, TX
281-487-7552

The Funky Monkey
607 Friendswood, Suite 27, Friendswood, TX
281-996-5007

Chapter 17

Health and Childcare

Chapter 17

Health and Childcare

Because finding all of the health resources available can be a maze of confusion, this chapter includes them all in one place. Read on to find state health resources, immunization information, pediatricians and more.

Health Organizations and Services

CHIP

1-877-KIDS-NOW (1-877-543-7669)

www.hhsc.state.tx.us/chip

The Children's Health Insurance Program (CHIP) is a national health insurance plan for children. Children qualify for CHIP based on family income and the number of members in the family. CHIP covers well-child exams, immunizations, health care provider services, prescriptions, hearing and vision exams, dental service and mental health services. Applications for CHIP are accepted during Open Enrollment. Call to find out dates for enrollment or visit their website.

Medicaid

1-800-252-8263

www.hhsc.state.tx.us/medicad

What is Medicaid?

The Texas Medicaid program pays medical bills for people

- who qualify for a category of Medicaid
- who have low income or cannot afford the cost of healthcare
- who have resources (assets) under the federal limit for the category of Medicaid

Texas has two types of Medicaid, Traditional and STAR. Under the traditional program, people receive medical care from any Medicaid provider. Under the STAR Program (State of Texas Assistance and Referral System), you are assigned to one provider who will manage all your healthcare needs. Both of the programs receive the same medical benefits. Please call or check online to find out which program you are eligible for.

Planned Parenthood of Houston

1-800-230-PLAN

www.pphouston.org

Planned Parenthood offers a variety of confidential services for women's health. They offer birth control and emergency contraception, pregnancy testing and counseling. They also test and treat sexually transmitted diseases. They offer screening and counseling for fertility, cancer and HIV/AIDS. Health and menopause exams are also performed. There is also an educational resource library.

For more information and clinic locations, you can check out their website. For medical questions, or to schedule an appointment with the nearest Planned Parenthood center, call their toll-free number.

WIC

1-800-942-3678

WIC is a special nutrition program that helps women, infants, and children. WIC provides nutritious food, nutrition education and counseling; breastfeeding support and counseling for pregnant and breastfeeding women. Eligibility is determined by income level, as well as, medical and nutritional need. Call their main number to find a WIC office near you or to obtain information about the program.

(For general eligibility guidelines, check our State and Community Resources Chapter).

Dental Assistance

Dental services for uninsured, low-income individuals and families.

Public Dental Health Clinic Locations:

Dental Branch
6516 MD Anderson Avenue, Houston, TX
713-500-4000

Northwest Dental Clinic
5668 West Little York, Houston, TX
281-447-2800

Pasadena Dental Clinic
3737 Red Bluff, Pasadena, TX
713-740-5000

SEARCH Health and Dental Clinic
2505 Fannin, Houston, TX
713-739-7752

Immunizations

The following information was obtained by Texas State Department of Health and the National Center for Disease Control.

State Vaccine Requirements for Texas School Entrance (Grades K-12)

- **DTP,DtaP, DT, Td:** 5 doses of any combination unless 4th dose was given on or after 4th birthday.
  Students 7 years or older: 3 doses of any combination.
  One does of Td required 10 years after last dose.
- **Polio (IPV):** 4 doses unless the 3rd dose was on or after 4th birthday.
- **Measles, Mumps, Rubella (MMR):** 2 doses of a measles-containing vaccine with the 1st dose on or after the 1st birthday.
  2nd dose by age 5 or entry into kindergarten
- **Hepatitis B:** 3 doses
- **Varicella:** 1 dose on or after 1st birthday.
  2 doses if vaccine given at 13 years or older.
- **Hepatitis A:** 2 doses on or after 2nd birthday for grades K-3 only.

For More Information

Anyone can download or request a free copy of the "Parents guide to Childhood Immunizations." This is a 94-page booklet introducing parents to 12 childhood diseases and the vaccines that can protect children from them.

Two ways for you to get a copy:

- Print your own copy at: www.cdc.gov/nip/publications/Parents-Guide
- Order a free booklet from the National Immunization Program on the same link. This printed bound version is available in English and Spanish and features children's drawings.

Immunizations are provided at the following locations:

Antoine Community Health Center
5668 West Little York Road, Houston, TX
281-447-2800

Harris County Health Department
1000 Lee Drive, Baytown, TX
281-427-5195

Humble Health Center
1730 Humble Place Drive, Humble, TX
281-466-4222

Laporte Health Center
1009 South Broadway, Laporte, TX
281-471-4202

Southeast Clinic
3737 Red Bluff Road, Pasadena, TX
713-740-5000

The Immunization Clinic
414B North Sam Houston Parkway, Houston, TX
281-260-6600

For more information visit:
www.immunizetexas.com

Immunization Links & Resources

American Academy of Pediatrics (AAP)

www.aap.org

The mission of AAP is to attain optimal physical, mental, and social health well being for infants, children, adolescents and young adults.

American Medical Association (AMA)

www.ama-assn.org

The AMA disseminates up-to-date information of health and medical practice, medical ethics and education to physicians and to the public.

Bill and Melinda Gates Children's Vaccine Program (Gates CVP)

www.childrensvaccine.org

Gates CVP was established to promote equal access to lifesaving vaccines worldwide. This site provides information on advocacy issues, clinical issues, service delivery, immunization financing, safe injections, other related organizations, etc.

Every Child By Two (ECBT)

www.ecbt.org

The goals of ECBT are to raise awareness of the critical need for timely immunization and to foster putting in place a systematic way to immunize all of America's children by the age of two.

Immunization Action Coalition (IAC)

www.immunize.org

This website has abundant useful information about immunization, immunization resources and their newsletter Needle Tips.

ImmTrac

1-866-624-0180

ImmTrac is a statewide immunization registry that electronically keeps track of your child's immunization record. This helps providers to see what immunizations your child has had and which immunizations are needed. ImmTrac can also print out shot records for your child's daycare or school and notify you when shots are due. Your child's information is only available to doctors, childcare centers and schools. Please call their toll-free number to find out how to register your child for ImmTrac.

National Immunization Program (NIP)

www.cdc.gov/nip

This is a comprehensive website that provides immunization information to the public and health professionals, including training, education materials, promotions, statistics, vaccine safety and disease surveillance.

National Network for Immunization Immunization (NNII)

www.immunizationinfo.org

Great information on vaccines and the diseases they prevent.

Texas Children's Hospital Immunization Help Line

832-824-2061

This is a wonderful resource to find out information on special immunization events in and around Houston, location of health clinics nearest you, and immunization requirements for your child's specific age. Information is in English, Spanish, and Vietnamese.

The Trouble Shooters/Health Mobile Unit Program

713-873-TOTS (8687)

Call to hear a recording of monthly schedules for mobile health clinics. Recordings are in English and Spanish.

Health and Education Resources

First Aid/CPR

The following organizations provide first aid training:

American Red Cross (Main Location)

2700 Southwest Freeway, Houston, TX

713-526-8300

(There are 14 other Houston-area locations, please call for a location near you.)

America's Finest CPR Training

16032 Drifting Rose Circle, Houston, TX

281-304-9320

American Heart Association

10060 Buffalo Speedway, Houston, TX

713-610-5000

Health & Safety Training Center
6250 Westpark Drive, Suite 203, Houston, TX
713-975-7360

Life Management Services
4022 Black Locust Drive
281-260-9488

Education for Specific Health Issues

American Cancer Society, Houston office
6301 Richmond Avenue, Houston, TX
713-266-2877
www.cancer.org
Information for employees, at work sites throughout the community, about support and assistance for cancer patients and their families.

American Heart Association, Houston office
10060 Buffalo Speedway, Houston, TX
713-610-5000
www.americanheart.org
Age-appropriate education for school-age children to teach them the importance of taking care of their hearts by eating healthy foods, exercising daily, and being tobacco-free.

Nutrition, education, and weight management programs specifically targeting how to make healthier food choices, the importance of exercise, and how to reduce fat intake.

American Red Cross, Central Houston
2700 Southwest Freeway, Houston, TX
713-526-8300
www.houstonredcross.org
HIV/AIDS prevention education for high-risk youth in correctional facilities, substance abuse facilities, group homes, alternative schools, and other community locations.

Education for Spanish speaking Latino community members in first aid, CPR, and HIV/AIDS. Culturally appropriate literature and materials are provided to participants.

Pediatrician Guide

How to Select A Pediatrician

Most parents and children develop close and lasting relationships with their pediatrician. If you select a pediatrician who matches your personality and needs, working together to keep your child healthy will prove to be an enjoyable experience.

Your pediatrician will become much more than a person who cares for your child when he or she is sick. Your pediatrician will be a friend who offers reassurance, advice and guidance throughout your child's years of growth and development.

Things to Consider

Before beginning the selection process, parents should think about what things are most important to them when choosing a pediatrician.

- Would you feel more comfortable dealing with an older doctor or a younger doctor?
- Would you prefer a male or female physician?
- Is it important for the doctor's office to be close to your home or work?
- Does your health insurance plan limit your choice of physicians?

When you've determined your preferences, there are several sources you can use to find the names of specific doctors. Your obstetrician, friends and relatives may all have suggestions and recommendations or, you may use a hospital's physician referral service. These services can find a pediatrician in your insurance plan and provide you with information about the doctor's training, board certification, office hours, and more.

Schedule an interview to meet the pediatrician you are considering. This introductory visit will help you determine whether you feel comfortable asking the doctor questions and whether his or her answers make sense to you. Many pediatricians will schedule an interview with you at no charge.

What Should You Ask the Office Staff?

It is not uncommon for parents to talk with a pediatrician's office staff as often as they talk to the doctor. You'll want to feel comfortable with your pediatrician's staff and ask them some important questions about the practice.

Here are a few suggestions:

- How many patients are usually seen in an hour?
- How long do patients usually wait to see the doctor?
- What are the office hours?

- Are there designated phone hours to speak to the doctor?
- Will I be able to speak with a nurse to seek routine information?
- Will my child have a primary physician, or do several doctors share patient care responsibilities?
- Is someone available to handle emergencies during evening or weekend hours?

What Should You Ask the Doctor?

Mothers and fathers have hundreds of questions about their child's health and development. Be assured that pediatricians are accustomed to answering lots of questions and most delight in sharing their knowledge and experience to help children start healthy lives.

When you talk with the doctor, don't be shy about asking questions. Pediatricians understand how important a child's health is to parents.

Here are possible questions to ask when interviewing a doctor:

- Is the physician certified by the American Board of Pediatrics or other specialty board?
- Where did the doctor attend medical school and receive postgraduate training?
- When hospitalization is necessary, does the pediatrician admit patients to a hospital specializing in pediatric care?
- What other members of the staff assist the doctor in caring for patients? What are their roles and qualifications?
- What are the doctor's views on issues like breastfeeding and bottle-feeding? Opinions vary among pediatricians, so it may be helpful to have a pediatrician who shares your same feelings.
- What are the doctor's views on well-baby care and early childhood development? Answers to these types of questions may tell you whether your philosophy of child-raising corresponds to the pediatrician's.
- Editorial provided by pediatric nurses from the St. Louis Children's Hospital Answer Line for BJC Health System.

Pediatrician Clinics

While there are countless pediatricians in Houston and surrounding areas, we have chosen to list only clinics. Most clinics have a larger staff, and after-hours care available.

NORTH

Conroe Pediatric Associates
404 Riverpointe Dr., Suite 100
Conroe, TX
936-441-8887

FM 1960 Pediatric Center Cypress Station Center
1250 Cypress Station Center
Houston, TX
281-440-1950

FM 1960 Pediatric Center Cypresswood Center
8111 Cypresswood, #104
Spring, TX
281-376-0707

Medical Plaza Pediatrics
1011 Medical Plaza Dr., Suite 220

Nanes Pediatrics
17030 Nanes, Suite 105
Houston, TX
281-440-4150

Sterling Ridge Pediatrics
6707 Sterling Ridge Dr., Suite A
The Woodlands, TX
281-296-2656

Woodlands Pediatric Associates
4545 Research Forest Dr., Suite A
The Woodlands, TX
281-367-5100
The Woodlands, TX
281-296-9119

NORTHWEST

FM 1960 Pediatric Center Copperfield Medical Center
8925 Hwy 6 North, Suite 451
Houston, TX
281-855-5300

FM 1960 Pediatric Center Lakewood Center
13215 Grant Road, Suite 100
Cypress, TX
281-374-7457

Katy Pediatrics
705 S. Fry Rd., Suite 120
Katy, TX
281-398-3100

Northwest Pediatric Clinic
1919 North Loop West, Suite 140
Houston, TX
713-869-1692

Pediatrics of Cy-Fair
11811 FM 1960 West, Suite 100
Houston, TX
281-970-2337

Spring Branch Pediatrics
8830 Long Point, Suite 605
Houston, TX
713-468-4071

NORTHEAST

Humble Pediatric Associates-Humble
18955 Memorial North, Suite 100
Humble, TX
281-348-7575

Humble Pediatric Associates-Kingwood
611 Rockmead Dr., Suite 600
Kingwood, TX
281-348-7575

Pediatric Associates of Kingwood
20035 W. Lake Houston Parkway, Suite 100
Kingwood, TX
281-359-1000

SOUTHWEST

Alief Children's Clinic
12121 Richmond, Suite 124
Houston, TX
281-589-9700

Ashford Pediatric Associates
14730 Barryknoll
Houston, TX
281-496-9700

Gulfton Pediatrics
5900 Chimney Rock, Suite Y
Houston, TX
713-661-2951

Houston Pediatric Associates
4110 Bellaire Blvd., Suite 210
Houston, TX
713-666-1953

Memorial Pediatric Associates
902 Frostwood, Suite 227
Houston, TX
713-467-4434

Midtown Pediatrics
2101 Crawford, Suite 214
Houston, TX
713-759-6888

Pediatricians of Sugar Land
2225 Williams Trace Blvd., Suite 108
Sugar Land, TX
281-491-3636

Pediatricians of West Houston
12000 Richmond, Suite 330
Houston, Texas 77082
281-493-2444

Pediatric Medical Group
4101 Greenbriar, Suite 100
Houston, TX
713-526-6443

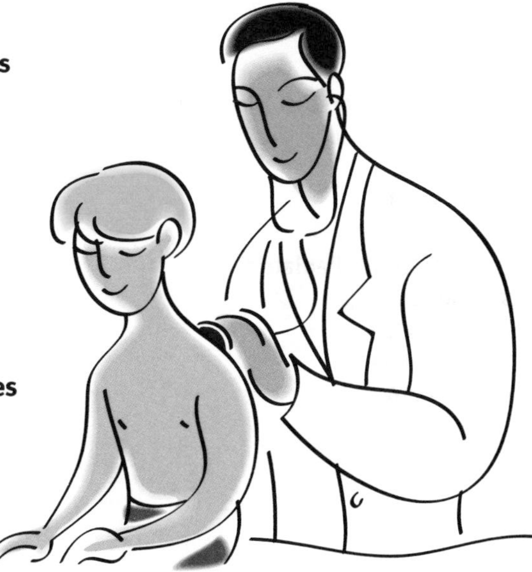

Piney Point Pediatric Associates
2450 Fondren, Suite 310
Houston, TX
713-781-7907

Post Oak Pediatrics
5757 Woodway Drive, Ste. 200
Houston, TX
713-782-4830

Town & Country Pediatrics
909 Frostwood, Suite 126
Houston, TX
713-461-6414

SOUTHEAST

Cullen Pediatric and Adolescent Health Center
5737 Cullen Blvd., Suite 200
Houston, TX
713-440-6539

Northshore Pediatrics
12605 East Freeway, Suite 200
Houston, TX
713-451-5555

Pediatric Associates of Baytown
4301 Garth Road, Suite 303
Baytown, TX
281-422-6678

Texas Children's Pediatric Associates
411 E. Parkwood
Friendswood, TX
281-242-3486

Texas Children's Pediatric Associates
3323 Burke Road
Pasadena, TX 77504
713-941-1177

Texas Children's Pediatric Associates
9330 Broadway, Building 300, Suite 312
Pearland, TX
281-412-5852
281-482-3486

Chapter 18

Pregnancy and Infant Resources

Chapter 18

Pregnancy and Infant Resources

Having a baby is one of the biggest events of your life. In this chapter you will find helpful information on community education, books, and support groups that can help you through your big event and beyond.

Community Education and Awareness Programs

March of Dimes
3000 Weslayan #100
Houston, TX 77027
713-623-2020
www.marchofdimes.org
www.marchofdimes.com/texas
The mission of the March of Dimes is to improve the health of babies by preventing birth defects and infant mortality.

Find information on birth defects, newborn screening, premature babies, weight gain during pregnancy, and almost anything else you would like to know about babies. They have an amazing pregnancy and newborn health education center on their website.

The March of Dimes organization sponsors many local events to raise awareness and money for research and programs to prevent premature babies.

National Center on Shaken Baby Syndrome
1-888-273-0071
www.dontshake.com
This is a referral and information center. They provide prevention information and community education classes. They also have professionals available for parents in crisis due to the stress of a baby.

Pregnancy Risk Line

1-800-822-2229

Information and assistance provided anonymously concerning substance use, misuse, and abuse during pregnancy.

Safe Riders

1-800-252-8255

www.dshs.state.tx.us/saferiders

This is a child passenger safety awareness program sponsored through the State of Texas.

If you have any questions about safety belts, car seats, or air bags you can call the number listed for information. On the website you can also find a list of car seat inspection stations in the Houston area. Find information on child passenger safety laws in Texas and a car seat shopping guide for children.

Vasa Previa Foundation

www.vpfu.org

To learn more about Vasa Previa please visit their website.

Vasa Previa occurs once in every 2,000-3,000 births. The fetal mortality rate is estimated to be as high as 95% if the condition is not prenantally diagnosed. The technology exists to detect Vesa Previa, but it is rarely diagnosed because prenatal screening for the condition is not the standard of care.

Vasa Previa Foundation was organized to promote the prenatal diagnosis and treatment of Vasa Previa. Their three main objectives are: 1. Educate the general public and medical community about how to detect and treat Vasa Previa. 2. Change standard procedures within hospitals and clinics to aid in the early diagnosis and treatment of Vasa Previa. 3. Provide support for those affected by Vasa Previa.

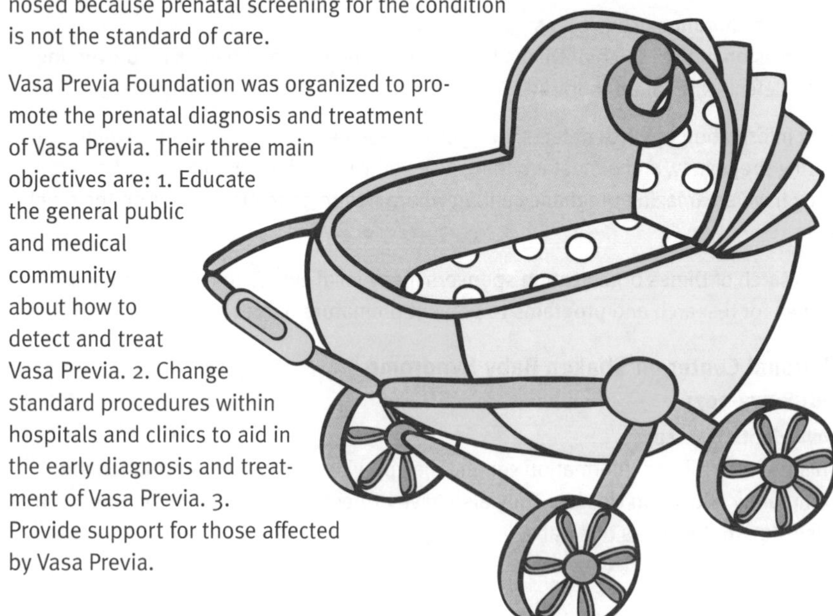

Grief and Loss Support Groups

Angel Watch

1-877-344-8600 (toll-free) or 713-592-5600

(Odyssey Healthcare will answer, just ask for Angel Watch)

Angel Watch is a perinatal hospice program that helps parents and families who are continuing pregnancies in which a probable lethal fetal abnormality has been diagnosed prenatally. It is currently a branch of Odyssey Healthcare and the only perinatal hospice program in the nation. It gives supportive care and guidance to families as they plan the medical management for their unborn infant and acts as a professional bridge for them as they transition from pregnancy, to parenthood, and then often to bereavement. In addition, it also helps families who lose their infants prematurely due to stillbirth or miscarriage. It uses the inter-disciplinary team efforts of physicians, nurses, social workers, Chaplains, bereavement counselors, and Child Life Specialists. It has two primary goals: 1. To support families through their experience in every way possible. 2. To promote a quality life for the child as long as that life may be. There is only a charge if hospice care is required after birth and many insurance companies provide reimbursement. Otherwise services are provided in home and without charge.

The Compassionate Friends (5 locations)

1-877-969-0010

www.compassionatefriends.org

The mission of The Compassionate Friends is to assist families toward the positive resolution of grief following the death of a child at any age. They also provide information to help friends and family cope with the loss and how to be supportive. There are five locations in Houston and surrounding areas. Please call the toll free number for a list of group leaders in your area.

H.A.N.D.-Houston's Aid in Neonatal Death

832-752-1919

www.hand.net

"This is a Houston based pregnancy and infant loss support group for parents whose babies have died any time from conception through late infancy. Our mission is to help parents cope with feelings of grief and isolation which accompany the loss of a baby." They offer group support meetings at multiple locations throughout Houston. Please call for information on meeting times and locations.

Share Parents Pregnancy & Infant Loss Support Group

281-376-7735

www.nationalshareoffice.com

Provides grief support for parents who have lost an infant to miscarriage, stillbirth, and newborn death. Groups are led by volunteer moms who have shared similar experiences. Hospital visits are available at the parent's request. They also provide training for hospital staff regarding bereavement. Every 2nd Saturday in October they sponsor "A Walk to Remember". Please call for more information about this event and to get on their mailing list.

SIDS Alliance

Greater Houston Chapter SIDS Alliance

713-924-1419

www.sidsalliance.org

First Candle/SIDS Alliance is a national nonprofit health organization uniting parents, caregivers, and researchers to government, business, and community service groups, to advance infant health and survival. They offer a grief support network, and crisis counselors that are available 24 hours a day.

Childbirth Education

Call your local hospital or ask your healthcare provider about prenatal, childbirth, and sibling classes and other programs that are available. Most hospitals in the Houston area offer a variety of prenatal classes FREE of charge or at a minimal cost.

Nativiti Women's Health and Birth Center

26614 Oak Ridge Dr.
The Woodlands, TX 77380

281-296-2333

www.nativiti.com

This facility offers childbirth classes, breastfeeding classes, and conscious parenting classes.

The Motherhood Center of Houston

3701 W. Alabama, Suite 230
Houston, TX 77027

713-963-8880

www.motherhoodcenter.com

This wonderful facility offers a huge variety of classes for expectant parents. Some examples are babysitting services, exercise classes, childbirth classes, seminars, and even support groups. Contact them for a detailed schedule and pricing.

Birthing Methods

The Bradley Method

1-800-4-A-BIRTH

www.bradlybirth.com

The Bradley Method teaches natural childbirth and views birth as a natural process. It is their belief that most women with proper education, preparation, and the help of a loving, supportive coach can be taught to give birth naturally. The Bradley Method is a system of natural labor techniques in which a woman and her coach play an active part. It is a simple method of increasing self-awareness, teaching a woman how to deal with stress of labor by tuning into her own body. The Bradley Method encourages mothers to trust their bodies using natural breathing, relaxation, nutrition, exercise, and education.

Lamaze

www.lamaze.org

This organization's vision is, " a world of confident women choosing normal birth." They believe normal birth is nature's simple way for the birthing process to happen. They teach women to be informed, confident, and supported through the birthing process. They believe in six practices for the normal birth process: 1. Labor begins on its own. 2. Freedom of movement throughout labor. 3. Continuous labor support. 4. No routine interventions. 5. Non-supine positions for birth. 6. No separation of mother and baby after birth with unlimited opportunity for breastfeeding.

Great Books

For Moms

Hot Mama- How to Have a Babe and Be a Babe – *Karen Salmansohg*

The Girlfriend's Guide to Pregnancy – *Vicki Lovine*

The Mother of All Pregnancy Books: The Ultimate Guide to Conception, Birth and Everything in Between – *Ann Douglas*

What to Expect When You're Expecting – *Heidi E. Murkoff*

Your Pregnancy Week by Week – *Glade B. Curtis, Judith Shuler*

For Dads

My Boys Can Swim! The Official Guys Guide to Pregnancy – *Ian Davis*

The Expectant Father- Facts, Tips and Advice for Dads to Be – *Armin A. Brott*

Websites

www.babycenter.com - Sign up for weekly e-mails about the stages and development of your pregnancy. There are a lot of great articles as well.

www.drspock.com - Helpful information on all the stages of raising your child

www.johnsonbaby.com - Parent learning center with great articles

www.houston.babyzone.com - This site has a lot of local information for your pregnancy and your baby.

Breastfeeding Resources

Birthcare

281-492-9796

www.mybirthcare.com

They provide all types of breastfeeding support. They specialize in personalized childbirth classes in the privacy of your own home. They can travel to most locations in the Greater Houston area. Please call for details.

Harris County Breastfeeding Coalition

Ben Taub Hospital
1504 Taub Loop
Houston, TX 77030

713-873-3252

www.bcm.edu/cnrc/hcbc/index.html

This coalition wants to increase breastfeeding awareness to all mothers. The website contains useful information on breastfeeding such as, articles, educational opportunities, and even information on breast-feeding friendly work environments. Check out one of their local meetings, and help support the cause.

La Leche League of Houston

www.ykc.com/LLLHouston

Helpline: 713-383-2819

This website lists local support groups that meet all over the Houston area. The list shows location, groups, meeting times, and leaders phone numbers who are available for help over the telephone.

NORTH

Breastfeeding Consultant Services, Inc.
Jane C. Van Nort
2151 F.M. 1960 W.
Houston, TX 77090
281-444-5115

The Parenting Center
Arnetta Dailey
19 Bitterwood Circle
The Woodlands, TX 77381
281-419-8816

NORTHWEST

A Baby's Choice
Georgia Crowhurst
11715 Goldstream
Tomball, TX 77377
281-216-5441

NORTHEAST

My Little Juel
Suzanna Juel
Kingwood, TX 77345
832-594-6969
www.mylittlejuel.com

SOUTHWEST

Baby Talk Breastfeeding Support
281-731-2803
281-565-Baby

SOUTHEAST

Add a Little Love
15810 Webelos St.
Friendswood, TX 77546
www.addalittlelove.com

Breastfeeding Phone Numbers

WIC Breastfeeding Hotline
1-877-942-5437

La Leche League of Houston
713-383-2229

Pregnancy Riskline
1-800-822-2229
Call if you have questions regarding medication or other substances that might affect your breast milk.

Breastfeeding Related Websites

www.aap.org/family/brstguid.htm
www.breastfeedingonline.com
www.hmhb.org
www.lalecheleague.org
www.lamaze.org
www.4women.org/Pregnancy

Ultrasounds

Fetal Vision
3007 Caroline St.
Houston, TX 77005
713-521-3551
www.fetal-vision.com
This facility specializes in 2D, 3D, and 4D ultrasounds. They offer several keepsake packages that include pictures, tapes, and cd's of your baby. Come see your baby before he is born.

First Sight Ultrasound
7000 Fannin M40
Houston, TX 70030
713-797-1000
www.firstsightultrasound.com
This is a full service prenatal ultrasound imaging center offering both diagnostic and keepsake ultrasounds. They offer "Geddes Keepsake" 4D ultrasound imaging that includes pictures, a tape, and a cd. You can bond with your baby before they are born.
See ad in back

PeekABaby
17284 Tomball Parkway
In the Willowbrook Mall
Houston, TX 77064
832-237-7335
www.peekababy3d.com
"Imagine the bonding that occurs when you first see your unborn child." Come and experience a truly unique 3D/4D ultrasound.

Chapter 19

State and Community Resources

Chapter 19

State and Community Resources

It is commonly stated that it takes a village to raise a child. This statement couldn't be more true. In this chapter you will find the programs and resources available in the "village." Browse through this chapter even if you don't think that you would utilize any of the programs and services, chances are you might know someone who can.

211 Texas United Way Help Line

Dial 211 or 713-957-HELP (4357)

This is one of the best resources in the state! Their trained specialists are friendly, helpful, and they have a vast database full of information that you need. They provide 13 Gulf Coast counties with instant information. Contact them to find local, nonprofit, state, government, health and human service information.

The operators are there to take your calls 7 days a week and 24 hours a day. Calls are answered in 6 different languages and they have access to translation in over 140 languages.

Child Abuse

Did you know...

- 1 in 3 girls and 1 in 5 boys will be sexually abused before the age of 18. (Prevention and Motivation Programs Inc., 2002)
- In 2003, 184 children in Texas died from abuse or neglect. (Texas Department of Protective & Regulatory Services)
- In 2002, Houston had 35,502 alleged child abuse victims (Texas Department of Protective & Regulatory Services)
- In America, every 6 hours a child dies from child abuse or neglect (Services to At-Risk Youth (STAR Program)

Child Protective Services (CPS)

713-394-4000

www.dfps.state.tx.us

CPS is a division of the Department of Family & Protective Services (DFPS). Their job is to investigate reports on child abuse and neglect. They also provide services to children and families, place children in foster care and adoptive homes. To find a CPS in your area, please visit the website or give them a call.

Justice for Children

412 Main Street, Houston, TX

713-225-4357

www.jfcadvocacy.org

National Child Abuse Hotline

1-800-4-A-Child (800-422-4453)

24 hour hotline and a secure website to file a child abuse report

Texas Abuse/Neglect Hotline

1-800-252-5400

www.txabusehotline.org

This is a confidential number that you can call , 24-hours a day, to report suspicions of child abuse or neglect, or you can file a report on their secure website.

Child Abuse Prevention Centers

The following centers have a common goal, to prevent and protect children from abuse and neglect. They offer several programs such as counseling, family support and parent resources. Some offer a safe haven for parents to bring their children to prevent abuse.

Children's Safe Harbor

412 West Lewis Street, Conroe, TX

936-539-3314- Main Office

936-441-2992- Metro #

www.childrenssafeharbor.org

DePelchin Children's Center (Main Campus)
4950 Memorial Drive, Houston, TX
713-730-2335
www.depelchin.org
There are 13 locations throughout Houston. To learn more about the services offered and to find a location nearest you, call or view their website.

Escape Family Resource Center
3210 Eastside Street, Houston, TX
713-942-9500
www.escapefrc.org

Family Outreach Center of Clear Lake/Bay Area
1300 Bay Area Boulevard, Houston, TX
281-486-8827
www.familyoutreachofamerica.com

Family Outreach Center of Montgomery County
610 North Loop 336 East, Conroe, TX
936-441-4733
www.familyoutreachoramerica.com

Domestic Violence/Rape

Did you know...

- Domestic Violence is the single most common source of injury to women. (Violence Prevention Center, 2002)
- 31% of American women report being physically or sexually abused by a husband or boyfriend at some point in their lives. (Commonwealth Fund Survey, 1998)
- In 1998, there were 7,914 rapes reported in Texas. (National Victims Center)
- 1 woman is raped every minute. (National Victims Center)

Domestic Violence Information Line
1-800-897-LINK
Gives referrals to shelters, counseling, advocates, etc.

National Domestic Violence Hotline

1-800-799-SAFE (7233)

24 hour crisis counseling and referrals to local agencies. Interpreters for most languages available.

Rape Safe Harbor 24 Hour Crisis Line

1-888-421-1100

Domestic Violence Centers

Domestic Violence centers provide shelter and protection for abused women and their dependent children. Programs are designed to help women and children move away from violence. Because most of the centers' addresses are confidential, the address listed is the administrative office. Please call to find out the location.

Aid to Victims of Domestic Abuse

2603 La Branch, Suit 100, Houston, TX

713-224-9911

www.avda-tx.org

Bay Area Turning Point

210 South Walnut, Webster, TX

281-286-5133-Office

281-286-2525-Hotline

www.bayareaturningpoint.org

Family Time

P.O. Box 893, Humble, TX

281-446-2615-Hotline

www.familytimefoundation.org

Fort Bend County Women's Center

14141 Southwest Freeway, Sugar Land, TX

281-494-4545-Office

281-342-HELP (4357)-Hotline

www.fortbendwomenscenter.org

Houston Area Women's Center
1010 Waugh, Houston, TX
713-528-6798-Office
713-528-2121-Hotline
www.hawc.org

Katy Christian Ministries Domestic Abuse Center
5011 East 5th Street, Katy, TX
281-391-5261-Office
281-693-7273-Hotline
www.ktcm.org

Montgomery County Women's Center
1600 Lake Front Circle, Suite 100, The Woodlands, TX
281-367-8003-Office
936-441-7273-Hotline
www.mcwcthewoodlands.org

New Horizon Family Center
313 South Highway 146, Baytown, TX
281-424-3300-Office
281-422-2292-Hotline

Northwest Assistance Ministries
15555 Kuykendahl Road, Houston, TX
281-885-4555-Office
281-855-4673-Hotline
www.namonline.org

The Bridge Over Troubled Waters
P.O. Box 3488, Pasadena, TX
713-472-0753-Office
713-473-2801-Hotline
www.thebridgeovertroubledwaters.org

The Victim Assistance Centre
1310 Prairie Street, Suit 77002, Houston, TX
713-755-5625-Hotline
www.thevictimassistancecentre.com

Women's Center of Brazoria County
P.O. Box 476, Angleton, TX
979-849-9553

Women's Resource & Crisis Center
P.O. Box 1545, Galveston, TX
409-763-1441-Office
409-765-SAFE (7233)-Hotline
www.galveston.comcrisiscenter

YWCA
3621 Willa Street, Houston, TX
713-868-9922
www.ywca.org
The mission of YWCA is to empower women and girls and to eliminate racism. They provide shelter for battered women, children's advocacy and intervention services, childcare, after school recreation, etc.

Emergency Shelters For Families

Did you know...

- 50% of all homeless women are fleeing a domestic violence situation. (Myra A. Sheehan, 1993)
- 24% of homeless people in the U.S. are employed with full-time or part-time jobs. (Ohio State University)

Coalition for the Homeless of Houston
www.homelesshouston.org
This website is a great resource that helps people find services and programs that offer shelter and living arrangements.

Emergency Shelters

Emergency Shelters provide emergency assistance and temporary housing for the homeless.

Star of Hope Transitional Living Center
6801 Ardmore, Houston, TX
713-748-7242

Star of Hope Women and Family Emergency Shelter
419 Dowling, Houston, TX
713-222-2220

The Harmony House
602 Girard Street, Houston, TX
713-223-8104

The Open Door Mission
5803 Harrisburg Boulevard, Houston, TX
713-921-7520

Ethnic/Minority Groups

Asians Against Domestic Abuse
P.O. Box 420776, Houston, TX
713-339-8300- Hotline
www.aadainc.org
Provides confidential support to the Asian American communities. Translation is available in many different Asian languages.

Chinese Community Center
9800 Town Park, Houston, TX
713-271-6100
www.ccchouston.org
A multi-ethnic organization that offers free job-training programs and classes.

Daya
5890 Point West Drive, Houston, TX
713-981-7645-Office
713-914-1333-Hotline
www.dayahouston.com
Daya serves Asian families in crisis by providing financial assistance, counseling, group support, and referrals. Services are fee.

Houston Area Urban League
1301 Texas Avenue, Houston, TX
713-393-8700

5320 Griggs Road, Houston, TX
In the Palm Center
713-845-2501
www.haul.org
A United Way agency working to enable African Americans and other minorities to gain self-reliance.

Food Assistance Programs

Did you Know...

- More then 750,000 Gulf Coast residents live in poverty. (Houston Food Bank)
- In 1998, Texas ranked 3rd in the nation for "food insecurity." (Center for Public Policy Priorities)

For food assistance or a referral to an emergency food pantry near you call 2-1-1 or 713-957-4357.

Houston Food Bank

3811 Eastex Freeway, Houston, TX
713-223-3700
www.houstonfoodbank.org
The Houston Food Bank distributes 27 million pounds of food each year to people in need. Each month they help 230,000 people who are hungry. They are currently serving 400 hunger-relief programs in 18 Houston area counties.

The Houston Food Bank provides a food pantry, shelters for the homeless, a safe place for the battered and abused, and nutritional sites for the children and elderly.

Food Stamps

www.fns.usda.gov/fsp
The purpose of food stamps is to end hunger and improve nutrition and health. Food stamps provide low-income households with the food they need.

Local food stamp offices can provide information about eligibility. USDA operates a toll-free number **800-221-5689** for people to receive information about the Food Stamp Program.

Texas Department of Human Services (Food Stamps)
713-767-2000
www.dhs.state.tx.us

Women, Infants, and Children (WIC)
800-942-3678 or 713-794-9090
www.dshs.state.tx.us
WIC provides nutritious foods for growing families along with healthcare information and help with breastfeeding. Call for clinic locations.

Who qualifies for WIC?
To qualify for WIC you must:

- Live in Texas. You do not have to be a US citizen.
- Have a family income less than WIC guidelines. A person receiving Medicaid or Food Stamps already meets the income eligibility requirements.
- Have a special nutritional need.
- Be in one of the following groups:
  - Pregnant
  - Breastfeeding
  - A woman who has had a baby within the last 6 months
  - A woman who has a child less than 5 years of age

Housing

City of Houston Homebuyer Hotline
713-522-4663
Offer help with down payment, closing costs, lower interest rates, tax credits and homebuyer counseling. Families with household incomes between $17,000 and $48,000 may qualify for home ownership.

Department of Housing and Urban Development (HUD)
713-313-2274
www.hud.gov
Sells properties at reduced prices to increase home ownership and access to affordable housing.

Habitat for Humanity
713-671-9993
www.houstonhabitat.org
A nationwide, non-profit builder of affordable homes. Offer interest-free loans in exchange for 300 hours of "sweat equity." You must be a first-time homebuyer and meet the household income eligibility requirements. Please call for details.

Housing Resource Center
713-578-2055
www.housingresourcecenter.org
Servicing Harris County to offer help with down payments, homebuyer counseling, affordable housing opportunities in Harris County.

Houston Housing Authority
713-260-0600
Provides housing for low-income residents in Houston.

YMCA
Cossaboom: 7903 South Loop East, Houston, TX
713-643-4396
Downtown: 1600 Louisiana, Houston, TX
713-659-8501

South Central: 3531 Wheeler, Houston, TX
713-748-5405
www.ymcahouston.org
These 3 YMCA locations in Houston offer affordable housing to international visitors, students, disabled, elderly and low-income individuals. Call the location nearest you for details.

Job Training Education/Assistance Programs

Dress For Success
3915 Dacoma Street, Suite A, Houston, TX
713-957-3779
www.dressforsuccess.org
Provide programs that help low-income women find a job and succeed in the workplace. Their programs provide assistance in becoming self-reliant.

G. E. D. Hotline
1-800-626-9433
Call and receive information on where and how you can take the G.E.D. high school equivalency exam in your area.

LDS Employment Center
16333 Hafer Road, Houston, TX
281-580-2564
www.providentliving.org
Computers available for job searches, job training and counseling.

Texas Workforce
1-800-735-2988
www.twc.state.tx.us
The Texas Workforce offers a wide variety of services to citizens of Texas, depending on your specific needs, such as:

- Child Care Services
- Community Resources
- Economic Information
- Financial Services
- Food Stamps
- Guide to Federal Government Benefit Programs
- Medical assistance Programs
- Training Services
- Unemployment Insurance
- Women and Infant Children (WIC)

View the website to find a Texas Workforce Center near you.

The Women's Home
607 Westheimer, Houston, TX
713-521-31503
www.thewomenshome.org
Services provided to help women in crisis regain self-esteem and become self-reliant. They offer educational and job training programs. Their goal is for the women to leave with a safe place to live and employment.

Women Helping Women

17515 Barnwood Drive, Houston, TX

281-631-9744

www.texaswomenhelpingwomen.org

Helping women in crisis become self-sufficient. They help train women with the skills thy need to have a job and help with job placement.

Legal Assistance

www.texaslawhelp.org

This is a wonderful online resource that offers free legal information and low-cost legal assistance.

Houston Lawyer Referral Service

1001 Fannin Street, Houston, TX

713-237-9429 or 1-800-289-4577

www.hlrs.org

Offer referrals, reduced-fee attorneys, an on call attorney available to answer your questions 24-hours a day.

Houston Volunteer Lawyer Program

712 Main, Suite 2700, Houston, TX

713-228-0735

www.ehvlp.org

Volunteers from the Houston Bar Association offer services to low-income individuals.

Chapter 20

Resources for Special Needs and Disabilities

Chapter 20

Resources for Special Needs and Disabilities

Having a child with special needs or disabilities requires parents to have additional resources at hand. Read on to find out about helpful programs and services in our community to ensure that your child utilizes the resources that are available.

Did you know . . .

- Almost 20% of all people with disabilities live in poverty households, which is twice the rate of people without disabilities.
- (Center for Technical Assistance and Training)
- The likelihood of abuse and neglect is between 1.6 and 3.9 times greater for children with disabilities.
- (U.S. Department of Health and Human Services)
- American Academy of Pediatrics studies on early child development have proven that a child's environment and what a child experience during their first few years of life significantly influence the development of their brain structure. By accessing specialized services for your child you will enhance and improve their abilities for the rest of their life.

Advocacy Organizations and Disability Programs

ADA Technical Assistance Center
1-800-949-4232
www.ada-infonet.org

Provides individuals and organizations with information relating to the Americans with Disabilities Act.

ARC of Greater Houston
3737 Dacoma, Suite E, Houston, TX
713-957-1600
www.thearcofgreaterhouston.com

ARC of Greater Houston is an organization of and for people with mental retardation and related development disabilities and their families. It is devoted to promoting and improving support and services for people with mental retardation and their families. The association also fosters research and education regarding the prevention of mental retardation in infants and young children. ARC advocates for people with disabilities and provides information to those seeking resources, support and services.

ADDA
Attention Deficits Disorder Association/Southern Region
12345 Jones Road, Suite 287-7, Houston, TX
281-897-0982
www.adda-sr.org

ADDA provides online information and resources about ADD or ADHD to assist parents, professionals and adults. Parents can find support groups, suggested reading material and much more. Information is in English or Spanish.

Down Syndrome Association of Houston
P.O. Box 303, Houston, TX
713-682-7237- English
713-382-4134- Spanish
www.dsah.net

This organization is a non-profit organization made up of families and friends of people with Down Syndrome. Their goal is to provide information and support to local Houstonians. They have monthly meetings, support groups, playgroups, as well as fun activities and events throughout the year.

Epilepsy Foundation of Southeast Texas
2630 Fountain View Drive, Suite 210, Houston, TX
713-789-6295 or 1-888-548-9716
www.epilepsyfoundation.org

This is a non-profit organization that provides services, education and programs to enrich the lives of children and adults with epilepsy. They have monthly meetings and fun and educational programs throughout the year. They provide service to 31 counties in Southeast Texas.

FEAT Houston

Families for Early Autism Treatment
1120 Medical Plaza Drive, The Woodlands, TX
281-348-7067
www.feathouston.org

FEAT is a non-profit corporation providing information and supporting families who are assisting children with Autism. They provide support groups for parents and have guest speakers and monthly meetings.

F2F

Family to Family Network
13150 FM 529, Suite 106, Houston, TX
713-466-6304
www.familytofamily.org

This network works with children and families, who have disabilities, by providing them with education, information, referrals, support and training. Their mission is to insure that children get good education and excel in life. They have a resource center with access to computers and a library, as well as, monthly get-togethers for children and their families.

MRNC

Mental Retardation Needs Council of Harris County
P.O. Box 924168, Houston, TX
713-680-8195
www.mrnc.hctx.net

The MRNC strives to improve the lives of people with mental retardation, and other related disabilities, and their families. They increase the publics understanding of people with disabilities and contribute with their participation in the community.

UCP of Greater Houston

United Cerebral Palsy of Greater Houston
4500 Bissonnet, Suite 340, Bellaire, TX
713-838-9050
www.ucphouston.org

UCP is a non-profit corporation that provides service to children and adults, who have Cerebral Palsy, and their families. They offer 6 major programs, summer camp and other fun events held throughout the year.

Camps for Special Needs

Camp for All
6301 Rehburg Road, Burton, TX
713-686-5666
www.campforall.org

Camp For All is a year-round camping facility for children with special needs. Their goal is to enrich peoples lives and for the children to gain self-esteem and independence. The camp provides activities and programs that meet the needs of all abilities, ages and interests. The programs offered are educational, fun and therapeutic. Activities include an animal farm, archery, aquatics, arts and crafts, biking, a challenge and rope course, fine arts, horseback riding, lake activities, nature trails, and sports. There are several different camps that take place throughout the year, please call or view the calendar online for upcoming events and camp dates.

Camp Janus
6301 Rehburg Road, Burton, TX (Camp For All)
713-686-5666
www.campjanus.org

Camp Janus is a yearly camping experience for children ages 5-18 who have recovered from a burn injury. The camp is free of charge and provides a fun, educational and therapeutic experience, as well as, self-confidence and new friendships. Activities include arts and crafts, fishing and swimming.

Camp Periwinkle
6301 Rehburg Road, Burton, TX (Camp For All)
713-807-0191 or 713-686-5666
www.periwinklefoundation.org

Camp Periwinkle is a camp for children with cancer and other life threatening illnesses and their siblings. It was created by the Periwinkle Foundation and Texas Children's Hospital. Camp Periwinkle is a weeklong camp that is free of charge for all participants, ages 7 –15, and patients at the Texas Children's Cancer Center.

The purpose of this camp is to provide children with fun and safe activities away from the everyday hospital life. Activities include archery, arts and crafts, baseball, biking, boating, campfires, dances, horseback riding, ropes course, and volleyball.

Camp Wenoweez

6301 Rehburg Road, Burton, TX (Camp For All)
713-686-5666
www.texaslung.org

Camp Wenoweez is a summer camp for children, age 8-12 years old, who have moderate to severe asthma. The Camp is held in Burton, Texas at the Camp for All facility. Children participate in outdoor physical activities, providing challenging opportunities in a medically safe environment. Activities include archery, arts and crafts, fishing, horseback riding, swimming, and daily education on asthma. The camp improves social skills, self-confidence and independence.

Camp YOLO

6301 Rehburg Road, Burton, TX (Camp For All)
713-807-0191 or 713-686-5666
www.periwinklefoundation.org

Camp YOLO was created by the Periwinkle Foundation and the Texas Children's Hospital Cancer Center. The camp is for teens, ages 13-18, who are dealing with adolescence and cancer. It provides the teens with fun activities as well as emotional support and a place to express their feelings and fears about cancer and other illnesses. The camp takes place two weekends each year and is free of charge for patients and their siblings.

Camp Xtreme

6301 Rehburg Road, Burton, TX (Camp For All)
979-289-3752 or 713-686-5666
www.campxtreme.com

Camp Xtreme is located at the Camp For All facility. It is a camp for young people, age 10-18, with physical disabilities. Activities include archery, basketball, canoeing, challenge courses, floor hockey, football, hand-cycling, kayaking, scuba diving, and water skiing. Camp Xtreme's goal is for children to develop independence through participation in activities and self-discovery.

Community Resources

Ronald McDonald House

1907 Holcombe Boulevard, Houston, TX

713-795-3500

www.rmhhouston.org

The Ronald McDonald House is a "home away from home" for families, of children being treated for cancer or other serious illnesses, who are traveling to Houston for medical treatment. They provide a comfortable home-like atmosphere to the families so that they can be closer to their children. The house is a 50-bedroom home located in the Texas Medical Center.

Shriners Hospital (2 locations)

6977 Main Street, Houston, TX

713-797-1616

www.shrinershq.org

The Houston Shriners Hospital is a 40-bed pediatric hospital that provides children, under the age of 18, orthopedic care at no charge. This hospital is one of 22 Shriners Hospitals throughout North America. They accept and treat children with routine and complex orthopedic problems and are known for their excellent work with children who have Cerebral Palsy. The physician's use the latest treatments and technology available in pediatric orthopedics, resulting in a shorter length of stay.

815 Market Street, Galveston, TX

409-770-6600

www.shrinershq.org

The Galveston Shriners Hospital is a 30-bed pediatric burn hospital that provides children, under the age of 18, care at no charge. The hospital is one of only 3 Shriners Hospitals that are dedicated to treating burns. The physicians treat children with acute burns and scaring and deformity from the result of a burn, as well as, children who need plastic surgery as a result of a burn.

Cole Therapy Center/ Cole Speech & Learning Center (2 locations)

11700 Louetta Road, Suite A, Houston, TX
281-379-4373
16835 Deer Creek Drive, Suite 120, Spring, TX
281-379-4373
www.colespeech.com

Cole Therapy Center offers language, speech, occupational and physical therapy services. Services are offered to children with Downs Syndrome, Cerebral Palsy, and other developmental difficulties. Services are available in your own home, school and daycares. Patients are served in Houston, Katy, Sugar Land and The Woodlands. Summer programs are also available.

ECI Keep Pace-HCDE

Early Childhood Intervention
11920 Walters Road, Houston, TX
281-397-4000
1-800-250-2246-Care Line
www.ecikeeppace.org

ECI Keep Pace is affiliated with Texas Early Childhood Intervention. They help children, from birth to age 3, who are developing later than other children their age. They serve Harris County and surrounding areas, as well as 13 local school districts. Therapy is available at your own home, school, or daycare. To find additional information and locations for your area, please view their website or call their care line.

Metropolitan Multi-Service Center

1475 West Gray, Houston, TX
713-284-1973
www.houstontx.gov

The Metropolitan Multi-Service Center provides special services for the community and people with disabilities and special needs. They offer several classes, recreation and sports for people of all ages.

Recreational Activities for Special Needs

Dionysus Theatre Troupe

5300 North Braeswood, Suite 527, Houston, TX

713-728-0041

www.dionysustheatre.org

This is a non-profit organization providing theatre experience, for children and teens, who are disabled. They write their own plays, usually about issues that the children are facing. They bring their shows to local schools and hospitals, as well as, teach theatre classes to all ages.

Dream Catcher Stables

P.O. Box 1454, Spring, TX

281-397-0849

Provides recreational and educational programs and horseback riding for individuals with disabilities and special needs.

Halter

Horses Assisting Learning Therapy Eyesight and Rehabilitation

P.O Box 5885, Katy, TX

713-705-0849

www.halter.us

Halter provides programs and activities, involving pet therapy, that help children and teens with special needs. Animals include miniature horses, rabbits, sheep, goats and cats. A popular program offered is the miniature horse-training program. This program provides children the opportunity to love, train and show a horse.

Illuminations Arts

1475 West Gray, # 176, Houston, TX

(Located inside The Metropolitan Multi-Service Center)

713-529-6910

713-529-6909- TTY

www.illuminationstheatre.org

Illuminations Arts is a theatre for people who are deaf or hard of hearing. They provide performing arts and artistic activities. Programs include Theatrical Interpreting, Shadow Interpreting, and American Sign Language

TAA

Texas Adaptive Aquatics
P.O. Box 41301 14999, Houston, TX
281-324-4653
www.taasports.org

Texas Adaptive Aquatics is a water skiing program for children, teens and adults with physical and mental disabilities. The program provides an opportunity for individuals to learn how to water-ski and to be able to get out of their wheelchairs and have fun. TAA takes place on Lake Houston. Equipment is supplied and instructors are there to teach courses to beginners, as well as, advanced water skiers.

The River Performing and Visual Arts Center

1475 West Gray, # 163 & #164, Houston, TX
(Located inside The Metropolitan Multi-Service Center)
713-520-1220
www.riverperformingvisualarts.com

This center provides year-round performing and visual arts programs to children ages 2-19 with special needs. They also have summer camps for children, ages 3-19, with disabilities.

Special Olympics of Texas

713-290-0049 or 1-800-876-5646
www.sotx.org

The Special Olympics mission is to provide year-round sports training and athletic competitions, in 20 Olympic-style sports, for children and adults with intellectual or physical disabilities. This gives them the continuing opportunities to develop physical fitness, demonstrate courage, experience joy, and participate in a sharing of skills and friendship with their families, other participating athletes and the community.

Special Olympics of Texas provides training to volunteer coaches who receive training in first aid, coaching techniques and the rules of the sports. They operate on a seasonal sport's calendar and offer training camps each season. The sports vary upon the season and have opportunities for athletes of all ability levels to participate.

Sports include: Aquatics, Athletics, Basketball, Bocce, Bowling, Cycling, Equestrian, Figure Skating, Golf, Gymnastics, Power Lifting, Roller Skating, Sailing, Soccer, Softball, Table Tennis, Tennis, Triathlon, and Volleyball.

Contact them or visit their website for a list of upcoming events.

Schools/Education

Texas Department of Assistive and Rehabilitative Services (ECI)

1-800-250-2246

www.dars.state.tx.us/ecis

ECI (Early Childhood Intervention) is a statewide program for families with children who have developmental delays and disabilities. They provide free assessments and evaluations to determine each child's need. They promote learning and development and provide support for families. Services are provided, by several agencies and organizations, for children up to the age of 3. To find a service program in your area, please call the 1-800 number or log on to their website.

Texas Department of State Health Services- Children with Special Health Care Needs

1-888-963-7111

www.dshs.state.tx.us

This is a Texas State organization that provides programs for children with disabilities and other special needs.

Region IV Education Service Center

7145 West Tidwell, Houston, TX

713-462-7708

www.esc4.net

Contact the Region IV to find any special schools, programs and services available for your child in the Houston area.

Avondale House

3611 Cummins, Houston, TX

713-993-9544

www.avondalehouse.org

The Avondale House is for children and young adults with Autism. They offer year-round school for children 3-22 years old, day habilitation services for teens and residential services for individuals aged 4-30.

Rise School of Houston

8080 North Stadium Drive, Houston, TX
713-532-RISE
www.riseschool.org

The Rise School of Houston provides early education to children with Down Syndrome and other developmental disabilities. They focus on toddler and preschool aged children, 6 moths – 6 years old, providing education and therapy. There are 6 different classrooms, of children based on age and educational needs.

The Arbor School

1635 Blalock, Houston, TX
713-827-8830
The Arbor School is a special education school for children and youth, grades kindergarten- 12th grade. There are a total of 37 students enrolled.

The Briarwood School

12207 Whittington Drive, Houston, TX
281-493-1070
www.thebriarschool.org

The Briarwood School is a school for children with developmental and learning disabilities, for children in kindergarten though 12th grade. It is a place that provides children with academic, emotional and social growth, as well, as self-esteem and independence. There are 3 separate "schools" in the Briarwood School. The Lower School is for children in grades K-6 who have been diagnosed with a learning disorder, the Middle and Upper School is for children in grades 7-12 who have also been diagnosed with a learning disorder, and the Special School is for people ages 5-21 who have developmental delays.

The Center/Caroline School

3550 West Dallas, Houston, TX
713-525-8400
713-525-8318- Caroline School
www.cri-usa.org

The Center provides service to children and adults with mental retardation and other developmental disabilities. The Caroline School, located within the Center, provides education for children, ages 1-9 years old, with severe health conditions and disabilities.

The Monarch School
1231 Wirt Road, Houston, TX
713-479-0800
www.monarchschool.org

The Monarch School is a non-profit private school for children 4-16 years old. They offer a unique learning experience, to children with special needs, by blending psychology and education together. They strive to meet the academic, emotional and social need of each child. The school offers 2 campuses: The Apprentice Campus and the Challenger Campus. Currently there are 75 students enrolled, 29 students at the Apprentice Campus and 46 students at the Challenger Campus.

Great Sports Sites

adaptiveadventures.org - Adaptive Adventures
disabledonline.com - Disabled Online
ushf.org – Handcycling Federation
healthnewsdirectory.com – Health News Directory
nscd.org – National Sports Center for the Disabled
narha.org – North American Riding for the Handicapped Association
ohiosledhockey.org – Ohio Sled Hockey
www.tbi-sci.org – Spinal cord injury queue
utahwintergames.org – Utah Winter Games
wheelersvanreantalsrentals.com – Wheeler Van Rentals
wildersnessinquiry.org– Wilderness Inquiry

General Disability Sites

www.chadd.org – Children and Adults with Attention Deficit/Hyperactivity Disorder

www.chasa.org – Children's Hemiplegia and Stroke Association

www.dec-sped.org – Division for Early Childhood – Advocates for children with special needs

www.discovertechnology.com- Offers computer classes and pen pals for people with disabilities

www.ehsnrc.org - Early Head Start National Resource Center

www.enablingdevices.com – This site offers battery operated switch toys and devices. Good site for purchasing assistive technology for an involved child

familyvillage.wisc.edu/index.htmlx – Disability related resources

www.familyvoices.org – information on how to contact senators

www.fathersnetwork.org – Support for father's raising children with Special Needs

www.fcsn.org – Federation for Children with Special Needs – family resources

www.handspeak.com – Animated sign language dictionary. Great site for learning or finding signs for many words

www.iamyourchild.org – Parenting information, order educational materials online

www.ideapractices.org – IDEA (Individuals with Disability Act) news

www.irsc.org – Internet Resources for Children with Special Needs

www.kotm.org – Kids on the move Early intervention program in Orem, Utah

www.ncd.gov – National Council on Disability

www.nectas.unc.edu – National Early Childhood Technical Assistance Center

www.nichcy.org – National Information Center for Children and Youth with Disabilities

www.our-kids.org- Support and information to parents with special needs children

www.preemies.org – Information on preemie development

www.rarediseases.org – Information on rare diseases

www.reedmartin.com – Special education law and advocacy strategies

www.specialchild.com – Disability awareness

www.specialfamilies.com – Robert Naseef, PhD. Psychologist, author and parent shares insights and experiences

ssa.gov/kids – Social Security information for parents

www.ucpa.org - United Cerebral Palsy Association – Family Center on Technology and Disability

Mental Illness

About 20% of American children suffer from a diagnosable mental illness during a given year according to the U.S. Surgeon General. Further, nearly 5 million American children and adolescents suffer from a serious mental illness (one that significantly interferes with their day to day life) Mental illness touches everyone's life. Learn more about the basic symptoms, treatments, and reources available to help.

Did you know...

- 45 million Americans suffer from psychiatric disorders – Surgeon General of the United States

- 1 in 5 will suffer from mental illness sometime in their life – National Institute of Mental Health
- Only 49% of people in need of mental health services are currently receiving treatment – Valley Mental Health

Common Mental Illness in Children

Anxiety disorders: Children with anxiety disorders respond to certain things or situations with fear and dread, as well as with physical signs of anxiety (nervousness) such as rapid heartbeat and sweating.

Disruptive behavior disorders: Children with these disorders tend to defy rules and often are disruptive in structural environments, such as school.

Pervasive development disorders: Children with these disorders are confused in their thinking and generally have problems understanding the world around them.

Eating disorders: Eating disorders involve intense emotions and attitudes, as well as unusual behaviors, associated with weight and/or food.

Elimination disorders: These disorders affect behavior related to elimination of body wastes (feces and urine).

Learning and communication disorders: Children with these disorders have problems storing and processing information, as well as relating their thoughts and ideas.

Affective (mood) disorders: These disorders involve persistent feelings of sadness and/or rapidly changing moods.

Schizophrenia: This is a serious disorder that involves distorted perceptions and thoughts.

Tic disorders: These disorders cause a person to perform repeated, sudden, involuntary and often meaningless movements and sounds, called tics.

Symptoms of Mental Illness in Children

General symptoms include:

- Abuse of drugs and/or alcohol
- Inability to cope with daily problems and activities
- Changes in sleeping and/or eating habits
- Excessive complaints of physical ailments
- Defying authority, skipping school, stealing or damaging property
- Intense fear of gaining weight
- Long lasting negative moods, often accompanied by poor appetite and thoughts of death
- Frequent outbursts of anger
- Changes in school performance, such as poor grades despite good efforts

- Loss of interest in friends and activities they usually enjoy
- Significant increase in time spent alone
- Excessive worrying or anxiety
- Hyperactivity
- Persistent nightmares
- Persistent disobedience or aggressive behavior
- Frequent temper tantrums
- Hearing voices or seeing things that are not there (hallucinations)

Causes of Mental Illness

Heredity (genetics): Mental Illness tends to run in families, which means the likelihood to develop a mental disorder may be passed on from parents to their children.

Biology: Some mental disorders have been linked to special chemicals in the brain called neurotransmitters. Neurotransmitters help nerve cells in the brain communicate with each other. If these chemicals are out of balance or not working properly, messages may not make it through the brain correctly, leading to symptoms. In addition, defects in or injury to certain areas of the brain also have been linked to some mental illnesses.

Nutritional Deficiencies: Some studies show that mineral deficiencies contribute to mental illness.

Psychological trauma: Some mental illnesses may be triggered by psychological trauma, such as severe emotional, physical or sexual abuse; an important early loss, such as the loss of a parent; and neglect

Environmental stress: Stressful or traumatic events can trigger a mental illness in a person with a vulnerability to a mental disorder.

Diagnosis

Diagnosing children can be particularly challenging. Many behaviors that are seen as symptoms can occur as a normal part of a child's development. These behaviors become symptoms when they "occur very often, last a long time, occur at an unusual age or cause significant disruption to the child's and/or family's ability to function." (WebMD)

Doctor's generally rule out any physical triggers before referring to a child or adolescent psychologist or mental health professional.

Treating Mental Illness

Mental disorders are like medical illnesses that require ongoing treatment with therapy or medication. Many of the medications used for children are the same ones used for adults. Creative therapies are often used such as play therapy or art therapy. These types of therapy are helpful for the child who might be having a hard time communicating their thoughts and feelings.

Progress is being made every day in the understanding and treatment of mental disorders. Many families have turned to naturalistic and homeopathic therapies with much success. When treating mental illness it is important to look at every aspect of the individual's life and try to make adjustments accordingly whether it be in diet, sleep, or any other external factors. Set your child up for success by creating an atmosphere to succeed and forming attainable goals.

Set realistic expectations for your child to avoid compounding the stress. Just as important, set realistic expectations for yourself. The journey is full of triumph and defeat. Ultimately as a parent, you will do some things right and some things wrong. Focus on the great small victories along the way. Small victories culminate in large progress for the child struggling with any disorder.

Educate your family and friends regarding your child's condition. The more they understand what you are dealing with, the more they can help. Some times people feel uncomfortable dealing with mental illness because they simply don't understand it. This creates uncomfortable stigmas. Often times the silence of friends and loved ones turns to ignorance that is more damaging than simply answering some hard questions.

Be your child's best advocate. Learn everything you can about your child's diagnosis, get online, buy books, research the medications that are prescribed. Don't be afraid to ask your doctor questions. Trust your instincts; no one knows your child better than you do, therefore no one should know more about their diagnosis than you do.

Can Mental Illness In Children Be Prevented?

Most mental disorders are caused by a combination of factors and cannot be prevented. However, if symptoms are recognized and treatment is started early, many of the distressing and disabling effects of a mental illness may be prevented or at least minimized.

Information on causes and symptoms obtained from WebMD

Reviewed by the doctors at The Cleveland Clinic Department of Psychiatry and Psychology. - Edited by Charlotte E. Gravson, MO, WebMO, May 2004.

Myths about Mental Illness

Myth: Psychiatric disorders are not true medical illnesses like heart disease and diabetes, People who have a mental illness are just "crazy."

Fact: Brain disorders, like heart disease and diabetes, are legitimate medical illnesses. Research shows there are genetic and biological causes for psychiatric disorders, and they can be treated effectively.

Myth: Mental illness is the result of bad parenting.

Fact: Most experts agree that a genetic susceptibility, combined with other risk factors, leads to a psychiatric disorder. In other words, mental illnesses have a physical cause.

Myth: Depression results from a personality weakness or character flaw, and people who are depressed could just "snap out of it" if they tried hard enough.

Fact: Depression has nothing to do with being lazy or weak. It results from changes in brain chemistry or brain function, and medication and/or psychotherapy often help people to recover.

Myth: Depression and other illnesses, such as anxiety disorders, do not affect children or adolescents. Any problems they have are just a part of growing up.

Fact: Children and adolescents can develop severe mental illnesses. In the United States, one in ten children and adolescents has a mental disorder severe enough to cause impairment. However, only about 20 percent of these children receive needed treatment. Left untreated, these problems can get worse. Anyone talking about suicide should be taken very seriously.

Myth: If you have a mental illness, you can will it away. Being treated for a psychiatric disorder means an individual has in some way "failed" or is weak.

Fact: A serious mental illness cannot be willed away. Ignoring the problem does not make it go away, either. It takes courage to seek professional help.

Myth: Addiction is a lifestyle choice and shows a lack of willpower. People with a substance abuse problem are morally weak or "bad."

Fact: Addiction is a disease that generally results from changes in brain chemistry. It has nothing to do with being a "bad" person.
-NARSAD's Scientific Council
National Alliance for research of Schizophrenia and Depression

Mental Health Resources

Child Builders

3800 Buffalo Speedway, Suite 310, Houston, TX
713-440-1155
www.childbuilders.org

Child Builders provides education and assistance to promote healthy child development. Their programs and services teach parents and children important skills to help them throughout life. Parents learn how to raise emotionally healthy children and children learn skills they will need to become good parents.

DePelchin Children's Center

713-730-2335
www.depelchin.org

DePelchin Children's Center provides mental health services to children and families in Fort Bend, Harris, Montgomery and Waller County. Services include counseling and treatment for emotionally disturbed children. There are 13 locations throughout Houston, please call or check online for a center near you.

MHA Houston

Mental Health Association of Greater Houston
2210 Norforlk, Suite 810, Houston, TX
713-523-8963-Office
713-522-5161-Information and referral line
www.mhahouston.org

MHA Houston is a non-profit United Way Agency that has been helping people, in the Greater Houston Area, for 50 years. They help people succeed in the world by providing better mental health care. They provide advocacy to the community and an Information and Referral Service. This service provides information about mental health problems and referrals to community resources.

NAMI

National Alliance for the Mentally Ill of Texas
1-800-633-3760
www.namitexas.org

NAMI Texas is a non-profit organization that provides advocacy, education and support to individuals affected by mental illness. They provide a variety of educational programs and support groups, as well as information to the public about mental illness. There 45 local affiliates in Texas. To find a location near you, please call or check their website for listings.

Books About Depression and Mental Health Issues for Kids

Help Me Say Goodbye

An art therapy and activity book for helping children cope with the death of someone special.

Ian's Walk: A Story about Autism

Grades 2-3. Appropriate as a read aloud story for younger children. A beautiful illustration of the complex feelings of resentment and love that children may feel when a sibling is "different."

I'm Frustrated (Dealing with Feelings)

Be sure to look up the entire series of "Dealing with Feelings" books by Elizabeth Crary for aids to teach your child about coping with various emotions. It also helps them distinguish between feelings and actions. Even more importantly the stories give kids several ways to cope with feelings by utilizing the "choose your own ending" format. They also allow parents and teachers to discuss other situations in a non-judgmental way.

Joev Plaza Loses Control

The adventures of a kid named Joey who has Attention Deficit Disorder.
2001 Newbery Honor Book

Just Because I Am

Ages 3-8. A great book to teach children about self-esteem.

Sad Days. Glad Days: A Story about Depression

Ages 5-8. A foreword by a medical professional introduces this sensitive bibliotherapeutic picture book about a child whose mother suffers form depression. There isn't much plot: Amanda Martha explains about the sad days, glad days and in-between days at her house, which are determined by how her mother feels. The story's ending is upbeat—but Hamilton offers no false promises to kids whose parents suffer from the illness.

The Face at the Window

Dora learns to overcome her fears of a mentally ill woman who lives in her community. This gentle and compassionate story is set in contemporary Jamaica, West Indies.

Together We'll Get Through This
This is the foundation book for the others in the Barklay and Eve Children's Book Series. This book recognizes and validates all kinds of losses that children may have, including divorce, moving to a different neighborhood, illness or death of pets and other loved ones. The book's message is that with love and support, we can get through anything.

Helpful Mental Illness Websites

www.aacap.org – American Academy of Child and Adolescent Psychiatry

www.anred.com – Anorexia Nervosa and Related Eating Disorders

www.dbsalliance.org – Depression and Bipolar Support Alliance

www.depressedteens.com - A resource for recognizing depression in teens

www.drada.org – Depression and Related Affective Disorders Association (DRADA)

www.drugdigest.org – Drug Digest

www.hopeandrecovery.org – Hope and Recovery

www.icmedia.com/mindprgm.htm – The Infinite Mind

www.mentalhealth.org – Mental Health Organization and Information Center

www.mentalhealthcommission.org – New Freedom Commission of Mental Health

www.nationaleatingdisorders.org – National Eating Disorders Association

www.nimh.nih.gov – National Institute of Mental Health

www.nmha.org – National Mental Health Association

www.nostigma.org – National Mental Health Awareness Campaign

www.Pfizer.com/brain – Pfizer Brain – The World Inside Your Head

www.surgeongeneral.gov – Surgeon General's Conference on Children's Mental Health

Chapter 21

Parenting Resources

Chapter 21

Parenting Resources

There are many resources in our community for parenting. We have listed some specific resources below. If you are looking for more information on parenting classes and groups, contact your local school district or university sponsored Continuing Education to obtain a list of classes and workshops.

Love and Logic
www.lovenadlogic.com

1-800-338-4065

If you are looking for easy ways to use techniques that will help you raise responsible kids who are fun to be around, you may want to attend *Becoming a Love and Logic Parent* class. Their books and seminars have been the most highly recommended from our Houston Mama's. You will learn the specific "how-to's", not just the theoretical concepts. Independent facilitators around the country present *Becoming a Love and Logic Parent* classes. Call for a list of facilitators in your area.

What is Love and Logic?

The Love and Logic Process:

- Shared Control: Gain control by giving away the control you don't need
- Shared thinking and decision-making: Provide opportunities for the child to do the greatest amount of thinking and decision-making.
- Equal shares of empathy with consequences: An absence of anger causes a child to think and learn from his/her mistakes.
- Maintain the child's self-concept: Increased self-concept leads to improved behavior and improved achievement.

The Rules of Love and Logic:

Rule #1:

- Adults take care of themselves by providing limits in a loving way.
- Adults avoid anger, threats, warnings or lectures.
- Adults use enforceable statements.
- Children are offered choices within limits.
- Limits are maintained with compassion, understanding or empathy.

Rule #2:

- Childhood misbehavior is treated as an opportunity for gaining wisdom.
- In a loving way, the adult holds the child accountable for solving his/her problems in a way that does not make a problem for others.
- Children are offered choices with limits.
- Adults use enforceable statements.
- Adults provide delayed/extended consequences.
- The adult's empathy is "locked in" before consequences are delivered.

Potty Training Solutions

1-866-202-2482

www.pottytrainingsolutions.com

Potty training can be one of the toughest stages of toddler hood! That is why we have included information, from this great online business, that offers many unique solutions to the potty training dilemma. They offer unique, hard to find potty training products, informational materials for parents and kids, educational books, videos and DVD's, as well as dolls and clean up items. They carry top lines such as Baby Bjorn, Gotz, Corolle, Primo, Mommy's Helper, Bummis and Thinkeroo.

Texas PTA

1-800-TALK-PTA

www.txpta.org

The Texas PTA's objectives are:

- To promote the welfare of children and youth in home, school, community, and place of worship.
- To raise the standards of home life.
- To secure adequate laws for the care and protection of children and youth.
- To bring into closer relation the home and the school, that parents and teachers may cooperate more intelligently in the education of children and youth.
- To develop between educators and the general public such united efforts as will secure for all children and youth the highest advantages in physical, mental, social and spiritual education.

The PTA has developed a new program called *How to Help Your Child Succeed.* Here are the key points of the program: 10 ways to foster your child's success.

Talk with your child. Talking early and often with your children helps them trust you as a source of information and guidance.

Set high but realistic expectations. Paying attention to your children's strengths, while acknowledging where they need assistance, can help children develop realistic self-expectations.

Build your child's self-esteem and confidence. Encourage your children to make choices even if it means making mistakes. This is how children learn and grow.

Keep your child healthy. Promote your children's physical, emotional, and social health.

Support learning at home. Show that education is important to you and that you value learning.

Communicate with your child's school. Communicate on a regular basis with the school to stay informed and involved.

Encourage exploration and discovery. By encouraging your children to develop their interests and seek opportunities to try new things you help them make the most of the world around them.

Help your child develop good relationships. All children want to fit in and belong. Helping your children develop friendships will go a long way to helping them build solid relationships as adults.

Keep your children safe. Teach your children safety procedures and how to avoid dangerous situations.

Participate in community service. Children's positive energy and talents can be acknowledged, beyond the classroom, when used to serve or help others.

From *How to Help Your Child Succeed*, a part of National PTA's Building Successful Partnerships program. *How to Help Your Child Succeed* is available as a two-part workshop in which participants learn more about the ten ways and how to put them into practice. To find out how to bring a workshop to your community and for more information on this program, contact Texas PTA or visit the How to Help Your Child Succeed area on the National PTA website: www.pta.org

Great Parenting Books

We talked to hundred of Houston Mama's like yourself and asked what their favorite parenting books and resources are. The top picks include:

Bringing Up Boys: Practical Advice and Encouragement for Those Shaping the Next Generation of Men- *by James C. Dobson*

Caring for Your Baby and Youth Child: Birth to Age 5- *by American Academy of Pediatrics*

Children's First Step- *by A. Lynn Scoresby*

Finding the Path: A Novel for Parents of Teenagers- *by Jeffrey P. Kaplan, Abby Lederman*

Girls Will Be Girls: Raising Confident and Courageous Daughters- *by JoAnn Deak, Teresa Barker*

Healthy Sleep Habits, Happy Child- *by Marc Weissbluth, M.D.*

How to Talk So Kids Will Listen and Listen So Kids Will Talk- *by Adele Faber, Elaine Mazlish*

Making The "Terrible" Twos Terrific- *by John Rosemond*

Parenting With Love and Logic: Teaching Children Responsibility- *by Foster W. Cline, Jim Fay*

Physical Activities for Improving Children's' Learning and Behavior- *by Billye Ann Cheatum & Allison A. Hammond*

Playful Parenting- *by Lawrence J. Cohen*

Raising Boys: Why Boys are Different-And How to Help Them Become Happy and Well-Balanced Men- *by Steve Biddulph*

Raising Confident Boys: 100 Tips for Parents and Teachers- *by Elizabeth Harley-Brewer*

Raising Confident Girls: 100 Tips for Parents and Teachers- *by Elizabeth Harley-Brewer*

Raising Your Spirited Child: A Guide to Parents Whose Child is More Intense, Sensitive, Perceptive, Persistent, and Energetic- *by Mary Sheedy Kurcinka*

Setting Limits with Your Strong-Willed Child: Eliminating Conflict by Establishing Clear, Firm, and Respectful Boundaries- *by Robert J. MacKenzie Ed.D*

Starting Smart- Creating Intelligent Kids- *by A. Lynn Scoresby*

The Baby Whisperer- by Tracy Hogg

The Happiest Toddler on the Block: The New Way to Stop the Daily Battle of Wills and Raise a Secure and Well-Behaved One- to Four-Year-Old- *by Harvey Karp, Paula Spencer*

Toddlers and Pre-Schoolers: Love and Logic Parenting for Early Childhood- *by Jim Fay, Foster Cline*

Helpful Websites

The following websites contain great information for parents and caregivers.

aap.org

babycenter.com

family.com

fatherhood.org

fathers.com

houston.babyzone.com

houstonkids.net

iamyourchild.org

parentcenter.com

parentingteenstoday.com

parentnetassociation.org

parentsoup.com

parenting.com

zerotothree.org

Chapter 22

Teens

Chapter 22

Teens

We have found some pretty great resources for Mama's that are wondering how to advise their teens on the ins and outs of dating. Your kids might come to think of you as the most resourceful mama in town when you can recommend hundreds of solutions to their dating dilemmas. The books we have recommended are available online.

Dating and Dances

The Dance Book: 555 Ways to Ask, Answer and Plan for Dances

Blair and Tristan Tolman

This book provides hundreds of creative ideas including: 218 ways to ask someone to a dance, 179 ways to say "Yes", 55 ways to say "No", 19 dinner ideas, 16 day dates or after the dance activities, 10 steps for planning a dance, and 68 dance theme ideas.

Some great ideas from this book include:
To Ask to a Dance:

Aluminum Foil - With parent permission, decorate your potential date's room with aluminum foil. Lay it on top of her bed, wrap it around her things, and tape it onto her door. Stick a poster on her door that says, "Don't FOIL me now! ALUMIN-ate my life and go to the dance with me!"

Fish - Fill her bathtub with water and put three live goldfish in it. Hang a poster over the bathtub which says, "If fishes were wishes, you'd have three. Would one of them be to go to the dance with me?"

Telephone Book - Obtain a telephone book and search through it to locate your first and last name. (Although you may not be listed in the telephone book, you will probably find two separate people with either your first or your last name.) Highlight your first name and your last name with a yellow magic marker. Leave a note on her car which asks her to the dance but doesn't say who it's from. Leave another note in her mailbox, one on her porch, and another on her bedroom door. Finally, leave the telephone book on her bed with a note which tells her that the mysterious note writer's name is highlighted inside the telephone book with a yellow marker. She must look through it to determine your identity.

To Answer YES to a Dance:

Briefs – Purchase a pair of the largest possible size of men's briefs. Write on them, "Let me be BRIEF: Yes!" Hang them in his room.

Christmas Lights – One evening when his is at home, arrange a string of Christmas lights on his front lawn so that it spells, "Yes!" Plug in the lights, ring the door bell, and hide. (Make sure you don't leave the home until he has seen the lights)

Marbles – Put a bunch of marbles in between the mattress and the fitted sheet of his bed. Include a message with them that reads, "Yes! I'm sure we'll have a MARBLE-ous time!"

To Answer NO to a Dance:

Band-Aids Adhesive Strips – Stick a bunch of band-aids all over a large piece of poster board. On the poster write, "I wish this was an "OUCHless" answer, but I'm HURT to say that I can't go to the dance with you!"

Chapstick Lip Balm – Purchase a tube of chapstick and give it to him with the following poem:

- I hope you're not CHAPPED
- But I have to say "No"
- But STICK around, please,
- And next time we'll go!

Mummy – Follow these instructions to make a mummy: first, make a dummy by stuffing some old clothing with straw or newspaper. Then completely wrap the dummy in toilet paper or strips of an old sheet. Pin a note to the mummy that says, "I'm sorry I can't go this time...I'm all WRAPPED UP!" Leave the mummy on his front doorstep.

Other Ideas from Houston Mama's

To Ask to a Dance:

Pop the Question – Leave helium balloons tied to the porch of your potential date's house. Before you fill the balloons with helium, fill them with confetti. In one of the balloons, place a piece of paper with your name on it mixed in with confetti. Leave a note that reads, "I'd POP if you'd go to the dance with me!"

Star Gazing – With permission from your date's parents, place glow in the dark stars spelling out your name on the ceiling of your potential date's bedroom. Leave a sign on his bed that reads, "It is written in the STARS for you to go to the dance with me." When he goes to bed that night, he'll find out who asked him to the dance by staring up at his ceiling.

Kiss the Ground – Place Hershey kisses all over his/her bedroom floor with a note that reads, "I'd kiss the ground you walk on if you'd go to the dance with me!" Replace one of the kisses flags with a strip of paper that has your name written on it.

The Lobster – Leave a live lobster on their porch with a note that reads, "I'd be in a real PINCH if you didn't go to the dance with me!" Leave a little note with your name on it in the lobster's claw!

To Answer YES to a Dance:

Depends – Buy a pack of "Depends" adult diapers and make a sign that reads, "You can DEPEND on me to go to the dance!"

To Answer NO to a Dance:

Ice Cream – Leave some ice cream and licorice ropes on his porch with a sign that reads, "I Screamed when you asked me, but I'm all tied up!"

Group Dating: 301 Ideas

Blair and Tristan Tolman

Why is group dating important? It provides safety, less social stress, and oftentimes more fun. Dating in groups helps teenagers develop social skills, make friends, and maintain high moral standards.

Why this book? This book is a compilation of hundreds of ideas for fun group dates. They can also be used for birthday parties, church activities, school activities, family reunions, or just get together with friends.

A few ideas:

Picture Mania

Divide the group into teams and let each team select a captain. Each team should have a chalkboard and some chalk. Give each team captain an identical set of cards, such as:

- Card #1 = RABBIT: ears, tail, nose, feet, body, eyes, mouth, and whiskers
- Card #2 = HOUSE: door, walkway, window, walls, chimney, roof, and garage
- Card #3 = SCHOOL BUS: windows, kids, driver, wheels, door, and exhaust

At the "Go" signal, each team captain calls out the first descriptive word on his first card ("ears"). The first person on his team runs to that team's chalkboard and draws a set of ears without knowing they are supposed to be rabbit ears. The captain then calls out the second word ("tail") and the second player runs to the chalkboard and adds his object to the picture. Continue in this fashion, drawing the words on the first card in order, until a team figures out what the object is supposed to be and calls it out. This team gets a point. Play additional rounds with additional cards for as long as you desire. The team with the most points at the end of the game wins.

Purse and Wallet Scavenger Hunt

For this scavenger hunt, write down a bunch of items that might be found in either a purse or a wallet. Couples play as teams. To begin, the host calls out an item. Couples scramble to find the item and race it to the host. The fastest couple to present the host with the correct item wins a point. Play by calling out a variety of items for as long as you desire. At the end of the game, the couple with the most points wins.

Red Flag Blue Flag

Each person ties a red and blue bandanna together and the group divides into two teams. Tuck the flags into the back pockets of each player; with the blue bandanna hanging out if that person is on the blue team the red bandanna hanging out if that person is on the red team. Everyone sneaks around the bushes of an outdoor playing area, trying to capture each other's flag. When a person captures the flag of a player on the other team he gives it back to that player who must reverse the color and join the other team, so that he is now hunting members of his previous color. The game is over when everyone is on the same color team.

Other Ideas from Houston Mama's

- Rent a U-Haul trailer and have a candlelight dinner
- Set up a projector and have a movie/pool party outdoors
- Go bungee jumping

Dating for Under a Dollar: 301 Ideas

Blair and Tristan Tolman

This book is a book for teenagers, young adults, youth leaders, or anyone looking for creative dates that don't cost a lot of money. No more evenings of "What do we do now?" This fun and easy-to-read book gives hundreds of ideas that can make a real difference. Those who use these fun and original ideas won't ever be able to go back to dinner and a movie. You will be given:

- 43 activities for large group dates
- 107 group dates
- 77 single or group dates
- 53 single dates
- 21 holiday dates

Cloud Breaking

On a cloudy day, take your date outside, spread out a blanket, and sit down. As you sit there, use your imagination to visualize objects in the clouds. Try to predict where the clouds will break and when they do, try to form new objects.

Wilderness Scrabble

Take a Scrabble game with you and your date somewhere outdoors. Play "Wilderness Scrabble" together; in which each word used must in some way relate to the surroundings that you are playing in. If it seems too difficult to create only words that have to do with nature, try using ten tiles instead of seven during the game.

More Date Ideas from Houston Mama's

Take a look at the Places to Go and Things to Do, Calendar of Events or the Great Outdoors chapter for lots of activities and events. Some other cheap date ideas include:

- Have a winter barbeque
- Check out the local museums
- Go to the library and read a book together
- Ride the Ferris Wheel at Kemah Boardwalk
- Have a picnic in the park
- Go see a movie at the Dollar Theater
- Go fishing
- Cook dinner together
- Have a scavenger hung

Continued from More Date Ideas from Houston Mama's...

- Play night games like "kick the can" or "Ghosts in the Graveyard"
- Host your own murder mystery dinner
- Play Frisbee golf
- Go ice skating
- Have a water fight
- Build a sandcastle at Galveston Island
- Fly a kite
- Go to a college football game
- Carve pumpkins
- Make gingerbread houses
- Play board games
- Go to an Astro's baseball game
- Go hit golf balls at the driving range
- Go on a walk on the beach
- Go to a drive-in movie
- Visit the zoo or the aquarium
- Do some star gazing
- Have a progressive dinner with some friends
- Go to the playground
- Take a craft class
- BE CREATIVE!

A Parent's Role in Dating

Be a Model for Healthy Relationships

How is your relationship with your spouse? Do you respect each other and model a strong friendship? Your relationship and behavior speaks far louder than anyone's words. Show your kids how you compromise, give and expect respect, care for, laugh with, and love each other. In turn they will seek out healthy respectful friendships and relationships.

Talk About Boundaries

This can be a tough topic, but it is on that you should all get comfortable with. At the appropriate time discuss sex and the surrounding issues. Make your teenager consider their standards and goals so that they have predetermined what their choices will be before they are in the thick of the situation. Encourage them to come to you with any questions. Instead of lecturing, discuss the topic openly so they will listen to your opinion; yet at the same time feel that they are making their own decisions.

Stay Involved

Know the who, what, when, where's and why's of your child's life. Make it a point to be around when your teenager, their friends and their dates are in your home. Invite them to spend time in your home often when you are there. Make your home a safe and involved place.

Help Them to Understand the Difference between Dating and Physical Affection

Dating is getting to know and understand someone and building a relationship with him or her. Dating does not mean that there are implied physical advances. Too often, a youth's understanding of a dating relationship is attached to the physical expectations instead of the deepened friendship.

Educate Them about the Signs of Abusive Relationships

Your teen should know that being manipulated, verbally put down, pushed or slapped, or being kept isolated from other relationships are all signs of an abusive relationship.

Teen Dating and Violence

One recent national survey found that 1 in 11 high school students said they had been hit, slapped, or physically hurt on purpose by their boyfriend or girlfriend in the past year. 1 in 11 students also reported that they had been forced to have sexual intercourse when they did not want to.

(Center for Disease Control and Prevention. Youth risk behavior surveillance-United States, 1999. In: CDC Surveillance Summaries, June 9, 2000. MMWR 2000; 49 (No. SS-5), p.8)

Typically the following behaviors are signs of a potentially abusive relationship:

- Extreme jealousy, yet the abuser claims that jealousy is a sign of love
- They exhibit controlling behavior
- Unpredictable mood swings
- Alcohol and drug use
- Explosive temper
- Isolates you from friends and family so they can have your undivided attention
- Shows hypersensitivity and uses force during argument
- Blames others for his/her problems/feelings
- Threatens to hurt or kill him/herself if the partner threatens to break up
- You are sometimes afraid of your partner
- You are often apologizing to friends or family for your partner's behavior

Teach your teenager that if they are in a dating relationship that in any way feels uncomfortable, awkward, tense or even frightening, they need to trust their feelings and get out of it. It could become, or may already be, abusive.

Remind them that they always have the right to say no. No boyfriend or girlfriend has the right to tell them what they can or should do what they can or should wear, or what kind of friends they should have.

To learn more about dating violence and how to help call the National Youth Violence Prevention Center 1-866-SAFEYOUTH (1-866-723-3968) or visit their website online. www.safeyouth.org.

Community Resources For Teens

Boys and Girls Clubs of Greater Houston
1520-A Airline Drive, Houston, TX
713-868-3426
www.bgclubs-houston.org

Provides after school recreation and team sports as well as teaching life skills and offering family support. Call for a location near you.

DePelchin Children's Center (main location)
4950 Memorial Drive, Houston, TX
713-730-2335
www.depelchin.org

Provides counseling for a wide range of issues such as problems at school, relationship conflicts with family or friends, teen pregnancy, depression, etc. They also offer shelter and school-based programs to children and teens in need. Please call or view their website to find other locations in and around Houston.

Teen Link Houston
713-529-TEEN
www.teenlinkhouston.org

This is one of the best resources for teens in Houston. It is often easier for teenagers to talk to someone their own age. They feel as though their peers can relate to them more than an adult can. Teen Link gives them a chance to do just that. It is a 24-hour crisis phone line for "teens to talk to teens." Teen Line volunteers are trained by counselors and are there to talk to other teens Mon-Fri 4-10pm and Sat-Sun 10am-11pm. During all other hours, a trained adult is there to listen and give council.

Wesley House (main office)
1410 Lee Street, Houston, TX
713-223-8131
www.wesleyhousehouston.org

Provides after school recreation, for teens, such as sports, scouting, tutoring, pre-employment training and computer training. There are 6 other centers in and around Houston, please call or view their website for locations.

YMCA
www.ymcahouston.org

Provides after school programs for youth to develop leadership skills, service, and personal development that give them positive opportunities which can lead to a successful and happy life. View their website for a location near you.

Crisis Hot Lines

24-hour hotlines providing counseling and education to youth and their family members:

Crisis Hotline
713-HOTLINE

Spanish Crisis Hotline
713-526-8088

Texas Youth Hotline
1-800-210-2278

Eating Disorders

Menninger Clinic
2801 Gessner Drive, Houston, TX
713-275-5000
Provides intensive treatment for both males and females struggling with eating disorders.

Texas Children's Hospital/GI & Nutrition Clinic
6621 Fannin Street, Houston, TX (11th Floor)
832-824-2575 or 713-798-8355
www.texaschildrenshospital.org

Provides treatment for weight management, anorexia and bulimia. Services help children and teens develop healthy exercise and eating habits.

The Healthy Weigh
2801 Bammel Lane, Houston, TX
713-622-6422
www.thehealthyweighonline.com

Provides nutritional counseling for teens and adults suffering from eating disorders.

Grief Support For Teens

Bo's Place
100050 Buffalo Speedway, Houston, TX
713-942-8339
www.bosplace.org

A group support center for children, teens and families who have lost a loved one.

Crisis Intervention of Houston/ S.O.S. (survivors of suicide)
3015 Richmond Avenue, Suite 120, Houston, TX
713-527-9864-Office
713-HOTLINE (468-5463)
www.preventsuicidenow.com

A support group for teens and families who have lost a loved one through suicide or for people who are having suicidal thoughts. Meetings are held in Northwest, Southeast and Southwest Houston. Please call for details.

Kidsaid
www.kidsaid.com

Kidsaid is a website designed for children and teens who are dealing with grief. Kids can talk with kids from all over the world, give and receive advice, gain support from kids their own age, etc. The website is owned and run by grief net (**www.griefnet.org**). It is a safe environment directed by a clinical grief psychologist.

Runaways

Boys and Girls Harbor

P.O. Box 848, Houston, TX

713-688-6262 or 713-688-6262

www.boysandgirlsharbor.org

A home for children who have been neglected, abused, or are in need of a home. Programs and counseling help children and teens gain social skills and responsibility.

Catholic Charities of the Diocese of Galveston-Houston

2900 Louisiana Street, Houston, TX

713-526-4611

www.catholiccharities.org

Provide temporary shelter for children and teen in crisis, crisis intervention, and family counseling. There are 6 other centers in and around Houston, please call for a location near you.

Covenant House

1111 Lovett Boulevard, Houston, TX

713-523-2231-office

1-800-999-9999-hotline

www.covenanthousetx.org

Services provided to homeless, runaway, and at-risk youth under the age of 21.

National Runaway Hotline

1-800-621-4000

24-hour hotline for youth providing crisis intervention, information and referrals.

Texas Runaway Hotline

1-888-580-HELP (4357)

24-hour hotline providing peer counseling to runaways and their family members.

Substance Abuse

Alcoholics Anonymous

713-686-6300

www.aahouston.org

Provide support groups for teenagers and families who have substance abuse problems. Meetings are held at several locations in Houston, please call or view the website for more information on when and where the meetings are held.

Bay Area Council On Drugs and Alcohol

1300A Bay Area Boulevard, Suite 102, Houston, TX

281-280-0800

www.bacoda.com

Services include information and education on substance abuse, prevention, intervention, counseling, etc. They provide service to Southeast Harris County, Galveston County, and North Brazoria County. Bilingual counseling is available.

Center for Success & Independence

3722 Pinemont Drive, Houston, TX

713-426-4545

www.tcsi.org

Provides residential treatment for teens with substance abuse problems.

Fort Bend Regional Council on Substance Abuse

10435 Greenbough, Suite 250, Stafford, TX

281-207-2400

www.fortbendcouncil.org

Services include drug and alcohol information and education, counseling, assessment, referrals, alcohol and drug abuse treatment programs, and youth intervention.

Houston-Clear Lake Counseling Center (2 locations)

1234 Bay Area Boulevard, Clear Lake, TX

281-334-0591

10497 Town and Country Way, Suite 216, Houston, TX

713-468-7577

www.houston-clearlakecounselingcenter.com

Licensed counselors provide services to teen and their families. Services include intervention, testing, treatment and rehabilitation.

Houston Council on Alcohol and Drugs

303 Jackson Hill, Houston, TX

713-942-4100

www.council-houston.org

A team of substance abuse prevention specialists and counselors provide youth and adolescent services. Services include substance abuse education, assessment, counseling, treatment and case management.

The Right Step
902 West Alabama Street, Houston, TX (central location)
1-877-627-4389
www.rightstep.com

Programs are designed for adolescents including detoxification, day treatment and outpatient treatment. There are 4 other locations that offer treatment for teens, please check online or call to find out the locations.

Skill Development or Employment

S.H.A.P.E. Community Center (Self-Help for African People Through Education)
P.O. Box 8428, Houston, TX
713-521-0629
www.shape.org

Offers after-school programs for teens up to 17 years of age. Activities include, job skills training and a youth leadership program in the summer.

Texas Workforce
1-800-733-5627
www.twc.state.tx.us

Job training for low-income youth age 16-24 years old. Call for a center near you.

The Work Source Youth Centers (YO Houston)
713-739-0800
www.yohouston.org

Offers vocational training and GED assistance for youth age 14-21 years or age. There are 4 different centers that offer a structured classroom and learning activities. Please call for eligibility requirements and locations.

Teen Pregnancy and Parenthood

(Also see Pregnancy and Infant Resources- Chapter 18)

Care Net Pregnancy Center of Northwest Houston
17776 Tomball Parkway, Suite 35B, Houston, TX
281-477-8200
www.carenetnw.com

Services include free pregnancy testing, maternal assistance and confidential counseling.

Foundation For Life
10900 Northwest Freeway, Suite 112, Houston, TX
713-263-8400
Offer free services including Emergency Aid (shelter, food and clothing), Medical aid (pregnancy testing, ultrasounds, prenatal care), confidential counseling and support.

Planned Parenthood
1-800-230-PLAN
www.plannedparenthood.org

Offers free or low cost pregnancy tests and birth control to teens up to 19 years of age.

Pregnancy Assistance Center North (2 locations)
115 North San Jacinto Street, Conroe, TX
936-441-6442
26402 I-45 North, The Woodlands, TX
281-367-1518
www.pacn.org

Services include free pregnancy testing, confidential counseling, parenting help and resources.

Pregnancy Care Center of Southeast Texas
1522 Sam Houston Avenue, Huntsville, TX
936-294-0404
www.pcctexas.org

Offers free pregnancy testing, counseling, and support to pregnant teens.

Pregnancy Help Center
1450 East Summitry Circle, Katy, TX
281-599-0909
www.phckaty.org

Services include free pregnancy testing, ultrasounds, sexual health education, counseling and support.

Pregnancy Hotline
1-800-550-4900
This hotline offers support, pregnancy information and referrals for medical care. Girls can also receive free pregnancy tests.

Chapter 23

Family Vacation Guide

Chapter 23

Family Vacation Guide

Whether you want to plan a family vacation or a getaway without the kids, Texas has so much to offer. We have a variety of recreation and unique getaways right in our back yard. You can really "get away " without having to go far.

In-State Vacation Guide

www.touringtexas.com

www.traveltex.com

www.gotexas.about.com

These are great online resources for locals and out-of-staters alike. Find information about the greatest destinations in Texas. Information includes lodging, restaurants, local attractions and more. These are really the best one-stop places that we have found to plan a fun vacation inside our great state of Texas.

Top Destinations

Listed on the following pages are some of the top destinations in the state. Because Texas is such a big state (the 2nd largest state in the U.S.), we decided to only list a few major vacation destinations. If you want to know more, visit one of the 3 websites listed above and find out more vacation ideas, where you can stay, what you can do, and how much it will cost.

Austin

Austin is located in Central Texas and is the capital of our state. It is a very beautiful city with valleys, hills and lakes running through it. The many lakes in Austin make this city a popular vacation spot for many Texans. Families love to go swimming, boating, and water skiing. Another popular place to visit is the state capital building, Governor's Mansion, Senate, and the House of Representatives. Sport enthusiasts love to watch University of Texas football, basketball and baseball games. While vacationing in Austin, make sure to stroll down Austin's famous 6th Street. This street is known for it's restaurants and live music, featuring every kind of music. Austin is considered to be the "Live Music Capital of the World."

Brenham

Brenham is an older, smaller town about 73 miles from Houston. It makes for a great day or weekend trip for the kids. It is known for being home of the Blue Bell Ice Cream. Take a tour of the creamery and watch the people and machines package the ice cream. Then visit the country store and ice cream parlor and enjoy a bowl of the delicious ice cream. The kids will love the Blue Bell Aquatic Center! It is a large outdoor pool with a 150 ft. long water slide, a banana split baby slide, ice cream cone float and an ice cream Popsicle walk-across. The best time to take a trip to Brenham is in the spring. The bluebonnets and wildflowers are in full bloom and cover the beautiful stretches of farmland. There is plenty of antique shopping in the historic downtown. Brenham is a great place to go for a day trip, however if you do choose to stay overnight, there are quite a few Bed and Breakfasts in town.

Corpus Christi

Corpus Christi is a popular tourist city in Texas. In fact, it is ranked the second most popular vacation spot in all of Texas. It is located on the Gulf Coast about 215 miles from Houston. The scenery and beaches are beautiful and with its mild climate, you can enjoy outdoor activities all year round. There are plenty of things to do in Corpus Christi. The beaches are a must! Vacationers love to swim, windsurf, parasail, scuba dive and fish in the beautiful water. When you want to take a break from swimming, there are lots of fun shops along the beach and waterfront seafood restaurants to dine at. One of the top ten attractions, in the state of Texas, is the U.S.S. Lexington. This is a museum on the bay, which offers great and informative tours of the ship. Another top ten attraction is the Texas State Aquarium. This is a wonderful place for kids to have a hands-on learning experience with different underwater species.

Dallas

Dallas is the number one destination for visitors in Texas, with world-class hotels, restaurants and shopping. It is about a 243-mile drive from Houston making the drive somewhat long, but well worth it! There is a lot to see and do in Dallas. Two major tourist attractions are both interesting and free of charge. One is to see the world's largest bronze monument. This monument includes more than 40 large long-horn steers, horses and cowboys, in a Texas cattle drive, moving across Pioneer Plaza. Another tourist spot is the John F. Kennedy Memorial at Dealy Plaza and the Dealy Plaza Museum. A favorite stop for kids is the Dallas World Aquarium. They will love the panoramic view of fish, stingrays, sharks, and sea turtles. There are many museums and art galleries to visit, along with, lots of shopping and dining. With over 7,000 restaurants, Dallas does not make it hard to find a good place to eat. If you happen to be there during football season, try and make it to a Cowboys game, or at least go by and see the famous Texas Stadium. If you are visiting Dallas in the fall, don't miss out on attending the State Fair. Each year the fair takes place late September-mid October and attracts more than 3 million visitors. It is the largest exposition in North America and features horse competitions, prize livestock, big name entertainers and lots of food and games. While in Dallas, if you have some spare time, take a drive 60 miles east to a town named Canton. It is home of the world's largest flea market. The flea market opens only one weekend per month, so be sure to find out which days it is.

Fredericksburg

Fredericksburg is a quaint town in the heart of the Texas Hill Country. It has been listed as the 11th most popular tourist town in the United States. It is a shopper's paradise, with over 150 shops! You will find antiques, clothing, gifts, jewelry, hand-made candles, and much more. Stroll down Main Street or take a tour on a horse-drawn carriage and take pictures of the beautiful historic churches and German style homes. Outdoor enthusiasts will love the wonderful, year-round outdoor activities, such as hunting, fishing, mountain biking and hiking. If you love fresh peaches, Fredericksburg is the place to be! 40% of Texas' peaches are grown in 60 local orchards. Peach season is mid-May to early August. If you are traveling there during that time, be sure to stop by some of the orchards. Make sure to take a drive 18 miles north of Fredericksburg to the Enchanted Rock State Park. This rock is the 2nd largest granite formation in all of North America. Families love to go hiking and have a picnic while enjoying the beautiful scenery. If you plan on staying for a few nights, Fredericksburg is famous for it's beautiful Bed & Breakfast Inns.

Galveston Island

Galveston Island is located 50 miles Southeast of Houston, making it an easy day or weekend getaway. Spend the day sunbathing on the 32 miles of beaches, swimming in the water, feeding the seagulls and pelicans, and fishing. Several of the beaches are equipped with playgrounds, picnic tables and volleyball nets. Take a stroll down the famous Strand and find plenty of souvenir shops, gift shops and restaurants. You can even rent four-wheel bikes and tour the area. There are many beautiful, historical homes to see located on the East End Historic District. One of the biggest tourist attractions in Galveston is Moody Gardens. Because there is so much to do here, it usually takes one full day. It is made up of 3 large glass pyramids, each with different activities for children to learn. There is also a restaurant, hotel, gardens and ice-skating rink located inside. If you don't find enough to do in Galveston, hop in the car and take a 30-minute drive north to the Johnson Space Center and watch real astronauts in action., or take a tour of the space center.

Kemah Boardwalk

Not far from Galveston and just a short drive north from downtown Houston is the little town of Kemah. Kemah has quickly become a favorite place for Texans and vacationers to come to. It is a great day or weekend getaway, with plenty of restaurants, shopping and waterfront activities for children and families. Just hanging out on the Kemah boardwalk is full of excitement! Activities include dancing fountains that kids love to run through, a carousel, huge Ferris wheel, a train to ride, arcade games, and a rock-climbing wall. If you're feeling adventurous, you can climb aboard Joe's Boardwalk Beast for an extremely fun and fast speedboat ride. Enjoy a nice lunch or dinner at one of the several restaurants. The Aquarium keeps the kids occupied with floor- to- ceiling aquariums, full of beautiful fish and other sea creatures, and divers who enter the tank to feed them. Every Thursday, during the summer, you can relax and listen to live bands and music during "Rock the Dock." If you chose to stay in Kemah over night, there are many accommodations to choose from.

New Braunfels

New Braunfels is 160 miles east of Houston. It was founded by Prince Carl, of Solmas-Braunfels, a region in Germany. Because craftsman and farmers from Germany settled in this town, locations and streets still have German names and German influence. Tourists enjoy eating at several German restaurants, New Braunfels Smokehouse being one of the local favorites. Other activities that families enjoy are the Natural Bridge Caverns and the Natural Bridge Wildlife Ranch, located between New Braunfels and San Antonio. The Natural Bridge Caverns is Texas' largest natural attraction and is open year-round. The Natural Bridge Wildlife Ranch is home to over 50 different animal species from all over the world. Families love taking a safari ride through the park to observe the animals. During the summer you can tube down the Guadulupe River or visit Schlitterbaun. Schlitterbaun is a nationally known water park, voted number 1 on The Travel Channel. Every fall New Braunfels hosts Wurstfest, one of the largest German festivals in America. This festival is a ten day "salute to sausage," filled with sausage making and sausage eating. If you are staying in New Braunfels during the months of February to November, take a short drive to the historic town of Gruene. Here you will find Market Days, where over 100 artisans showcase their handcrafted jewelry, pottery, etc.

San Antonio

San Antonio is home of the world-renowned Alamo, one of the most visited historical sites in The United States. You can take a tour of the Alamo and visit their gift shop for souvenirs. Relive history at the IMAX, located inside the River Center Mall, and watch a 48-minute movie about the Alamo. The Alamo is a short walk from the famous River Walk, located near downtown. Visitors enjoy strolling around the river, shopping at the River Center Mall, and eating at the many sidewalk cafés. A great way to tour the area is by boat. Relax, and enjoy the beautiful scenery and architecture, as a tour boat takes you around the river and explains the history of San Antonio. Some other activities that families enjoy is the San Antonio Zoo (one of the largest zoos in the country), Fiesta Texas Six Flags Theme Park, Splashtown Water Park, and Sea World (the world's largest marine life park).

South Padre Island

South Padre Island is known for it's beautiful beaches and warm gulf waters. Because of the gulf breezes, it has become the number one destination for windsurfing. If you don't know how to windsurf and would like to learn how, lessons and boards are available at most of the local shops. If you prefer other water sports, jet skies, wave runners and surfboards are also available for rent. Paddleboats and bumper boats can be rented for the kids. South Padres Island is also home of the best fishing spots in Texas. The waters are filled with speckled trout, flounder and red fish. It is also a great place to go horseback riding on the beach. Pony rides are available for children under 4 years old. There are plenty of wild life refuges, museums and restaurants on the island as well.

Weekend Getaway Guide

Do you need a romantic getaway from the kids but can't find the time or money to fly away to Hawaii for the week? Try a cozy little bed and breakfast for a night or a weekend getaway. You'll be surprised at how many charming and original escapes exist in Houston and surrounding areas.

North

Heathers Glen

200 East Phillips, Conroe, TX
936-441-6611
www.heathersglen.com

This bed and breakfast is a beautiful three-story Victorian estate, with several themed suites and guest rooms. Each room comes with a private bath and TV. The suites, and several of the other rooms, come with a Jacuzzi tub, VCR, coffee maker, refrigerator and microwave. A continental breakfast is served each morning in the privacy of your own room.
Rates: $125 - $195

Janeves Old Town Bed & Breakfast

2438 Spring Creek Drive, Spring, TX
281-288-8888
www.janevesbedandbreakfast.com

This bed and breakfast is a quaint little house with sleeping accommodations for 4 guests. The kitchen is fully equipped with a refrigerator stocked with complimentary beverages. In the mornings a continental breakfast, coffee, and tea is available. There is a TV, VCR, CD player, books and magazines for you to use, along with complimentary gourmet chocolates and bubble bath. The back yard has a private patio and gazebo with paths leading to secluded gardens, streams, waterfalls and ponds.
Rates: $95

McLachlan Farm

24907 Hardy Road, Spring, TX 77383
281-350-2400
www.macfarm.com

McLachlan Farm is a secluded bed and breakfast, making you feel as though you are miles away from Houston. The house is a quaint country house with wrap around porches and swings. There are 6 rooms, all with queen or king size beds, private baths, and bathrobes, Two of the rooms are brand new loft suites. Each suite comes with a private entrance, Jacuzzi tub for two, a fireplace, and private balconies. A gourmet country breakfast is served every morning. Be sure to ask about their special occasion package.
Rates: $90 - $175

Downtown

Bogarts on the Boulevard

1536 Heights Boulevard, Houston, TX
713-802-1281
www.bogarts.org

This is your one stop place for rest and relaxation! Bogarts on the Boulevard is not only a bed & breakfast, it is also a salon and day spa. You don't even have to leave your place to get a massage or facial. There are 6 guest suites all with a private bath, cable TV, VCR, phone, miniature fridge, a goose down comforter and pillows. Each guest has access to the outside pool and hot tub. Breakfast is served every morning.
Rate: $115-$250

Hidden Oaks Bed & Breakfast
7808 Dixie Drive, Houston, TX
713-640-2457
www.hiddenoaksbnb.com

Hidden Oaks is a beautiful plantation style home built in 1927. There are 3 suites, each suits comes a king size bed, sitting room, private bath, phone, free wireless Internet, TV, VCR, CD player. One of the suites is like it's own apartment, equipped with it's own kitchen, appliances, coffee maker, dinning room table, and dishes.
Rate: $125-$175

Patricia Bed & Breakfast Inn
1200 Southmore Boulevard, Houston, TX
713-523-1114
www.texasbnb.com

This bed & breakfast is a beautiful 3-story mansion built in 1919. It is conveniently located near downtown Houston, in the Museum District. This colonial-style home has 3 bedrooms and 2 suites to choose from. All of the rooms are spacious and have their own private bathroom, robes, telephone, cable TV, and VCR. The suites have a sitting room adjacent to their bedroom, some with a two-person whirlpool tub. Breakfast is served daily in the dinning room. Specialties include their homemade pina colada poppy seed bread and French toast with marmalade.
Rates: $100-$150

Robin's Nest Bed & Breakfast Inn
4104 Greenly Street, Houston, TX
713-528-5821
www.therobin.com

This inn is a Victorian farmhouse built in 1898. There are 6 rooms, each with a queen size bed, private bath, cable TV, phone, and mini refrigerator. Two of the suites just opened and have whirlpool tubs for two and a private entrance. For you early risers, a continental breakfast is served each morning before 9am. From 9 – 10am a full, made from scratch, breakfast is served. The owner received culinary lessons, from a chef in Paris, so the breakfasts are wonderful!
Rates: $89 - $175

Sara's Bed & Breakfast

941 Heights Boulevard, Houston, TX

713-868-1130

www.saras.com

Sara's Bed & Breakfast is an 11-bedroom house located 5 minutes from downtown Houston. There are 3 suites and 8 guest rooms; all rooms come with a queen or king size bed, a private bath, TV, VCR, telephone, and robes. Each room is named after a city or town in Texas. The suites come with a sitting room and private balcony. A full breakfast is offered Tuesday through Sunday, in the Garden Room, and a self-serve breakfast on Mondays and major holidays. Breakfasts are changed daily.

Rate: $70-$200

Sycamore Heights

245 West 18th Avenue

713-861-4117

www.sycamoreheights.com

Sycamore Heights is located in the heart of the historic Heights. There are 3 large suites, each with a queen size bed, private bath, sitting room, phone, cable TV, and VCR. A continental breakfast is served every morning.

Rate: $75 - $95

The Lovett Inn

501 Lovett Boulevard, Houston, TX

713-522-5224

www.lovettinn.com

The Lovett Inn is located in Montrose, near the Museum District. It is a beautiful colonial style home with 10 rooms to choose from. Each room comes equipped with a desk, telephone, answering machine, iron and ironing board and hair dryer. Most of the rooms have their own private balcony, microwave and mini refrigerator. There is a library to relax and read a book, an outdoor pool and hot tub, magazines and newspapers to read, games to play, and a continental breakfast served daily.

Rate: $95-$150

Galveston

Coppersmith Inn

1914 Avenue M, Galveston, TX
409-763-7004
www.coppersmithinn.com

This bed and breakfast a two-story, five-bedroom house. Each room comes with a king or queen size bed, private bath, TV, VCR, DVD player, and CD player. Guests enjoy the free movies and beautiful Coppersmith Gardens. A full country breakfast is served each morning. Honeymoon and anniversary packages are available. Ask about their fall and winter discounts.
Rates: $100 - $175

Grace Manor Bed & Breakfast

1702 Post Office, Galveston, TX
409-621-1662
www.gracemanor-galveston.com

The Grace Manor is a Victorian home within walking distance to the Galveston Strand. Beautiful gardens, full of all kinds of different flowers, surround the house. There are 4 spacious rooms all with a king size bed, a private bath with Jacuzzi or claw-footed tub. The Hospitality Room has a refrigerator, filled with bottled water and soda, homemade cookies, chocolate, coffee and fresh juice for all the guests to enjoy. A gourmet breakfast is served daily in the dinning room and is accompanied by soft music and candles.
Rates: $99 - $199

Normandy Inn Bed & Breakfast
1101 23rd Street, Galveston, TX
832-347-3621
www.normandyinngalveston.com

Normandy Inn is a beautiful three-story house built in 1905. There are 6 large suites to choose from, each with a private bath and a unique view of Galveston. Breakfast is served each morning. Guests especially love the fresh peaches from the Inn's orchard.
Rates: $80- $200

The Inn @ 1816 Post Office
1816 Postoffice, Galveston, TX
409-763-7004
www.inn1816postoffice.com

This Inn was built in 1886 and is located in the heart of the Galveston East End. It is a Victorian home with antique furnishings. There are 6 guestrooms to choice from, as well, as a game room with a pool table and board games. Bicycles are provided to tour the island or take a ride on the beach. Arrangements can be made for a horse-drawn carriage ride or a gourmet picnic. Coffee, tea, appetizers and refreshments are available throughout the day and a gourmet breakfast is served every morning in the dining room.
Rates: $115 - $195

The Queen Ann Bed & Breakfast
1915 Sealy Avenue, Galveston, TX
409-763-7088
www.galvestonqueenanne.com

This bed and breakfast has been featured in several magazines, including Southern Living. It is located within walking distance of the histories downtown Galveston. There are 6 rooms decorated with beautiful antiques. Hot tea and cookies are available throughout the day in the dinning room. A homemade breakfast, served on antique china, is offered daily in the dinning room and is accompanied by soft music and candlelight. Ask about their customized packages and getaway specials.
Rates: $105 - $185

Kemah

A White Texas Pelican Bed and Breakfast

408 A. Bay Avenue, Kemah, TX
281-358-3900
www.awhitetexaspelican.com

This bed and breakfast is a two-story contemporary home located on Galveston Bay. The rooms have a beautiful view of the sunset and boats sailing by. It is a short walk from Kemah Boardwalk and just a few blocks from the beach. Located outside is a 250-foot private pier to fish off. There are 3 rooms located in the main house and 2 rooms and a loft in the Caribbean cottage. Each room has a private bath and TV. A Jacuzzi is located on the back porch and golf carts are available for the guests to use. A continental breakfast is served daily.
Rates: $ 60- $250

The Captains Quarters

7C1 Bay Avenue, Kemah, TX
281-334-7010
www.captsquarters.com

This bed and breakfast is along the banks of the Galveston Bay. It is a beautiful house with large porches and a beautiful view of the bay. There are 4 rooms, all decorated with different themes and each with a nice view. Breakfast is served dockside every morning, while watching the boats go by.
Rates: $50 - $160

Kemah Boardwalk Inn

#8 Kemah Waterfront, Kemah, TX
281-334-9880
www.kemah.com

The Boardwalk Inn is a beautiful 52-room Hotel, located in the center of Kemah Boardwalk. Each room faces the boardwalk and has a private balcony overlooking it. Rooms vary from guestrooms to suites. All rooms have TV's, phones, a coffee maker with complimentary coffee, an iron and ironing board, hair dryer, soaps and lotion. The guest rooms have a king or 2 double beds and a private bathroom. The suites have 3 private balconies overlooking the boardwalk, a dinning room with a wet bar and mini refrigerator, a living room, 1 ? baths and a master bedroom with a king size bed. Ask about their Sunday rate special.
Rates: $139 - $189

Other Vacation Ideas

If your not in the mood for a bed and breakfast or you can't be away from the kids for too long, or whatever the reason may be, why not try a romantic dinner cruise. It doesn't get more romantic than eating and dancing under the stars with your significant other. Some even offer a boat and breakfast. This is an overnight stay aboard a luxurious yacht with breakfast served in the morning.

At the Helm

Kemah Boardwalk Marina
281-334-4101
Book a romantic overnight stay aboard a luxury motor yacht. A continental breakfast is included.
Rates: $250 per couple

Island Princess Charters

Kemah Boardwalk Marina
281-332-5757
www.islandprincesscharters.com

Book a fun and unique "Boat and Breakfast" for two or a romantic "Sunset Cruise" on board a private motor-yacht. Choose from 2 yachts, the Island Princess or the Odyssey.
Rates: $75 per person

Lighthouse Charters

Kemah Boardwalk Marina
281-316-1254
www.lighthousecharters.net

Enjoy a "Boat and Breakfast," a romantic overnight stay aboard a luxury motor yacht. Breakfast is provided by one of the restaurants on the boardwalk. Rates vary depending on the day selected.
Rates: $125 - $165 per couple

Majestic Ventures

League City

281-333-3080

www.majesticventures.com

Take a dinner cruise on one of three beautiful yachts. Or sail to one of the restaurants on the bay, enjoy dinner at the restaurant and sail back to port. Price varies depending on the day selected.

Rates: $45.95 - $59.95 per person

Star Fleet

Kemah Boardwalk Marina

281-334-4692

www.starfleetyachts.com

Cruise around Clear Lake and Galveston Bay while having a romantic dinner. Following dinner, listen to the music and dance under the stars. Cruises are only offered on Valentines Day, July 4th, Memorial Day and New Years Eve.

Rates: $69 - $99 per person

Chapter 24

Just for Mom

Chapter 24

Just for Mom

Everyone needs a way to plug into their community. If you're feeling isolated, cooped up, wishing you could meet more moms to relate to, or are simply looking for a great way to be more involved with your community, try joining a local Mom's Group. You can meet amazingly diverse people and form lasting friendships. From support groups to play groups, you can find just about anything through a Mom's Group.

Local Mom Groups

Houston Area Mommys

www.groups.yahoo.com/group/houstonareamommys2004

A group for new moms or soon-to-be moms in Houston and surrounding areas. Being a new mom can sometimes be overwhelming and with that comes anxiety. This is a great place to have conversations about pregnancy and parenthood and to exchange ideas. Couples are welcomed and encouraged to join. Members due occasionally get together to "meet and greet." The group started on April 17, 2004 and now has 56 members.

M.O.M Club (Mothers of Multiples)

A support group for mothers of twins or more. Offer monthly meetings, playgroups, etc. There are several groups in and around Houston. Here is a list of several that we found. Check out the websites for more information.

- Bay Area: **www.houstontwins.com**
- Bellaire Area: **www.bellairemoms.org**
- Katy Area: **www.kapom.org**
- Kingwood Area: **www.kamom.com**
- Northwest Houston Area: **www.nwhmom.org**

Mommies in Texas

www.groups.yahoo.com/group/mommiesintexas

This is a group for both stay-at-home moms and work-outside-of-home moms from all over Texas. It is a place for moms to talk, share parenting ideas, and form friendships. Currently 102 members actively participate through this Yahoo group that was founded February 8, 2002. For more information, please check out their site.

MOM's Club International (Moms Offering Moms Support)

www.momsclub.org

MOMS Club is an international group that provides a great network of support and friendship to "stay at home" mothers. They meet during the day when mothers need the support the most. Your children are welcome to come to the club meetings and babysitting services are offered. There are local coordinators that are available for advice, ideas and help.

MOMS Club is a nonprofit corporation so the dues to the local chapters are only $15-30 per year. Registration fees for the chapters are only $30 per group or $2 per member per year. There are several MOMS Clubs in and around Houston. Check out their website to find locations near you.

Moms Meet Up Group

www.moms.meetup.com

Meet local moms to talk about kids and parenting, share experiences, and to find advice and support. There are over 723 groups worldwide participating in 16 countries. You can either find a "meet up group" or start a "meet up group" in your area.

M.O.P.S (Mothers of Preschoolers)

www.mops.org

MOPS is a support group for all moms raising preschoolers. Infancy to kindergarten are filled with unique needs, MOPS helps moms through these times with monthly or weekly meetings, support and friendships. MOPS was organized in 1973 and there are now over 3200 groups across the United States and in 33 countries around the world. There are over 71 groups in and around Houston. Hop online to find a group near you.

Mothers & More

Northwest Houston Seventh Day Adventist Church
7126 Spring Cypress Road, Spring, TX
866-841-9139 ext 3204
www.members.tripod.com/nwhmothersnadmore

Mothers & More is a national nonprofit organization dedicated to improving the lives of mothers. They focus on mothers' needs as individuals and members of society and promote the value of all the work mothers do. This mothers group meets on the 2nd Tuesday of each month at 7:30 pm in Spring, Texas at the Northwest Houston Seventh Day Adventist Church. There are 30 members and it has been going strong for about 5 years now. They offer regular evening meetings, guest speakers, mom's night out, family outings, playgroups, book clubs, seasonal events, fundraising events, and much more. They have no religious affiliations.

Parents Without Partners

www.pwphouston.org

Parents Without Partners is a non-profit, international organization for single parents and their children. It provides support and friendship to parents who never married, or lost a spouse through death, divorce, or separation. There are many organizations throughout Houston and the annual dues are around $45.00.

Texas Military Moms

www.groups.yahoo.com/group/txmm

This group is for moms whose significant other is currently serving with the US Military and is either from Texas, or stationed in Texas. Many of these moms have found friends to laugh with and cry with, during this difficult time. Since the group began on March 25, 2004, the membership has grown to 23 members.

Workout Facilities

There are so many fitness centers out there that we decided to highlight a few "Mama's only" facilities. While most gyms are designed for both male and female, several of them have a "women's only section" located in the gym. To find a traditional workout facility in your area, check your local yellow pages.

Curves for Women

1-800-848-1096

www.curves.com

This is an international chain of workout facilities made just for women seeking to loose weight. It is a program with 30-minute workouts 3 times a week around any schedule that you are currently using. The price and the hours vary at all locations. The company started in 1992 and there are already over 8,000 Curve locations. Due to the many locations in Houston and surrounding areas, (over 50 locations) we did not list them all here. The full list of locations can be found on their website under "Locations," or call 1-800-848-1096.

Ladies Workout Express

1-800-833-LADY (5329)

www.ladyofamerica.com

Ladies workout Express is a facility for women only and a franchise of Lady of America (see information in next listing). They specialize in weight loss, offering circuit training, personal trainers and nutritional counselors. They also have senior programs and youth programs for teens (ages 13-19). The price and hours vary by location. Because of the large number of Ladies Workout Express locations in and around Houston, we did not list them here. Please call or view them online for details.

Lady of America

1-800-833-LADY (5239)

www.ladyofamerica.com

Lady of America is a full service ladies only fitness center Their facilities include personal training, aerobics, circuit training, cardio machines, free weights, Pilates, locker rooms, multi-screen video systems, weight lose and nutrition programs, and child care. The membership fee and hours vary upon the location selected. Because there are so many Lady of America locations in Houston and surrounding areas, we did not list them all here. Please call 1-800-833-LADY or check out their website to find locations near you.

Memorial Athletic Club for Women

14520 Memorial Drive, Houston, TX

281-558-6691

www.fitmac.com/macwomen.htm

This women's only facility is located next to the Memorial Athletic Club & Aquatic Center. Instructions and programs are specialized to fit women's needs. They offer Pilate programs, personal training, cardio machines, weights, 2 aerobic studios, health and fitness lectures and teen programs. After exercising, you can shop at the Apparel Boutique for exercise and outerwear clothing. All female members have access to the Women's Center and the Memorial Athletic Club. Membership fees vary depending on the type of plan selected.

Hours: Mon-Thu 6:30am-8: 30pm, Fri 6:30am-6:00pm, Sat 8:00am-3:00pm

Shapes for Women

10760 Grant Road, Houston, TX

832-237-1990

www.shapesforwomen.com

Hours: Mon-Thu 7am-8pm, Fri 7am-5pm, Sat 9am-12pm

Price: 1 time enrollment fee $49.00 and $29.95 (+Tax)/month

Shapexpress for Women

4854 Beechnut, Houston, TX

713-663-6444

www.shapexpress.com

Hours: Mon-Thu 6:30am-9:00pm, Fri 6:30am-7:00pm, Sat 8:00am-12:00pm

Price: Varies on the package selected

Slender Lady of Cypress

11732 Grant Road, Cypress, TX
281-257-2444
Hours: Mon-Thu 8am-7pm, Fri 8am-6pm (closed 1pm-3pm for lunch), Sat 9am-12pm
Price: $31.10/month

Beauty and Day Spas

In the unselfish world of motherhood, there seems to be a notion that going to the spa is a lavish, self-indulgent affair and that taking time out to be pampered, spoiled, and thoroughly looked after is over-indulgent.

If it will make you feel any better, we are including some of the benefits of what you'll get from a little pampering once in awhile so that you can feel like you've got a legitimate excuse to go and take some time for yourself. Going to a spa can actually have therapeutic effects. These include:

- soothing tense and sore muscles
- cleaning, toning and nourishing the skin
- detoxifying the body to enhance the immune system
- stimulating circulation to ease conditions like arthritis and rheumatism
- relieving anxiety, anger and depression
- calming allergies and easing symptoms of diabetes, migraines and asthma
- improving flexibility
- increasing the body's energy flow
- healing emotional distress
- enhancing body-mind awareness
- improving spiritual focus and clarity

Now you have the perfect excuse! If you can't find one that fits listed above, make one up! Don't know where to go? Try any of these local spas and we're sure you'll be glad you did!

NORTH

A Bella Day Spa

25907 Oak Ridge Drive, The Woodlands, TX
281-367-9557
www.abelladayspa.com

Price Range: Massages starting at $65.00/HR
Unique: Quaint home setting

Bellagio Day Spa & Salon
3329 FM 1960 West, Houston, TX
281-440-3772
www.bellagiodayspa.com

Price Range: Massages start at $70.00/HR
Unique: Italian scenery and faux finishes

Derma Technique Day Spa
5460 FM 1960 West, Houston, TX
281-580-4130
www.dermatechnique.com

Price Range: Massages starting at $70.00/HR
Unique: A day at the spa with lunch included starting at $210.00
See ad in back

Elegant Spa & Salon
25710 I-45 North, The Woodlands, TX
281-364-0088
www.gotomyspa.com

Price Range: Massages starting at $65.00/HR
Unique: Hot Stone Therapy Massage $75.00

Hawaiian Retreat Day Spa
8765 Spring Cypress, Spring, TX
281-376-2223
www.hawaiiandayspa.com

Price Range: Massages starting at $70.00/HR
Unique: Pre-mommy massage $70.00/HR

Serenity Day Spa
7620 Louetta Road, Spring, TX
281-655-1922
www.serenitydayspa.com

Price Range: Massages starting at $65.00/HR
Unique: Voted “Best Day Spa” in North Houston

NORTHWEST

D'Elegance Salon & Day Spa

20940 Katy Freeway, Katy, TX
281-646-8001
www.delegance.com

Price Range: Massages starting at $70.00/HR
Unique: Voted one of Houston's Top 10 Day Spas

Josephine's Day Spa & Salon

1127 Eldridge Parkway, Suite 1008, Houston, TX
281-870-0083
www.josephinesdayspa.com

Price Range: Massages start at $99.00/75 min
Unique: Maternity massage is $105.00 for 75 minutes

Utopia Day Spa

12155 Jones Road, Houston, TX
281-890-4SPA
www.utopia.com

Price Range: Massages starting at $70.00/HR
Unique: pre-natal massage $85.00/HR

NORTHEAST

Moriri Salon & Day Spa

19 North Main St, Kingwood, TX
281-360-2296
www.moririhair.com

Price Range: Massages starting at $60.00/HR
Unique: Pre-natal massage $60.00/HR

Studio North Salon & Spa

2249 Northpark Drive, Humble, TX
281-359-0104
Price Range: Massages starting at $55.00/HR
Unique: Prenatal massage $65.00/HR

SOUTHWEST

D'Elegance Salon & Day Spa

10001 Westheimer Road, Houston, TX
713-784-0050
www.delegance.com

Price Range: Massages starting at $70.00/HR
Unique: Voted one of Houston's Top 10 Day Spas

Figaro Salon & Spa

4200 Westheimer, Suite 116, Houston, TX
713-952-4414
Price Range: Massages starting at $70.00/HR
Unique: Luxurious and elegant

Natures Way Day Spa & Salon

5000 Westheimer Road, Houston, TX
713-629-9995
www.natureswaydayspa.com

Price Range: massages starting at $80.00/HR
Unique: Pre-natal massage $85.00/HR

Sanctuary d'Sante

3637 West Alabama, Houston, TX
713-622-7722
www.sanctuarydsante.com

Price Range: Massages start at $80.00/HR
Unique: Offer several Mother/Daughter packages

Sensia Studio and Japanese Day Spa

1711 Post Oak Boulevard, Houston, TX
713-627-0070
www.sensiastudio.com

Price Range: Massages start at $75.00/HR
Unique: First Japanese Day Spa in Houston. Signature treatment is the Scen-Tao-Warm Stone Massage $80.00/HR

Spa Roma
19832 Southwest Freeway, Sugar Land, TX
281-341-0054
www.sparomatexas.com

Price Range: Massage prices starting at $75.00/HR
Unique: Pregnancy massage $80.00/HR

Tovas Hair Salon & Day Spa
1409 South Post Oak Lane, Houston, TX
713-439-1035
www.tovas.com

Price Range: Massages starting at $75.00/HR
Unique: Featured in W Magazine as Houston's best Day Spa

Trellis Spa At The Houstonian
111 North Post Oak Lane, Houston, TX
713-685-6790
www.trellisspa.com

Price Range: Massages starting at $100.00/50 minutes
Unique: Just-For-Mothers-To-Be Services: Pre-natal Massage $110.00/50min, Vitamin C Facial $110.00/50 min, Foot Rescue $60.00/HR

T'Salta Urban Spa
34 South Wynden Drive, Houston, TX
713-680-0626
www.tsalta-houston-day-spa.com

Price Range: Massages start at $80.00/HR
Unique: The Spa Teaser (for spa "first-timers") $180.00 for 2 hours/includes a mini-massage, mini-facial, makeup application and hairstyle. A little of everything!

Uptown Day Spa
1141 Uptown Park Boulevard, Houston, TX
713-961-0950
www.uptowndayspa.com

Price Range: Massages start at $85.00/HR
Unique: Carries an exclusive line of French hair and skin products

Urban Retreat Day Spa & Salon

2329 San Felipe Street, Houston, TX
713-523-2300
www.urbanretreat.com

Price Range: Massages start at $75.00/HR
Unique: Pre/Post Operative Massage is medically proven to reduce swelling & bruising. $45.00-$85.00, face/30 min & body/60 min

White Lotus Center & Spa

3540 Highway 6 South, Sugar Land, TX
281-325-1053
Price Range: Massages start at $55.00/HR
Unique: All first time clients receive 20% off for service

SOUTHEAST

Balmori's Day Spa

West Broadway/Silverlake Plaza II Shopping Center, Pearland, TX
281-412-4118
www.balmorisdayspa.com

Price Range: Massages starting at $70.00/55 minutes
Unique: Bambino Massage (for expectant mothers) $65.00/25 min or $95.00/55 min

Bergamos Spa Retreat

313 East Edgewood Drive, Friendswood, TX
281-992-3775
www.bergamossparetreat.com

Price Range: Massages start at $80.00/50 minutes
Unique: Couple "date night" massages the 1st Fri & Sat night of the month from 6-9 pm.

Beyond Beaute Day Spa & Wellness Center

2805 Center Street, Deer Park, TX
281-930-1734
www.beyondbeaute.com

Price Range: Massages starting at $72.00/HR
Unique: Signature Ayurvedic Pedicure $60.00

New You Day Spa
20801 Gulf Freeway #3, League City, TX
281-316-3614
www.newyoudayspa.com

Price Range: Massages starting at $50.00/HR
Unique: Mention their website and receive 20% off your first visit

Skin Care Retreat
2020 Broadway Street, Pearland, TX
281-412-4118
www.skincareretreat.net

Price Range: Massages starting at $65.00/HR
Unique: New Technology Oxygen Facial $75.00

DOWNTOWN

Indulgence Day Spa & Hair Salon
8 Chelsea Boulevard, Houston, TX
713-942-7888
www.indulgencespa.com

Price Range: Massages start at $70.00 for 50 minutes
Unique: Have your next birthday party or bridal shower here. For parties with 8 or more guests have the whole spa to themselves, lunch and tea included.

Sunset Body Works at The Rice Hotel
909 Texas Street, Houston, TX
713-223-5900
www.sunsetbodyworks.com

Price Range: Massages starting at $75.00/HR
Unique: Offer monthly specials

GALVESTON

The Spa at Moody Gardens/The Moody Gardens Hotel
Seven Hope Boulevard, Galveston, TX
409-741-8484
www.moodygardenshotel.com

Price Range: Massages starting at $95/50 minutes
Unique: The Secret Garden Teen Spa, offering spa services just for teens.

Chapter 25

Chapter 25

Emergency Phone Numbers

911 for Fire, Medical Emergency, Child Abuse

Poison Control 1-800-222-1222

HARRIS COUNTY

Houston Fire Department
713-247-5000

Houston Police Department
713-222-3131

Harris County Sheriff's Department
713-221-6000

FORT BEND COUNTY

Richmond Fire Department
281-232-6871

Rosenberg Fire Department
281-342-6131

Richmond Police Department
281-342-2849

Rosenberg Police Department
281-342-5566

Fort Bend County Sheriff's Department
281-341-4617

GALVESTON COUNTY

Galveston Fire Department
409-766-2145

Galveston Police Department
409-797-3702

Galveston County Sheriff's Department
409-766-2322

MONTGOMERY COUNTY

Montgomery County Fire Marshall
936-538-8288

Montgomery County Sheriff's Department
936-760-5871

Conroe Fire Department
936-760-4688

Conroe Police Department
936-756-5588

A

Animals, 1, 4, 9, 12, 14, 217, 227, 240, 370, 413

B

Bowling, 1, 18, 24, 60, 245, 252, 259, 371

C

D

E

Miniature Golf, 17, 19-23, 44, 253, 260, 264

Museums, 1, 5, 15, 27, 209, 211, 397, 411, 414

Music, 19, 22, 110-111, 113-126, 129, 133, 136, 173, 181, 192-193, 202, 209, 212, 219, 222, 245-246, 255, 261, 264, 274-278, 280-287, 410, 412, 418-419, 422

N

Nature Centers, 1, 7

O

P

Paintball, 1, 30-32, 263

Parks, 1, 7, 9, 39, 42-46, 50-51, 55, 59, 62-67, 72, 110, 180, 239, 263, 281
Parks, 1, 7, 9, 39, 42-46, 50-51, 55, 59, 62-67, 72, 110, 180, 239, 263, 281

Pregnancy, 326, 337, 339-346, 391, 400, 405-406, 425, 434

Q

R

S

Sports, 3, 34, 36, 49, 57, 59-67, 72-73, 75-110, 167, 198, 216, 227, 256, 265, 361, 366, 369, 371, 374, 400-401, 414

T

Theatres, 252, 254

W

Y

Advertiser Index

NOW ONLINE!
The Houston Mama's Handbook
A Reference Guide for Mothers in Houston
The Houston Mama's Handbook
visit us on the web at:
www.houstonmama.com

Coupon Code: Get One

Your Next Copy

Coupon Code: 50HB

Any Product in
our online store!

Coupon Code: OSHB

on your next order.

Coupon Code: FSHB

inflatable
party zone!
Birthday Parties
Team Parties
Church Groups
Mom's Groups
PUMP IT UP
"The Inflatable Party Zone"
PUMP IT UP is a large indoor play arena for kids of
all ages featuring huge inflatables reserved
for your very own private party or group event.

THE WOODLANDS
536 Sawdust Road
The Woodlands Texas
281-465-4747
KATY
923 South Mason Road
Katy, Texas
281-829-5711
KINGWOOD
23810 HWY 59 N
Kingwood, Texas
281-359-5515
HOUSTON
7620 Katy FWY #415
Houston, Texas
713-686-7867
CY. Fair
10910 W. Sam Houston PKWY N. #100
@ Fallbrook, Houston, Texas
281-469-4205
WWW.PUMPITUPPARTY.COM
1-866-476 JUMP

SUPPORT YOUR
LOCAL MAMA
An online marketplace for enterprising mama's
shop www.supportyourlocalmama.com to support your local mama

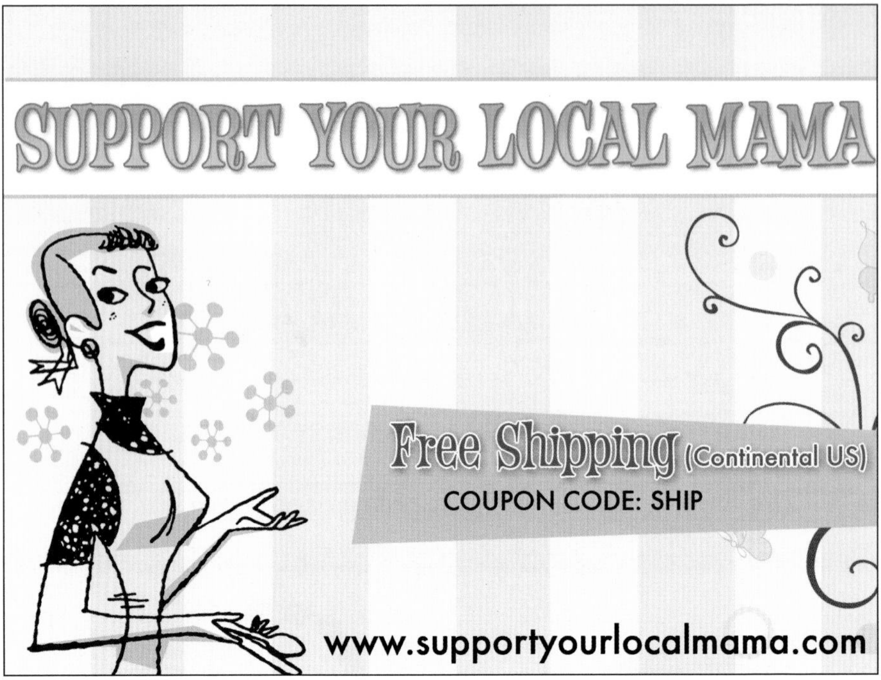
SUPPORT YOUR LOCAL MAMA
Free Shipping (Continental US)
COUPON CODE: SHIP
www.supportyourlocalmama.com

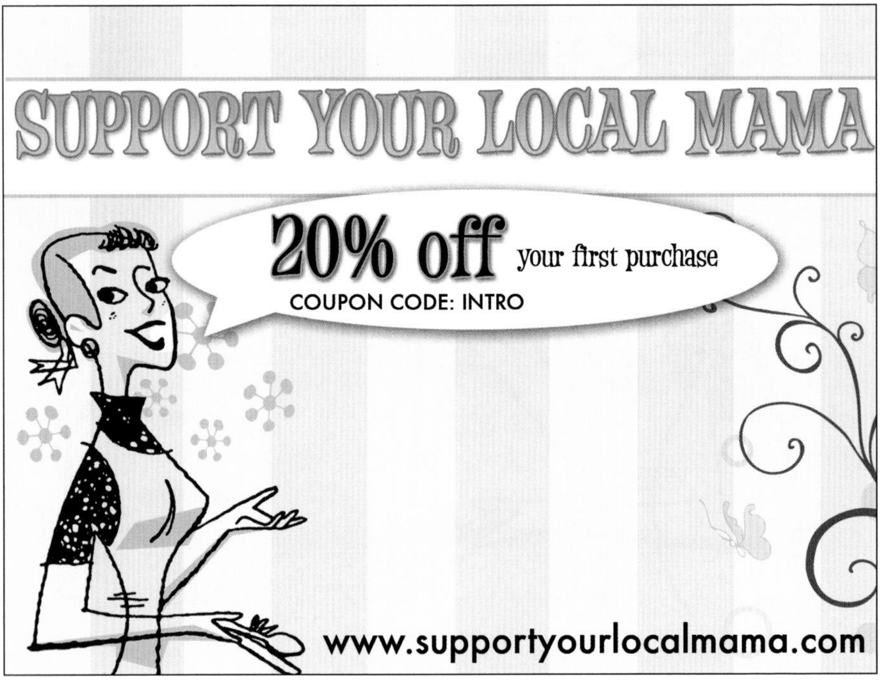
SUPPORT YOUR LOCAL MAMA
20% off your first purchase
COUPON CODE: INTRO
www.supportyourlocalmama.com

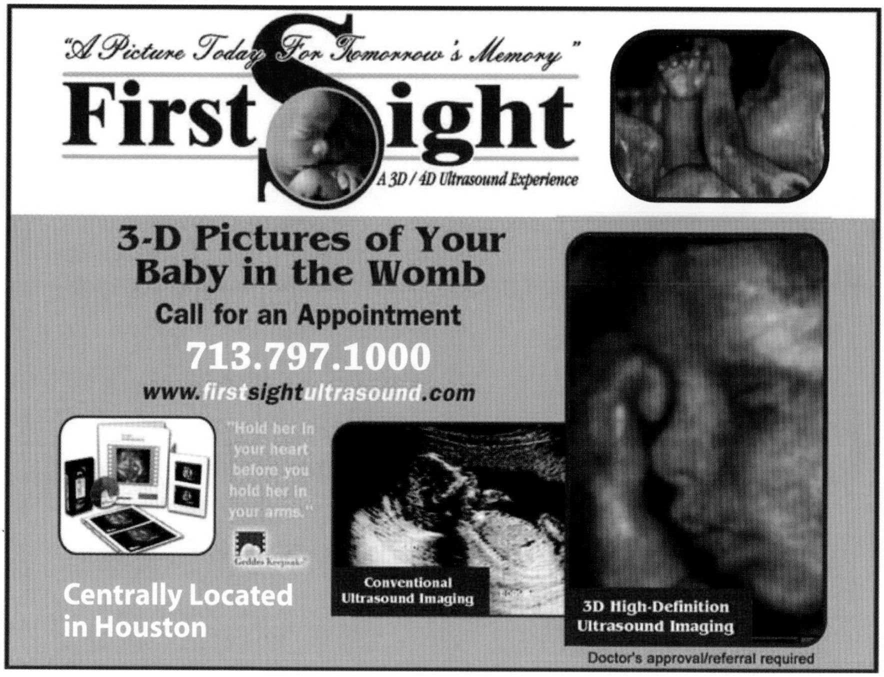
"A Picture Today For Tomorrow's Memory"
First Sight
A 3D / 4D Ultrasound Experience
3-D Pictures of Your Baby in the Womb
Call for an Appointment
713.797.1000
www.firstsightultrasound.com
"Hold her in your heart before you hold her in your arms."
Centrally Located in Houston
Conventional Ultrasound Imaging
3D High-Definition Ultrasound Imaging
Doctor's approval/referral required

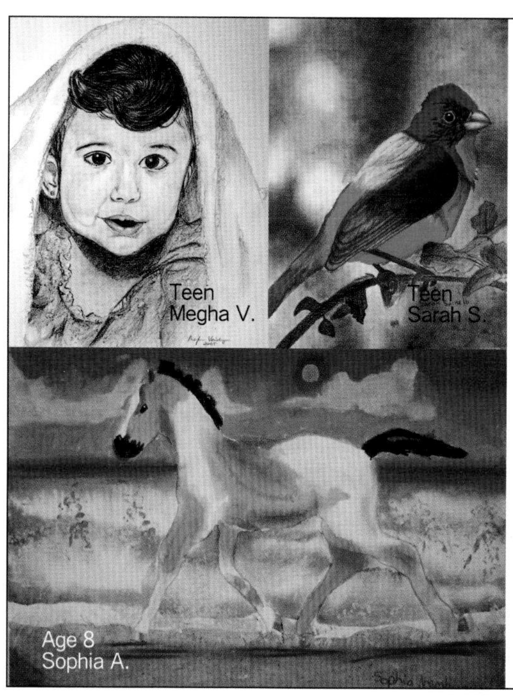

Teen Megha V.
Teen Sarah S.
Age 8 Sophia A.
Every Child has an Artist Within.
Under the direction of nationally acclaimed artist Thomas S. Cleveland a Master Designer for the U.S. Mint your child or your inner-child will develop that artist.
Adult, Teen, & Children
Day, Evening, After School & Saturday Classes
Spring Break & Summer Camps
Scout Badges and Birthday Parties
Individual instruction in a group setting.
Enroll & Start Anytime!
the Artist Within STUDIO SCHOOL
281-370-9336
12710 GRANT RD, CYPRESS, TEXAS 77429
ARTISTWITHIN.NET

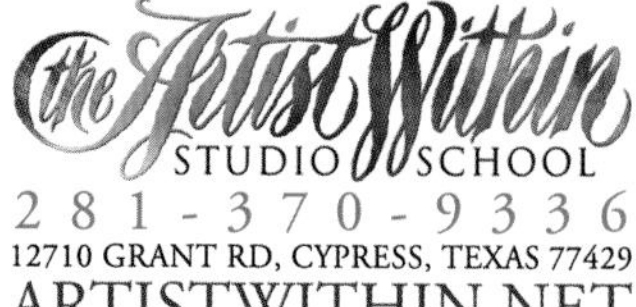

FREE
FREE
Moms-To-Be
Gift Certificates Available
A 3D - 4D Ultrasound Experience
"The Photo of a Lifetime"
A Picture Today For Tomorrows Memory
FREE Photo Brag w/Gold Package
Call for an appt 713.797.1000
First Sight
DOCTORS APPROVAL/REFERRAL REQUIRED
FREE
FREE

AERODROME
ICE SKATING COMPLEX
We have the
COOLEST
birthday party
in town!
8220 Willow Place North
Houston 77070
(FM-1960 @ SH-249)
281-84-SKATE

STEPPING STONES
SCHOOL
Enrollment Special!
(First Week Free admission by mentioning this ad)
Offering a Path to brighter, healthier and happier children
* Large shaded playground & soccer field
* Spacious and colorful classrooms
* Academic Scholastic curriculum
* Summer swimming in our pool
* Experienced staff and low ratios
* Computer, dance & music classes
* Gymnastics, P.E. & art classes
* Houston's healthiest whole foods menu, organic milk and 100% fruit juice
Ages 18 Mos.-Kindergarten
Full Time ($125-$135)
Part Time/Afterschool
Care Available
11250 S. Wilcrest (near Beltway 8 & 59) • (281) 988 9855
www.steppingstoneshouston.com

Introducing Dream Dinners

Because meal time is *family* time.

Dream Dinners lets you choose 12 wonderful entrees you assemble once a month and then take home and serve to your family in the weeks ahead.

Dream Dinners.
All the Ingredients for a great meal!

870 S. Mason Rd. Suite 104
Katy, Texas
832.969.0690

www.dreamdinners.com

Birthdays
Families
Any Size Group

Pony Rides • Train Rides
Hay Rides • Petting Zoo

281-859-1616
www.oilranch.com

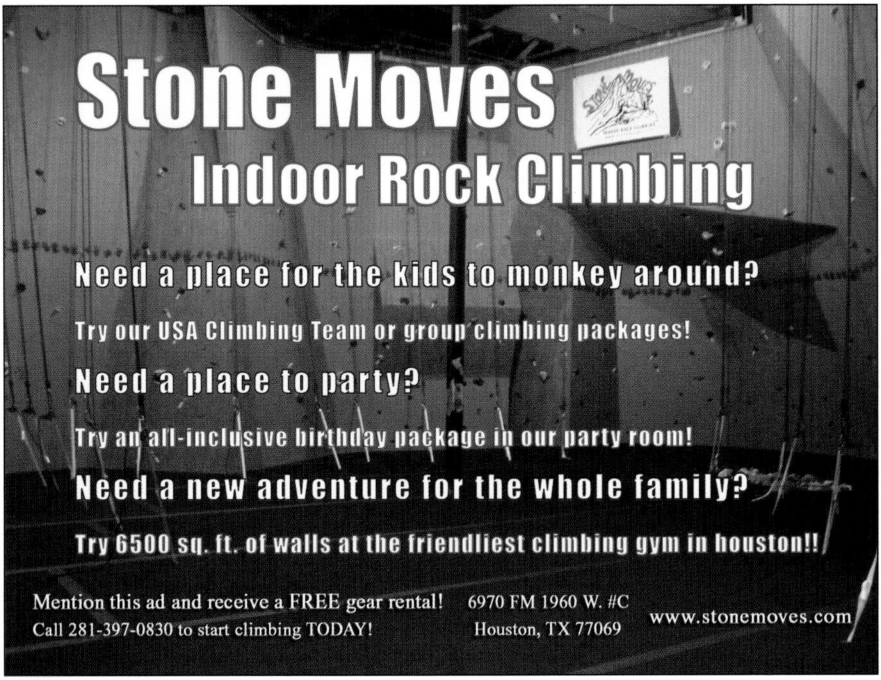

Stone Moves

Indoor Rock Climbing

Need a place for the kids to monkey around?

Try our USA Climbing Team or group climbing packages!

Need a place to party?

Try an all-inclusive birthday package in our party room!

Need a new adventure for the whole family?

Try 6500 sq. ft. of walls at the friendliest climbing gym in houston!!

Mention this ad and receive a FREE gear rental!
Call 281-397-0830 to start climbing TODAY!

6970 FM 1960 W. #C
Houston, TX 77069

www.stonemoves.com